THE EARLY DAYS OF
CHRISTIAN SOCIALISM
IN AMERICA

THE EARLY DAYS OF
CHRISTIAN SOCIALISM
IN AMERICA

BY

JAMES DOMBROWSKI

OCTAGON BOOKS

A DIVISION OF FARRAR, STRAUS AND GIROUX

New York   1977

Copyright 1936 by Columbia University Press

Reprinted 1966
by special arrangement with Columbia University Press

Second Octagon printing 1977

OCTAGON BOOKS
A DIVISION OF FARRAR, STRAUS & GIROUX, INC.
19 Union Square West
New York, N.Y. 10003

LIBRARY OF CONGRESS CATALOG CARD NUMBER: 66-17511
ISBN 0-374-92223-3

Printed in USA by
Thomson-Shore, Inc.
Dexter, Michigan

To E. J. K. *in Friendship*

PREFACE

THERE is a generally accepted belief today that Christianity
has a vital concern with the world of everyday social relationships. In one sense there is nothing new in this secular interest of religion. A dual reference of religion is implied in the
two great commandments of Jesus. The founder of Christianity,
both by precept and by example, pointed his followers to a
proper relationship to God their Father and to men their
brothers: Christianity never lacked an ethical emphasis. Revolutionary changes have, however, occurred in the content ascribed to the Christian ethic, and to understand the modern
social emphasis in religion one must study it against its historical background. Such study is, unfortunately, made difficult because the meager literature in this field deals almost exclusively
with the period subsequent to 1900. One reason for this restricted
viewpoint has been the false assumption that the Social Gospel
first arose shortly after the turn of the century, with the work
of the denominational social-service commissions. These commissions, however, must be regarded as a product of antecedent
social forces. One purpose of this study is to make a modest
contribution to an understanding of contemporary social movements in religion by an examination of certain aspects of social
Christianity in the last three decades of the nineteenth century.

The author gratefully acknowledges his indebtedness to Professor Herbert W. Schneider, of Columbia University, for his
generous criticism and advice in the preparation of this volume;
to Professors Harry F. Ward and Reinhold Niebuhr, of Union
Theological Seminary, to whom the author owes his initial interest in this field; to Mrs. Sue Fay Hinckley, Ralph Albertson,
John Chipman, and George Herbert Gibson, Jr., for the use
of letters, unpublished manuscripts, and historical material
concerning the Christian Commonwealth Colony; to Herbert
Gleason, Paul Bellamy, Graham Taylor, John Bakeless,

Francis G. Peabody, and Richard T. Ely for magazine files, letters, and references; to the library staff of Union Theological
Seminary and of Columbia University for their courteous assistance in the assembling of material.

J. DOMBROWSKI

HIGHLANDER FOLK SCHOOL
MONTEAGLE, TENN.
June 1, 1936

CONTENTS

THE EARLY DAYS OF
CHRISTIAN SOCIALISM
IN AMERICA

INTRODUCTION

THE development of a social emphasis in American Christianity is not to be explained by attributing it to a single factor, either in the traditional body of Christian thought or in the social situation within which it was elaborated. It was not merely the result of American activism, as one student of the problem has indicated; neither was it a product of the ethical implications inherent in the social teachings of the prophets or the New Testament, as others have believed. It was not the continuation of a social interest occasioned by the slavery controversy or a reflection of the rebirth of the Christian Socialist movement in England. The Social Gospel movement cannot adequately be placed in history by a "nothing but" phrase. It came as a consequence of the impact upon religious thought of widely differing factors including those named above: eighteenth-century humanitarianism; liberal tendencies in theology as represented by Maurice, Bushnell, Munger, and Gladden; an inherent concern for social justice; gains made in social psychology and in sociology as illustrated by the work of Ward, Small, Giddings, James, and Dewey; the influence of a group of political economists and journalists writing with religious presuppositions, such as Colwell, Ely, Commons, Lloyd, and Bellamy. Finally, it was in part a defense mechanism called forth by the attack upon religion of labor leaders, socialists, and reformers, many of them deeply religious, and all concerned with the problem of social change: for example, Robert Owen, Saint-Simon, Karl Marx, and Henry George.

Probably the most important factor in the development of a social emphasis in American Christianity was the pressure exerted by an expanding labor movement. The Civil War had given an impetus to the organization of labor, and by 1870 there were thirty-two national trade-unions in the United States. Each city had its trade assembly, labor press, and workingmen's library. The panic of 1873 and the industrial difficulties of the seventies brought widespread unemployment and suffering attended by desperate strikes, such as the great railroad strike of 1877. The end of the decade found labor in a critical condition with only 18 percent of the national trade-unions surviving.[1] During the eighties there were indications of the growth of an aggressive and determined labor organization. The Knights of Labor, organized in 1869, reached the climax of its influence in 1886, when it had one million members.[2] In 1886, the year of the Haymarket riot, there were sixteen hundred strikes, involving six hundred thousand men, and Carol D. Wright estimated that one million men were unemployed. Then came the panic of 1893. The following year, the country was aroused by the Pullman strike and the sympathetic strike of the American Railway Union headed by Eugene V. Debs. The disturbances of the industrial world had their political counterpart in third-party movements. The Labor Reform Party, founded in 1872, was absorbed in 1878 into the Greenback Party, which united the Eastern proletariat and the Western farmer. The Union Labor Party, founded in 1888, was supported by the West and the South. In 1892 the Populist or People's Party—registering dissatisfaction with watered stocks, high rates, crop liens in the South, mortgages in the West, and unemployment and poverty in the industrial centers of the East—polled more than one million votes.[3]

During this period, criticism of religion by labor leaders, socialists, and reformers, as well as the alienation from the church of large numbers of workers, put religion on the defensive.[4] It gave added significance to the coupling of Christian ethics and apologetics in the early courses in ethics at Princeton and Union Theological Seminary. Labor leaders charged religion with in-

---

[1] Harold U. Faulkner, *Economic History of the United States*, pp. 589-90.

[2] The Knights of Labor did not require all of its members to come from the ranks of labor. In its membership were a number of intellectuals and ministers, including the Reverend W. D. P. Bliss, the Reverend James O. S. Huntington, and the Reverend W. L. Bull.—*The Dawn* (1890).

[3] Faulkner, *op. cit.*, p. 604.

[4] "The working-men are largely estranged from the Protestant religion. Old churches standing in the midst of crowded districts are continually abandoned because they do not reach the working-men."—S. L. Loomis, "Modern Cities and Some of Their Problems," *Theological Seminary Bulletin* (1887), p. 10.

difference to their struggle for improved conditions or with actual hostility to the trade-union movement. While the early struggles of labor were in progress, there was no Maurice or Kingsley heard in the American church world.[5] Here and there a working-class preacher with a proletarian congregation would give voice to the aspirations of the workers, but almost no prominent churchman, with the exception of Wendell Phillips, was sympathetic to the workers' movement. The liberal preacher Henry Ward Beecher said in 1877:

God has intended the great to be great and the little to be little . . . The trade union, originated under the European tradition, destroys liberty . . . I do not say that a dollar a day is enough to support a working man . . . But it is enough to support a man! Not enough to support a man and five children if a man insist on smoking and drinking beer . . . But the man who cannot live on bread and water is not fit to live.[6]

When he said this, the Reverend Mr. Beecher had a salary of $20,000 a year and an income of about this same amount from his lectures. At the same time, as Paxton Hibben remarks, the burden of four years of the depression following the panic of 1873 was being borne on the backs of labor, when three million out of a total population of forty-five million were unemployed, and whole families were starving.[7]

Labor leaders criticized religion on four counts: first, that it was conservative, viewing society with its class distinctions as a result of an unalterable edict of Providence; second, that it taught meekness and submission to authority, rather than revolt in the face of oppression and injustice, and offered the re-

[5] This resolution was introduced at the Second Industrial Congress representing seven states held in New York in 1847: "Resolved: That while we fully appreciate the labors of all in behalf of suffering humanity, we are constrained to declare, more in sorrow than in anger, that the great body of the so-called Christian Church and clergy of the present day are fearfully recreant to the high and responsible duties placed upon them. That they sustain the blood-stained banner of capital and fraud in their crusade against labor, and have themselves become the fiercest of the vanguard brood that gorge upon the veins of honest industry and injustice; therefore we would warn them that if they would have those principles which they preach, and by which they profess to be governed, influence the people of this country, they must infuse into their teachings and practice more of truth, justice, and regard for the rights of humanity."—George E. McNeill, *The Labor Movement*, p. 210.
[6] Paxton Hibben, *Henry Ward Beecher, an American Portrait*, p. 236.
[7] *Ibid.*

wards of a life in the next world as compensation for the lack of well-being and happiness in this world; third, that its ethical pretensions with respect to brotherhood were steeped in hypocrisy, since it proffered charity instead of economic equality and justice; fourth, that its vested interests and dependence upon the wealthy ruling class made it inevitably an instrument for promoting the ends of the bourgeois group and explained its failure to take the side of the workers in any of the major industrial disputes in the United States.

Many labor leaders, while disavowing ecclesiastical religion, were professed followers of Jesus:

And now we feel at liberty to ask the indignant follower of the lowly Nazarene what he and his like have meant by this two thousand years of cant about the Fatherhood of God and the Brotherhood of Man? What kind of a brotherhood? A brotherhood in which the brother with a weaker body or less cunning brain shall be fed on poorer food and wear inferior clothing and live in a less desirable house? Is this the mouse your mountain has brought forth after all these centuries of labor? Nay, gentlemen, you are not in earnest. You have found for yourselves that physical comfort and well-being which you are afraid would be so harmful to others, and now in your easy chairs, in your comfortable parlors, you have forgotten your mission—if you ever had one . . . The world is weary of your pretenses . . . And now it requests you to step aside and give room to earnest men and sincere women who really believe in, and labor to realize, that doctrine of human brotherhood which you have preached so long in sniffling tones, and which in your hearts you have always despised.[8]

Such attacks upon religion did not go unanswered. In 1879 Professor Roswell D. Hitchcock of Union Theological Seminary issued a small volume scarcely aimed to conciliate the ranks of labor, to increase the understanding of socialism among the bourgeois audience to whom presumably the book was directed, or to soothe the passions aroused by industrial conflict. The more radical form of socialism which he designated as communistic socialism should be treated summarily, he said:

Today there is not in our language, nor in any language, a more hateful word than Communism. In Paris seven years ago, in Pittsburgh last year, in Berlin this year, it meant, and still means, wages without work, arson, assassination, anarchy. In this shape of it, the

[8] William L. Lewis, *Ten Blind Leaders of the Blind*, p. 190.

instant duty of society, without taking a second breath, is to smite it with the swiftness and fury of lightning.[9]

Apparently the professor was not a pacifist. At about the time when Professor Hitchcock's book appeared, the Reverend J. H. Rylance, rector of St. Mark's (Episcopal) Church, New York, was acknowledging the validity of the charge that the Church had become a bourgeois institution in these words:

. . . our religion, instead of cementing the social structure, is too often a disorganizing element, the churches having come very generally to recognize and to pander to caste distinctions, making costly provision for the wealthy and refined, while to the outcast multitudes we fling the mere scraps and crumbs from our ecclesiastical tables, thus alienating the hearts of the common people, while some we have filled with bitter scorn.[10]

The Reverend Mr. Rylance in a series of sermons in 1879 dealt sympathetically with the problem of socialism.

The charity and philanthropy sponsored by the religious institutions, to which the apologists of religion pointed as evidence of its concern for human welfare and as a refutation of the charges of socialists, was cited by labor leaders as a major reason for the alienation of workers from religion. It was a device, they charged, for denying justice. W. B. Prescott, president of the International Typographical Union, one of the oldest and strongest Internationals, ascribed his own defection from religion to this policy. While disavowing all ecclesiastical religion, he called himself

. . . an ardent admirer of Christ and his teaching. . . . Poverty hovered over my youthful days, and I happened to be located in a wealthy Presbyterian parish, and at my mother's behest attended church and Sunday-School, the wealthy managers of which, apparently not relishing the ragged and ill-fitting clothes of the worshippers from our district built a mission in that neighborhood, actuated by much the same motives that now moves a man to build a shelter for his dog in the back yard. This and many other acts of a similar nature I resented, and it took very few years for me to see that I was not wanted, except to afford some an opportunity of assuming a patronizing attitude toward us, and consequently became a derelict. . . .

[9] Roswell D. Hitchcock, *Socialism*, p. 24.
[10] J. H. Rylance, *Communism, not the Best Remedy*, p. 10.

This policy is largely responsible for the inability of the evangelical churches to hold the masses.[11]

Professor John R. Commons, on the basis of information from social workers and labor leaders in several states, wrote in 1894 that Christianity was strong in promoting charity but weak in promoting justice. Religious and professional groups, listed by social workers in the order of their willingness to assist charitable work, were listed in exactly the reverse order by labor leaders with respect to their interest in labor. Professor Commons's query to the social workers read: "From which of the following classes, according to your observation, come the best and most persistent workers in charities and correction, and in what proportions?" The answer of a secretary of the charity organization of a western city was typical of the replies received from social workers: Protestants, 65 percent; Catholics, 10 percent; Jews, 10 percent; Unitarians, 12 percent; Ethical Culturists, 3 percent. The question addressed to the labor leaders asked for a rating of these groups according as they supplied the "best, most persistent advocates of the cause of labor." The reply of Samuel Gompers, president of the American Federation of Labor, was typical of the answers of the labor leaders:[12] 1. Members of ethical societies; 2. Unitarians; 3. Non-believers; 4. Catholics; 5. Protestants; 6. Jews; 7. Ministers; 8. Physicians; 9. Lawyers.

The expansion of the social movement in religion follows a line of development parallel to that of the social sciences, especially sociology. The introduction in 1876 of Professor William Graham Sumner's course at Yale is usually named as the beginning of sociological instruction in the United States. Lester F. Ward's book *Dynamic Sociology*, the first important work in sociology by an American author, did not appear until 1883. Sociology was introduced at Michigan in 1881, at Indiana in 1885, at Colby in 1889, at Bryn Mawr in 1890, and at Harvard in 1891. Professor Edward A. Ross began his teaching at Indiana in 1891, Professor Albion W. Small instituted the department of sociology at the new University of Chicago in 1893, and

[11] W. B. Prescott, letter to John R. Commons, quoted in *The Kingdom*, June 22, 1894, p. 158.   [12] *Ibid.*

one year later Professor Franklin H. Giddings was called to
found the department at Columbia.[13] Of the seven theological
institutions that began to give lectures in social ethics in 1892-93,
five called them lectures in sociology, either with a qualifying
ecclesiastical adjective—as *Christian sociology* at Chicago Theological Seminary, Meadville, and Hamilton, or *ecclesiastical
sociology* at the Divinity School of the University of Chicago—
or unmodified, as at the Episcopal Theological School at Cambridge. The *Seminary Student,* published by the students of
Union Theological Seminary, announced in 1893 the organization of a society for the discussion of social problems. The subjects to be examined were "the nature and methods of sociological study and the minister's relation to the problems of the
day." At the second meeting, the name was changed to "Sociological Society." [14] The extent to which sociology had penetrated
the theological curriculum by 1892 is indicated by its inclusion
as a regular division of the subject of Systematic Theology in
Philip Schaff's *Theological Propaedeutic,* published in that year.

Professor Ely's articles on the relation of religion to social
problems, which appeared in the religious press during the
eighties, were an important factor in directing the interest of
religion toward sociology. He had claimed on the authority of
the commandments of Jesus equal importance for sociology
and theology. Half of the time of theological students, he said,
should be devoted to the study of social science. Seminaries
should be the chief intellectual centers for the study of sociology.[15] The fact that some teachers of sociology approached
the subject with ethical and religious presuppositions, further
stimulated the interest of the clergy in the subject. Professor
Small, trained in theology at Newton, and influenced by Ely,[16]
had said, "Jesus was, after all, the profoundest economist." [17]
Later, as editor of the *American Journal of Sociology,* he intro-

[13] The action of Columbia probably was due to the example of Chicago, according to Professor Giddings.—Albion W. Small, "Fifty Years of Sociology in
the United States," *American Journal of Sociology,* XXI (1926).
[14] *Seminary Student,* I, 155.
[15] Ely, *Social Aspects of Christianity,* p. 17.
[16] John Lewis Gillen, "The Development of Sociology in the United States,"
Publications of the American Sociological Society, XXI (1926).
[17] Albion W. Small, in *The Dawn,* November, 1890.

duced a series of articles on religion and sociology, to which
Shailer Mathews contributed. Professor John R. Commons
wrote, "The object of sociology is to teach us how to love our
neighbors." [18] "A Great Need—Sociological Seminary" was the
title of an article, published in 1895 by the Reverend Samuel
Zane Batten, secretary of the Brotherhood of the Kingdom.[19] In
1892 Professor Commons, then at Oberlin, issued a *Popular
Bibliography of Sociology* containing a list of about one hundred
titles on general sociology, the state, pauperism, charities, family, labor, crime, prisons, remedies, etc., arranged to give the
"general reader, especially the Christian minister and worker,"
a list of the best available books on important sociological problems. The Reverend Samuel W. Dike started a department of
"Sociological Notes" in the *Andover Review* in 1886, following
up his article in 1884 on the sociological approach to the religious problems of the country town. He discussed the social
movement in religion as if it were entirely confined to an academic interest in sociology and warned against an expansion of
the subject too hasty for sound scholarship.

The well-defined anti-religious bias of Lester F. Ward, the
most influential American writer in the pioneer days of sociology, probably was an incentive to the study of sociology by
religious leaders, even if they turned to it with no more worthy
purpose than to make use of it in apologetics. On the positive
side, Ward's emphasis on the importance of the psychic factor
in social change supported the minority group interested in
social reform. As a follower of Comte, Ward criticized religion
on similar grounds. Religion diverted attention from science,
from the material and rational processes in which alone progress
was to be sought. Like Marx, Ward looked upon a cosmology
which assigned historical events to the will of a Deity or to the
unfolding of the Absolute as the basis for a justification of the
existing order, nullifying confidence in the possibility of a
rational control of social forces. For the same reason, he was
opposed to that academic champion of *laissez-faire* economics

[18] John R. Commons, *Social Reform and the Church.*
[19] Samuel Z. Batten, "A Great Need—Sociological Seminary," *The Kingdom,*
June 4, 1890.

and the Spencerian evolutionary theory (which regarded society as a product of unconscious spontaneous forces over which man had no control), William G. Sumner, who stated his views thus:

If this old world is as bad as they say, one more reflection may check the zeal of the headlong reformer. It is at any rate a tough old world . . . All its wry and crooked gnarls and knobs are therefore stiff and stubborn. If we puny men by our arts can do anything at all to straighten them, it will be only by modifying the tendencies of some of the forces at work, so that after a sufficent time, their action may be changed a little and slowly the lines of movement may be modified. This effort, however, can at most be only slight, and it will take a long time. In the meantime spontaneous forces will be at work, compared with which our efforts are like those of a man trying to deflect a river, and these forces will have changed the whole problem before our interferences have time to make themselves felt . . . Everyone of us is a child of his age and cannot get out of it . . . The things which will change it are the great discoveries and inventions, the new reactions inside the social organism, and the changes in the earth itself on account of changes in the cosmical forces . . . The men will be carried along with it and be made by it. The utmost they can do by their cleverness will be to note and record their course as they are carried along, which is what we do now, and is that which leads us to the vain fancy that we can make or guide the movement. That is why it is the greatest folly of which a man can be capable, to sit down with a slate and pencil to plan out a new social world.[20]

The word *dynamic* in Ward's title *Dynamic Sociology* expressed the potential creative factor in man's relation to his environment. Progress was to be achieved by bringing social forces, human institutions, under intelligent control. Man is not only capable, said Ward, of modifying social institutions, but it becomes his duty to adapt such instruments to his needs, radically changing them, if need be;

When we remember that it [government] is designed to conserve whatever interest society may possess, it seems not too much to say that the most advanced governments of the world are less perfectly adapted to their highly complicated functions than are the least advanced governments to the simplicity of the interests intrusted to their charge. Government, therefore, is not only holding back, but is itself going backward.

[20] William Graham Sumner, "The Absurd Attempt to Make the World Over," *War and Other Essays,* pp. 209-10.

It therefore becomes the interest and the duty of society, throwing off the yoke of government in the odious sense of this ill-conceived term, to establish a truly progressive agency.[21]

Both the religious and secular development of sociology were indebted to eighteenth-century humanitarianism and later positivism. The influence of these ideas of the Enlightenment was felt directly through the new theology and indirectly through the part it played in the new subject of "social science."
The first important American book on this subject was Henry C. Carey's three-volume work, *The Principles of Social Science* (1858-60). As early as 1868, a disciple of Carey and of Stephen Colwell, the Reverend Mr. Thompson,[22] taught a course in social science at the University of Pennsylvania. Professor Thompson described his early courses thus:

I change every year the ground traversed so as to keep the subjects fresh to myself. I generally give my lectures as foot-notes to the newspapers. But I also include more general topics of social science—such as Communism, Socialism, Organization of Charity, Prison Discipline, the Elevation of the Working Classes, the Temperance Problem, the Public Education.[23]

Other early courses in social science were given by Perry at Williams (1865), by Laws at Missouri (1876), by Sumner at Yale (1872), by Mayo-Smith at Columbia (1878), and by Sanborn at Cornell (1865). Out of the material for these early courses came the later sociological courses in social problems. They also provided the models for early seminary courses in ethics, Christian ethics, social ethics, and Christian sociology.
Humanitarianism and philanthropy were prominent features

[21] Lester F. Ward, *Dynamic Sociology*, p. 250.
[22] Professor Robert Ellis Thompson, born in Ireland in 1844, educated at the University of Pennsylvania, licensed to preach by the Reformed Presbytery of Philadelphia, and ordained in 1874. Tolman says his work in sociology began in 1874; Bernard credits him with a course in social science in 1868; and *Who's Who in America*, material for which is furnished by the subjects themselves, states that he was a member of the faculty of the University of Pennsylvania from 1868 to 1892, being successively professor of Latin and mathematics (1868-71), professor of social science (1871-81), and professor of history and literature (1881-92). He also lectured at Harvard, Princeton, and Yale. His Stone Lectures at Princeton Theological Seminary, on "Christian Sociology," were published in 1891 under the title *De civitate dei: The Divine Order of Human Society*.
[23] F. B. Sanborn, "The Social Sciences, Their Growth and Future," *Journal of Social Science*, XXI (1886), 9.

of the American Social Science Association,[24] the parent organization of most of the social science societies in America, organized in 1865. The title of the secretary's report for 1894, "The Commonwealth of Social Science," is significant. The report is permeated with the spirit of the Enlightenment:

> But do we not behold the fable of Saint-Pierre [25] turned into the fact of American life—sixty millions of people in United States and Canada, fulfilling, with slight qualifications, the ideal conditions that the eighteenth century laid down for a blissful republic? Here is universal toleration; here the amalgam of races; here the domestic peace and the contempt of foreign conquest. And here, which is more to our purpose, is the grand international exhibition of the social sciences in full operation, unfettered by traditions and precedents, and escaping easily from the dominion of vested and petrifying institutions.[26]

Clergymen were attracted to the work of the Association by its emphasis on philanthropy and charity and by its friendly attitude toward religion.[27] The report for 1884 of the secretary, Professor Sanborn of Cornell, closed with these words:

> We thus return at the close of our session to that which was the beginning of social science—the revelation of God to man through institutions and precepts [Hebrew charities had been under consideration] hallowed by age venerable even in misapprehension and error . . . for we cannot too often consider and repeat that the origin of every science and pre-eminently of the social sciences is divine.[28]

The conferences of the Association were reported by clergymen in the progressive religious press. Gradually the term "social science" was purged of the taint of infidelity given to it by the work of Comte and Spencer.

[24] The American Social Science Association, modeled on the English organization of similar name, grew out of activities of the Massachusetts Board of Charities (founded in 1863) in its efforts to collect material on poverty, industry, insanity, pauperism, crime and disease. A special committee was charged with the evangelical mission of propagating courses in social science.—*Encyclopedia of Social Reform.*

[25] The French philanthropist who wrote *Paul et Virginie,* 1789.

[26] F. B. Sanborn, "The Commonwealth of Social Science," *Journal of Social Science,* XIX (1894), 4.

[27] The early membership roll lists sixteen members bearing the title "the Reverend." Not all clerical members, however, used the title.

[28] *Ibid.*

I

THE PHILOSOPHY OF SOCIAL CHRISTIANITY
IN AMERICA, 1870-1900

SOCIAL Christianity, as it emerged into the proportions of a movement in the last two decades of the nineteenth century, had a decidedly antitheological bias. It regarded the preoccupation of religion with theology as a major cause of indifference to questions concerning social justice. Ethics were judged to be of more importance than dogma. When theological writing appeared, it was with the purpose of "humanizing theology." [1]

Social Christianity emphasized the immanence of God. The transcendence of God was neglected or denied. This development may be attributed largely to the influence of nineteenth-century science. The major intellectual concept of the past century is the doctrine of evolution. This biological idea was regarded as having made all supernaturalism intellectually disreputable. God was to be found only in physical facts, and the facts were given by natural science. In attempting to "reconcile" natural science and religion, John Fiske, Henry Drummond, and Lyman Abbott reduced God to an immanental factor in the process of evolution. Instead of the Holy and unapproachable Being before Whom man worshipped in awe and reverence, God became a mere point of reference to explain a vague humanitarianism. In the eighties Francis G. Peabody, of Harvard University, an early exponent of social Christianity, wrote of God as the "central cosmic energy" responsible for all social reform. God, as an active agent within the social order, was a guarantor of progress, and the assurance of a steady movement in history toward a co-operative society.

One effect of this emphasis on immanence was to destroy the

[1] *Cf.* the chapter on the "New Theology" in Theodore Munger's *Freedom of Faith.*

distinction between the secular and the religious world. A dualism between the spiritual and the secular is impossible to maintain in a monistic world. When God was identified with the temporal world the eternal became confused with the temporary. Social Christianity acted here as popularizer. It gave an added impetus to the secular trend in religion which attained prominence in the Renaissance and was accelerated by the Enlightenment.

It is significant that the Social Gospel had a correlative existence with Calvinism. It showed its greatest strength in the countries where Calvinism was most deeply entrenched. Thus, to some extent, the "this-worldly" emphasis of Calvinism produced a social Christianity opposed to the "other-worldliness" of Lutheranism and the "next-worldliness" of Catholicism. Withdrawal from the world, the religious ideal of the mystical or pietistic religious groups, was rejected in favor of participation in the world with a view to transforming it. Orthodox Christianity had tended to regard the world as a mere temporary dwelling place for the soul *en route* to the heavenly abode. As an escape from life it gave rise to the Marxian criticism that religion was an opiate of the people. The Social Gospel, on the other hand, insisted that life on the earth was not to be regarded as preparation for some future existence. The good life was to be realized here on the earth. God's will was to find complete fruition. In some respects this was a reaffirmation of the Puritan ideal of a theocracy.

The one term which served as the most characteristic symbol of the social movement in Christianity was the "Kingdom of God." With the Ritschlians, advocates of the Social Gospel tended to restrict religion to ethics. Religion had for its function the establishment of the Kingdom of God on earth. Exception was taken to the Catholic interpretation of the Kingdom as synonymous with the Church; to the idealistic view that the Kingdom was located within another world or the next world; and finally to the pietistic interpretation of the Kingdom as existing within a body of believers. The Kingdom of God, given a purely ethical interpretation, meant the transformation of this world into a just and righteous society. Much importance was attached to the words of Jesus, "Thy will be done on earth as it is in Heaven."

This ethical interpretation of the Kingdom implied a change in the idea of eternal life. It ceased to have a purely eschatalogical meaning. As in the thought of Maurice, it was regarded as a function of life upon the earth. "Eternal" signified a quality of life, not duration. To know God, to seek truth, and to practice righteousness is eternal life.

The traditional ideas of the fall, the atonement, and sin received new interpretations. The traditional notion of sin ceased to have meaning when personality was discovered to be largely a public product. It seemed to follow obviously that the individual was not to be charged with responsibility for his vices. The development of social psychology changed the attitude of many persons toward criminals and promoted a relativistic ethic. Attention was turned toward the understanding of the antecedents of wrongdoing, now denominated "anti-social action." It follows, too, that if man is not to be charged with responsibility for his vices, neither is he to be credited with his virtues. As man's vices ceased to be looked upon as a reflection of individual defection of an ancient ancestor, so virtue ceased to be regarded as a free gift of God's grace. Goodness and evil tended to disappear in the abstract as men came to appreciate the social nature of religion and the social structure of personality. There remained society, consisting of individuals who behave in concrete fashion under the stress of social factors, capable of manipulation and control. Students of theology in social science courses in the seminaries learned to look upon criminals as pathological patients rather than as mere sinners, as the victims of social forces for which society was more responsible than the criminal himself. The treatment prescribed aimed at redemption to useful citizenship by patient and scientific treatment rather than by punishment administered under the pressure of a revengeful and retributive idea of justice.

The legalistic notion of the atonement was rejected. A society which had renounced the idea and the practice of retributive justice could not accept a doctrine of the atonement in which that idea was implicitly ascribed to God. The Social Gospel movement, however, placed more, not less, importance on the cross. In the passion of Jesus was seen the crowning achievement of a life spent freely in the service of man, the symbol for all time of the social passion that should characterize all human relationships. Social forces responsible for the death of Jesus were analyzed and found to be still operative in human society. Thus, in the sense that all men were accomplices, albeit involuntarily, in the brutalities or sinfulness of a society which put the innocent to death, exploited the weak, and used military forces to keep subject nations and races in their places, everyone might be said to share the guilt for such wrongdoing. In this sense of social responsibility for the wrongs of society, the concept of original sin was rehabilitated. But the term is unsatisfactory, for it carries the connotation of human nature as something given, whereas the tendency is to regard it as a product of social conditioning.

The most prominent feature of the Social Gospel is its emphasis upon the saving of society rather than upon the salvation of individuals. Leaders of the movement regarded it primarily as a revolt from the excessive individualism of Protestant theology. The appeal to the conscience of the individual, used by Reformation theologians to discredit papal authority, had laid the basis for religious anarchy. For three hundred years Protestant theology had stressed the relationship of the individual soul to God. But nineteenth-century science had destroyed the notion of society as an aggregate of discrete units and had substituted the concept of a social organism. Thus the idea of an individual abstracted from all social relationships had no corresponding reality. It followed that the salvation of the individual soul ceased to have meaning. Obviously there could be no salvation of the individual apart from that of society as a whole. It was this idea that gave the "Social" Gospel its unique significance. Professor Thompson wrote, "We have come to the end of a great era of mere individualism in religion, in politics, in economics. John Wesley, Adam Smith, and Jean Jacques Rousseau were the prophets of that age." [2]

[2] R. E. Thompson, *De civitate Dei*, p. 8.

In popularizing the notion of the saving of society rather than the individual, the Bampton Lectures of Canon Fremantle, *The World as the Object of Redemption*, were of great importance. They pointed out the ethical and religious significance of an organic view of society. Protestant theology, he said, with its undue emphasis on justification through faith and its preoccupation with the relationship of the individual soul to God, had contributed to the indifference concerning the saving of society. It had negated the influence which Christians should have on the organization of the Christian life and the influence which a Christian society or a society with the Christian spirit would exert on its members. "It had not dared to think of a saved and living society even as an object of hope." The Catholic Church more than the Protestant Church had retained this notion of a Christian society; yet it had never made the achievement of such a society a primary end of the Church—rather, it had set up the contrast of the heavenly city of Augustine, where the earthly city is merely the inn preparing the traveler for the better realm, and it had attempted to overlay society with Christian forms under the control of the clergy. "The main object of effort," he said, "is not to be found either in the saving of individual souls out of a ruined world, or in the organization of a separate society destined always to be held aloof from the world, but in the saving of the world itself." [3]

It is a curious fact that while the leaders of the Social Gospel attacked the individualism of Protestant theology, they themselves never completely transcended that tradition. Men such as Josiah Strong, Samuel Z. Batten, Francis G. Peabody, and Shailer Mathews wrote voluminously on the subject of the social teachings of Jesus, elaborating endlessly the social theme already so admirably stated by Canon Fremantle; yet in the end they remained individualists. At the conclusion of Shailer Mathews' *Social Teachings of Jesus* he wrote that if Christianity is to choose between the changing of society and the changing of individuals, it will choose the latter. Thus the so-called Social Gospel, as represented by many of its leading advocates, denied the major concept implicit in its title. This individualistic ap-

[3] Canon Fremantle, *The World as the Object of Redemption*.

proach to the problem of social reform was the more remarkable in view of the optimistic estimate of human nature which was a characteristic feature of most of the Social-Gospel literature. At this point the movement drew heavily upon the ideas of the Enlightenment with its optimistic conception of man's inherent goodness and perfectibility.

The result was that in its estimate of human nature social Christianity substituted eighteenth-century humanitarianism for the orthodox conception of "total depravity." The Christian orthodox position of the innate sinfulness of man and his need for grace went by the board. All imperfections and brutalities of man were attributed to social maladjustments which would yield easily to correction when once exposed to the light of reason and Christian idealism. The lag between the good envisaged and the lesser good actually achieved in terms of personal and social relationships was given an easy external interpretation. Human nature became evil or anti-social only when it was corrupted by society or ignorance.

The problem of evil ceased to be a stumbling block to the religious mind. There was almost no appreciation of the tragic incompleteness of life. It was naïvely assumed that given a better social state, a co-operative commonwealth, or even an adequate program of religious education, it would follow automatically that man would attain to all his ethical and aesthetic aspirations.

At one point only was there affinity between this optimistic view of human nature and the pessimistic attitude characteristic of traditional religious thought. Both regarded human nature as something given rather than as a product of social development. But Augustinian Christianity looked upon the raw stuff of personality as something essentially evil, while social Christianity held it to be good and perfectible. Thus social Christianity at this point had more in common with the ideas of Rousseau and the Enlightenment than with the main stream of Christian thought.

Granted this major assumption of the Social Gospel, that human nature in its given state was essentially good and only became corroded by external pressure from a corrupt society, then logically it would seem to follow that in seeking to improve the quality of life, one should attempt to reorganize and reform the social setting of human nature rather than to change or to convert human nature *per se*.

There was considerable unconscious hypocrisy in the early Social-Gospel movement, as there is in every religious movement with high ethical pretensions. Such hypocrisy arises with the assumption of a higher degree of disinterestedness than actually exists. The Social Gospel failed to do justice to the element of self-interest which always insinuates itself into every ethical pretension, whether of the individual or the group. Social Christianity claimed to transcend all temporal, provincial, and special interest and to prescribe an impartial justice for social conflicts. It overlooked the fact that the Church itself was predominantly a middle-class institution and that its pronouncements were colored by the special interests of that class. Hypocrisy arises not so much because of special pleading, for such an expression of self-interest when properly qualified is merely a desirable and an inevitable expression of the will to live; hypocrisy arises when the presence of such an increment of self-interest is unrecognized by a group which lays claim to an absolute disinterestedness.

The nature of this self-interest was manifest, for while citing the Kingdom of God on earth as the goal of social Christianity, whenever its outlines became concrete it could be observed to have curious similarity to the bourgeois world of the nineteenth century. Religious sanction was given only to those ethical attitudes indigenous to a bourgeois world.

Maintaining that they drew their inspiration and authority from the Scriptures and from Jesus, leaders of the movement abstracted from these sources notions in harmony with middle-class liberalism. Writers such as Shailer Mathews and Lyman Abbott stressed the parable of the mustard seed but tended to ignore the warnings of Jesus to the rich. In the vague beginnings of a militant labor movement, early leaders of social Christianity saw only the mutterings of an envious and greedy mob instead of the birth pangs of a new society. That such writers spoke of the "threat" of organized labor or the "threat" of socialism is evidence of the extent to which they conceived of the interests of religion as identical with the interests of the ruling class. To the rich and the powerful they addressed words of soft counsel, advising greater generosity to the poor; and to the poor they advised patience, submission, and the habit of looking for compensation for present trials in the next world. Religion, said Professor Thompson to his comfortable middle-class audience, must remind the poor . . .

that all this (deceitfulness of riches) is the shallow and outward judgment of those who look on appearances, and that no real good in life is denied to the humblest condition, while many of the best are possible to them alone, such as the constant mutual helpfulness and kindly service which are the monopoly almost of poor families and neighborhoods. It has to insist that this life is but the fore-court and preparation for another in which all inequalities are re-dressed, and the rich man who found his good things in purple, fine linens, and sumptuous fare, will have reason to envy the poor man who had to do without them and to find his good things in another quarter.[4]

For the most part leaders of the Social Gospel were liberals advocating an ethic of charity consonant with a conservative and aristocratic society and based on the assumption of a permanently class-divided world. In an early article in the *Bibliotheca sacra* Professor John Bascom speaks of the "wickedness" of an equalitarian society for it would destroy the essentially religious office of almsgiving. In his popular text *Christian Ethics* Newman Smyth, Professor Tucker's associate at Andover Theological Seminary, declared that charity is the highest attainable ethic. "The use and devotion of wealth to the broadest and highest human utilities is the supreme social obligation of the rich, which justice requires and which love expects." [5]

That the Church itself lived on the crumbs of philanthropy was responsible to no small degree for its giving to middle-class ethics a certain absoluteness. Thus, instead of critically examining the sources of great fortunes, Josiah Strong wrote that it is the duty of some men to have a "great deal of money" for their capacities for money-making were given to them by God and by

---

[4] Thompson, *op. cit.*, pp. 259-60.
[5] Newman Smyth, *Christian Ethics*, p. 463.

exercising them they enhance the possibilities of charity.[6] He quoted with evident approval the testimony of a man who had given fifty thousand dollars to a Christian College. "I cannot tell you what I have enjoyed; it is like being born into the Kingdom." [7]

The optimism of the Social Gospel concerning human nature united with the doctrine of evolution led to an optimistic interpretation of history. In the writing of Washington Gladden, references appeared often to a principle of progress, and his work was typical of almost all of the other exponents of social Christianity: Peabody, Strong, Mathews, Batten, Sprague, Taylor, Ely, and Bliss. "On the whole," wrote Gladden quoting H. G. Wells, "and nowadays almost steadily—things get better. There is a secular amelioration of life, and it is brought about by Good Will working through the efforts of men." [8] Gradually, but inevitably, the idea grew that the individualism of *laissez-faire* economics would give way to a society founded on good will and mutuality.[9]

New technical conditions of modern industrial society, with the social problems involved, were regarded with equanimity. Improved methods of transportation and communication were considered an indication that the world was being knit together. Steam and electricity would make the world a neighborhood and every man a neighbor, wrote Josiah Strong.[10] History, revelation, and science taught that the end of man was a perfect society, the New Jerusalem of the book of Revelation come down to earth. Francis G. Peabody saw in the humanitarian movement of reform a manifestation of a "social energy" implied in the teachings of Jesus. Let the Church turn this energy of Christian idealism and enthusiasm into the struggle for a new society, and the New Jerusalem would come automatically.[11]

Advocates of the Social Gospel borrowed from professional economists the idea of an evolutionary natural law that promoted economic equality. The general effect of this notion was a com-

[6] Josiah Strong, *Our Country*, p. 198.
[7] *Ibid.*, p. 221.
[8] H. G. Wells, quoted by Washington Gladden, *Recollections*, p. 312.
[9] *Ibid.*, p. 313.
[10] Strong, *The New Era*, p. 345.
[11] Francis G. Peabody, *Jesus Christ and the Social Question*, p. 358.

placent acquiescence in the *status quo* and an unwarranted optimism concerning the future. Henry C. Carey was quoted, "labor
is so rewarded out of the joint product of the two forces (capital
and labor) that there is a tendency toward equality of condition
among all classes." Professor Thompson concluded, therefore,
and his attitude was typical of the majority of the humanitarians
and liberals in the Social-Gospel movement, that the task of
religion is to reconcile individuals and conflicting groups, to
make them conscious of the unity of their interests, and to evoke
a motivation of good will among all men. The arguments for
such optimism were judged to be especially cogent in America.
Whereas the exploitation of the workers and peasants in Europe
was such that radical change might be necessary to insure a
modicum of justice to the workers, no such conditions existed
here. Put an American in the place of a European peasant, wrote
Strong, and there would be a revolution within twenty-four
hours. To be an American and an Anglo-Saxon in this generation
was to "stand on the mountain-top of privilege." [12] The entire
course of history was a moral development, exemplified in the
gradual emancipation of the masses. History was interpreted as
a steady unfolding and development of democracy in the course
of which Christian principles were made explicit. According to
Abbott the sequence was: Hebrews, Constantine, the popes,
Luther, America, paternalism, individualism; and tomorrow
there would be fraternalism.[13]

Reliance upon biological concepts rather than upon ideas
gained from a realistic analysis of economic facts obliterated
for liberals the fundamental truth of the divisive character of
capitalistic society. This contributed to their confusion in developing a proper technique for social change. It resulted in an
erroneous assumption of an underlying harmony of interests
between the working class and the owning class. On the basis of
this *a priori* judgment, liberal Christianity in the nineteenth
century took the position that the function of religion in time
of industrial conflict is to act as impartial arbitrator. At most, its
task was the promotion of a spirit of good will and brotherhood
among all classes.

[12] Strong, *Our Country,* p. 102.
[13] Lyman Abbott, *The Evolution of Christianity,* p. 188.

The church is tempted alternately to side with each party to the great dispute which divides modern society. On the one side lie wealth, social influence, the command of the means to carry out great schemes for the promotion of the cause of Christianity; on the other side lie the numbers for whose welfare the church itself exists, and whose indifference or hostility may seem likely to be overcome by a hearty partisanship for their interests and wishes. It was the former temptation which prevailed a generation ago; it is the latter which is unbalancing many of the brightest spirits now. Each is equally mistaken.[14]

This dependence on good will alone as a technique of social change led to futility. It failed to do justice to the vicious character of the struggle inherent within a society divided into an owning class and an exploited class; and again it overlooked the rôle which self-interest played in individual and group action.

The failure to appreciate the place of interest in shaping ethical concepts made it impossible to appreciate the place of economic power in politics. American democracy was judged to be the expression of Christian brotherhood. "The ballot of the millionaire or of his brother carry the same weight . . . influence depends upon wealth and position but political power does not" wrote Lyman Abbott.[15]

The futility of Christianity in effective social action was heightened by the influence of the "historical movement" in religion which paralleled the rise of historical science in the nineteenth century. When it was found that Christianity has a history, that it is possible that the religion of Jesus has little in common with the form of religion practiced in His name, and that the ethical ideals of religion have been conditioned by the culture of each succeeding age which embraced it, the idea gained currency that the failure of Christianity to make its ethical ideal effective in society was due to an impure interpretation of the teachings of Jesus. Christianity had been appropriated by Constantine and had been corrupted ever since. Now let the pure ethical teachings of Jesus be recovered through scientific research; let them be made known to the world, and a rebirth of dynamic ethical religion would follow, transforming society. Instead of overcoming the world, Christianity had been overcome

¹⁴ Thompson, *op. cit.*   ¹⁵ Abbott, *Christianity and Social Problems*, p. 46.

by the world. The pure form of apostolic religion, as it was before it had become tarnished by the accretions of theological dogma and ritual, must be proclaimed by Christianity. The failure of Christianity to make the New Jerusalem concrete in this world was charged to the eclecticism of historic Christianity. It was thought that ethical difficulties were psychological and not objective. It was the Christian ideal, now turned aside from the pure ethics of Jesus, that was at fault; not the economic process.

This good-will ethic tended to abjure all considerations of the objective conditions of society. Pathological social conditions, it was said, were due to an inadequate ethical ideal, whereas the real truth of the matter was to be found in the character of social life. The attempt to replace the each-for-himself psychology of capitalism without first changing the economic base of capitalism would be to defy all that had been made known of the springs of human action. While paying lip-service to the mutuality of Christianity, men could not make their actions comply with that ideal so long as self-survival and the needs of their families demanded action along contrary lines. Not many men will affirm an ideal at the expense of self-extinction and disloyalty to family obligations, which is involved in attempting to live according to the precepts of the Sermon on the Mount in a society based on ruthless competition for profit.

The Social Gospel exhibited less political realism than either proletarian radicalism or profound prophetic religion, which places a truer estimate upon the refractory and obstinate nature of self-interest. Proletarians who have suffered at the hands of ruthless power entrenched in an industrial system and who have tried all of the avenues of moderation and of moral suasion, conclude that such power will continue to utilize its control of society to increase its advantage until finally justice can only be achieved by a violent revolution in which the sources of power are brought under the control of workers. Also, highly ethical religion, such as that of the Old Testament prophets and the religion of Jesus built upon them, sees human society from the perspective of a holy and just God who forgives man but also judges him. He forgives seventy times seven, until society reaches such proportions of injustice and sin that God in His righteousness destroys it and lays the the citadels of power low. Thus the prophet and the profoundly religious soul is always pessimistic with regard to the present; but he differs from the cynic or complete pessimist by his hopeful attitude toward the future. He is optimistic because of his confidence that God will form a better society out of the ashes of the present world.

Among Christian socialists the concept of gradualism had the effect of toning down the idea of socialism until it meant little more than a vague organic unity of the race. Under this interpretation of the term anyone who granted the validity of some measure of interdependence and mutual obligation among men might call himself a socialist. Even Professor Hitchcock, of Union Theological Seminary, a bitter foe of scientific socialism, on occasion called himself a socialist. The work of the Reverend W. D. P. Bliss and the Reverend Philo W. Sprague, the two most important writers in the Society of Christian Socialists, shows the influence of the contemporary ideas of evolution, progress, and positivism. They assumed that in society the operation of natural law makes progress inevitable. Ultimately, the necessary operation of this law would make the achievement of a socialist society a certainty. It was a point of view which prompted piecemeal reform. Under this conception every slight gain in working conditions or labor legislation was heralded as a step toward the Kingdom of God. Christian socialism came to be regarded as a method; the social goal was all but lost to view. All of the emphasis was upon gradualism. Socialists, wrote Sprague, "are more evolutionists than revolutionists." [16] Socialism would evolve, "naturally, as a growth, a development, a stage in social evolution." [17]

When the good-will ethic was translated into a practical strategy it took the form of upholding law and order and opposing all forms of rebellion and revolt. The net result was that social Christianity was delivered into the hands of the ruling class as one more instrument for keeping the proletarian group quiescent. Here again the Social Gospel gave evidence of its middle-class origin and background. A bourgeois society always

[16] Philo W. Sprague, *Christian Socialism*, p. 32.
[17] *Ibid.*, p. 10.

emulates peace, harmony, and good will and makes a virtue of submission to authority. A proletarian group emphasizes justice, to the point of rebellion if need be, and regards revolt against tyranny and injustice as a higher ethical standard than arbitrary resignation and meekness of spirit. It makes much of righteous indignation. A powerful ruling class usually resorts to violence in suppressing insurrection and rationalizes its abuse of a rebellious minority by an appeal to the necessity of maintaining law and order. It is not noted that behind such an argument is a gratuitous assumption that the interests of the ruling class coincide with the general interest; nor does it take into consideration that no peace founded on injustice can be enduring. Whenever the privileges or livelihood of a considerable minority are abrogated or abridged, there will be rebellion. In such a situation high religion will choose justice rather than peace.

The middle-class emphasis of the Social Gospel on law and order also failed to take account of the extent to which the local and national forces of government were dominated by the ruling financial interests. During the period under observation troops and legal machinery were used indiscriminately by local and Federal authorities to protect property rights and to maintain the *status quo* under the guise of maintaining law and order. But the implications of this fact were not appreciated. The truth of Lenin's remark that a bourgeois government is the executive committee of the capitalist class had not yet been realized.

Further testimony to the confusion of the Social Gospel at this point is seen in the occasional affirmations of the priority of justice over peace, a preference which is disregarded when planning a strategy for social change. "War," said Washington Gladden, "is a great evil. . . . But it is not the greatest evil. The permanent degradation of men who do the world's work would be a greater evil." [18] Then he characterized capitalism as a system under which workers are reduced to a permanent state of degradation; but when he came to consider the practical job of changing that system, he fell back upon the bourgeois fallacy of thinking that it could be done by moral suasion, by resorting to "reason and good will." [19]

[18] Washington Gladden, *Recollections,* p. 312.   [19] *Ibid.,* p. 304.

This fallacy based on moral and rational optimism, so characteristic of social Christianity, which ignored the obstinate resistance with which intrenched interests fought off all efforts to qualify its power, is the more remarkable when coupled with a realistic analysis of social forces. Men like Francis G. Peabody and Shailer Mathews, who theorized about the social struggle and never came to grips with practical situations, of course, had almost no inkling of the real facts involved in radical social change. On the other hand, Washington Gladden, Wendell Phillips, and W. D. P. Bliss, men actively identified with the labor movement, seemed to appreciate the tenacity with which a dominant economic class retains its advantage, and the violence to which it would resort whenever its prerogatives were challenged in serious fashion. These men frankly admitted that industrial life is a form of war, and recognized that whatever gains labor had been able to make in wresting privilege from the owning class had come through labor unions. The advantages, they acknowledged, were proportioned among the workers in direct ratio to the strength and militancy of their organizations, and they tacitly recognized the necessity for coercion. "If war is the order of the day, we must grant to labor belligerent rights," wrote Gladden.[20] The plain implications of this analysis cried for an active co-operation on the part of ethical idealists with labor groups seeking social change. Gladden was one of the worst offenders in promoting the opposite point of view. Instead of frankly recognizing the struggle and throwing in the lot of religious forces with the workers, to give practical ethical direction to the former, social Christianity held aloof from the struggle or else counseled patience and moral suasion.

It would be an injustice, however, as the following pages will bear out, to say that all the members of the Social-Gospel group were theorists who refrained from active participation in the day-to-day struggles of workers. There were a few men whose actions, like those of Bliss, belied their own philosophies, who gave their support to labor in defending and enhancing its position through strikes, boycotts, and legislative coercion.

[20] *Ibid.*, p. 301.

Was it (the Pullman strike) wise? . . . We emphatically say yes! Must America slowly sink to European and Asiatic conditions? There was no help save by workingmen standing together and declaring one majestic no! . . . Congress would not help and the church only talks and that not very plainly . . . The strike was costly but it was worth it. Only by standing together can workingmen possibly to-day gain their rights.[21]

In this statement and in other statements it was implicitly recognized that while it might be possible for the individual to transcend interest and attain to some measure of disinterestedness, this was not to be expected in group relations. A face-to-face ethic was not to be relied upon in social conflict. Nor could the mere appeal to the good will of the employer be counted upon to achieve justice. Justice would not be handed down from above. The appeal to good will must be supplemented by some measure of coercion exercised by the organization of the oppressed group. Unfortunately, however, these obvious inferences, from concrete situations and personal experience, did not form the basis for Bliss's social philosophy. There was a wide discrepancy between his actions and his theories.

The man of the entire Social-Gospel group who saw most clearly the nature of the problem involved in social change was the Reverend George D. Herron, by far the most able man prominent in the early days of the movement. He rejected the subjectivist approach to social change. The appeal to motivation, he said, was not sufficient, for the most ruthless social injustice was often perpetrated by "good" people. He pointed out the paradox of a brutal society composed of good men and explained how a society of good people might yet be greedy, vicious, and godless in many of its operations.[22] The merit of his position was that he saw with clear insight how economics conditioned ethical attitudes. "How can we obey Christ's law of love," he asked, "when every industrial maxim, custom, fact and principle renders that law inoperative." [23] Thus the primary task of religion, he wrote, was to revolutionize that economic

[21] W. D. P. Bliss, *The Dawn*, VI (1894), 7-8.
[22] George D. Herron, *The Larger Christ*, p. 31.
[23] Herron, "The Social System and the Christian Conscience," in *The Kingdom*, August 18, 1898.

base of society. The daily activities of men in their normal relations with their brothers must be made consistent with the operation of brotherhood. The economic structure within which these activities operated, must be changed. The drive for private profits must be replaced by concern for the welfare of the entire body of workers; then the premium now placed on the acquisitive anti-social traits of human nature would give way to mass approval of social tendencies in society.

With the exception of a small minority represented by George D. Herron, it may be said that the dominant philosophy of proponents of the Social Gospel in the eighties and nineties was liberalism, which carried over as the major emphasis of the movement until the World War. For a definite program religious liberalism borrowed from the reform movement in politics. It reached its climax in the Progressive Movement of 1912 when churchmen went to the polls singing "Onward Christian Soldiers." That liberalism, not radicalism, was the rallying point of social Christianity is partly to be explained by a reference to the social environment of the movement. The economic situation in the United States during the last three decades of the nineteenth century was more conducive to liberal than to radical thought. Radical philosophies originated in Europe, where class lines were more sharply drawn and where the policies of preemption had been more rigorously developed. It was more difficult in the United States to demonstrate the need for a revolutionary program. An expanding economy kept alive the hope of the underprivileged that they could rise into the favored classes. People still believed that capitalism would in time bring prosperity, wealth, and abundance to all. The American worker and farmer still refused to accept the idea that his social status was fixed permanently. A few writers such as Henry George, Henry D. Lloyd, and George D. Herron were pointing out the drift of events, that class lines were becoming more sharply defined, that the logic of the inherent contradictions within capitalism was leading inevitably to more and more concentration of wealth, to the enrichment of the few at the expense of the masses. But there were few who apprehended the cogency of their arguments.

II

STEPHEN COLWELL: NEW THEMES FOR THE
PROTESTANT CLERGY

IN THE early days of the social movement in American Christianity the most important works were written not by clergymen but by writers in the field of political economy. One of the earliest significant books to treat the problems of an industrial order viewed from the perspective of the Christian ethic was written by Stephen Colwell, wealthy Philadelphia manufacturer and trustee of Princeton Theological Seminary, who divided his time between industry, religion, and the study of political economy. He was the first of a distinguished line of students in the field of political economy, including Richard T. Ely, Henry George, Edward Bellamy, and Henry D. Lloyd, whose works resulted in a unique development within American Christianity known as the Social-Gospel movement.

As early as 1851 Stephen Colwell published a book, *New Themes for the Protestant Clergy,* discussing the relation of religion to the political and economic order. The book exhibits the influence of the author's wide reading in European literature and suggests the influence of Saint-Simon, Comte, and Sismondi.[1] Christianity, the author stated, had become so overlaid with theology and critical studies that it was no longer honestly entitled to be called by the name of its founder. The Church and the clergy had taken on the character of bourgeois institutions— complacent, comfortable defenders of the existing order. The edge of their critical ethical faculties had been dulled by financial endowments. They had concentrated their energies on luxurious churches from which the poor were excluded and had concerned themselves almost exclusively with confessions, prayer

[1] An appreciation of Sismondi's work appeared in Colwell's preliminary essay for Matile's translation of Frederick List's *National System of Political Economy* (Philadelphia, 1856).

books, theology, faith, and doctrine, all of which are irrelevant
to the essentially ethical function of Christianity. Their purpose
was to make religion operative in human relations, to develop a
social economy consonant with the teachings of Jesus.[2] The economic order then existing, exalting profits above human values,
had nothing in common with Christianity.

This buying at the cheapest rates, not regarding the hardship to him
who sells, and selling at the dearest rate possible, not regarding the
interest of him who buys—this position in trade or in society which
makes it not only the interest, but the natural course, of everyone
to prey upon his fellowmen . . . is well fitted to carry selfishness to
its highest limits . . . This idea of considering men as mere ma-
chines for the purpose of creating and distributing wealth, may do
very well to round off the periods, syllogisms, and statements of
political economists; but the whole notion is totally and irreconcil-
ably at variance with Christianity.[3]

Colwell saw in the vague stirring of revolt among the workers
of the world a natural and desirable reaction against injustice.
He cautioned "stern Christian conservatives" not to denounce
them. "Let the voice of Christian ministers be heard addressing
them in tones of kindness and encouragement." [4]

The lack of faith in so-called infidels, often might be traced,
he said, to a passion for the welfare of humanity which had been
outraged by the failure of organized religion to lend assistance
to their work of reform. He named Paine as an example. "They
find Christians arrayed against their plans, and they immediately
array themselves against Christianity." [5] He was writing three
years after the publication of the Communist Manifesto, although there is no evidence that he was familiar with it, and
before the appearance of *Das Kapital;* yet he had an appreciation of how ethical attitudes were conditioned by interest.

It is plain that the institutions of this world, political, social, commercial, and industrial, we had almost said religious, partake little
of the spirit of Christ; and yet his ministers and disciples are its most
noted and uncompromising defenders. Is it because these ministers
and disciples are so well treated by the world, that they are in such
strict league with it, and are so prompt to take its part? [6] [Rulers

[2] Stephen Colwell, *New Themes for the Protestant Clergy,* p. 244.
[3] *Ibid.,* pp. 240-41.   [4] *Ibid.,* p. 221.
[5] *Ibid.,* p. 267.   [6] *Ibid.,* p. 198.

are not the chief obstacle to reform, but:] . . . Large classes of men are interested everywhere in preserving the existing order of things intact—All change in their estimation threatens some sacrifice of position, or power, or wealth, or influence on their part . . . They mould literature and public opinion.[7]

Colwell was not a socialist and preferred the method of Christian "charity"—a term which he used in the sense of brotherliness, not as mere almsgiving—yet he saw in socialism's demand for social justice and in its criticism of capitalism a position which seemed to have much in common with Christianity. Therefore he was anxious to make common cause with it.

We look upon the whole socialist movement as one of the greatest events of this age. We believe no man can understand the progress of humanity or its present tendencies who does not make himself, to some extent, acquainted with the teachings of socialism, and does not watch its movements. It is regarded by many, especially by Protestant divines, as a war upon Christianity. This betrays ignorance . . . it is stubborn and wicked conservatism which is rooted to one spot in this world of evil, refusing to believe in anything better, scouting humanity as a dream, not conceding to Christianity the trimuphs which are assured by its own promises, offering to Christ this present world as now exhibited, or none,—not perceiving that the social, political, and commercial institutions of the present day, founded on and sustained by a selfishness heretofore unequalled are the great barriers to the progress of Christianity. The works of socialists have exposed this hideous skeleton of selfishness—they have pursued it with unfaltering hatred; and this constitutes our main obligation to them . . . they have burst away from the chains of superstition, false morals, and false social science. Who is able to instruct them? . . . It does not meet the objections which they offer when the Catholic priesthood say to them that they must not oppose the authority of the church, that the church will take care of them, that she will make up in alms what they be wanting for their sustenance from the avails of industry. Nor is the case made better when they are told by Protestants that their position is the one assigned them in the order of Providence, which cannot be changed nor resisted without fatal consequences; that their misery and suffering are the natural results of that depravity inherent in human nature and inherited from our first parents, and that we can no more banish wretchedness and poverty than we can eradicate original sin. Neither do the political economists meet the case by urging that the laws of trade are founded upon the very nature of things . . . and that these

[7] Colwell, *Politics for American Christians*, p. 15.

laws cannot be altered because their working may not be equally favorable to all. . . . It would be a useful task to glance over pages thus in contrast, and entertain our readers with socialists pleading the cause of humanity, and Christians taking the part of wealth and power.[8]

While the work of Colwell was received with scorn by his professional religious contemporaries, it served the purpose of drawing attention to the neglected social obligations of Christianity, particularly to industrial problems, at a time when all of the ethical indignation of the North was directed against the slave-holding South, and when the only criticism of wage slavery from religious sources came from the South. His book precipitated a vigorous debate. A second edition was required at once. The criticism from religious quarters was not entirely hostile. The Reverend E. W. H. Ruffner published a small book, *Charity and the Clergy,* defending Colwell. "Socialism," Ruffner wrote, "has no essential connection with any anti-Christian idea." [9]

[8] Colwell, *New Themes,* pp. 359-63.
[9] In the next few years Colwell published two more books reiterating the thesis of *New Themes: Politics for American Christians; a Word upon Our Example as a Nation, Our Labor, Our Trade, Elections, Education and Congressional Legislation* (1852), and *The Position of Christianity in the United States in Its Relations with Our Political Institutions* (1854).

III

HENRY GEORGE, A PROPHET OF SOCIAL JUSTICE

AS AN obscure compositor and journalist, eking out a meager existence on the Pacific coast under the constant pressure of extreme poverty, Henry George gave little evidence that he would one day become a great prophet, and perhaps America's greatest social philosopher. His wife pawned her trinkets. He printed labels on a job press to barter for wood, food, and milk. When his second child was born and the doctor told him mother and child were starving, he asked the first well-dressed man he met for $5.00. Had the man refused, gentle Henry George was prepared to knock the man down.

It was natural that Henry George should have attracted religiously minded people to his standard, for he founded his theories of social reform upon a religious base. Starting with his interest in social justice he elaborated a religious philosophy of ethical theism. God was the spiritual reality behind the universe from which emanated the urge toward justice. A happy turn of mind and combination of personal qualities equipped Henry George for his task. He perceived the truths established by modern psychology relating to the social sources of personality. Progress, therefore, was not merely a question of improving human nature, as the traditional religionist of his generation believed, but of changing society. He saw with a clear eye the importance of economic relationships as primary factors in a developing culture.

Henry George looked at life through the eyes of a Hebrew prophet. He was appalled by the suffering and poverty of his generation. His religious and social ideas are to be interpreted against this personal background of deep concern with the struggle to attain social justice. He had no interest in theory *per se.* Ideas, either in the field of political economy or religion, were to be judged instrumentally according to their efficiency in assisting man to achieve a more just society.

The name of political economy has been constantly invoked against every effort of the working classes to increase their wages or decrease their hours of labor. Take the best and most extensively circulated text-books. While they insist upon freedom for capital, while they justify on the ground of utility the selfish greed that seeks to pile fortune on fortune, and the niggard spirit that steels the heart to the wail of distress, what sign of substantial promise do they hold out to the working man save that he should refrain from rearing children? [1]

The religious faith of Henry George came to him as the result of his inquiry into the causes of poverty. His Scotch and English parents were intensely religious. Morning and evening prayers were part of the family routine. This early religious environment had a profound effect upon his entire life. His naturally religious piety was offended, however, in early youth by the seeming irreconcilable facts of a beneficent Deity and the suffering and want of workers.

It was not until he had completed his analysis of the economic activities of man and had discovered that the degradation and poverty of men was caused not by God's providence but by man's violation of the will of God that his faith was restored. As a result of his study *Progress and Poverty* he said: " . . . out of this inquiry has come to me something I did not expect to find, and a faith that was dead revives." [2]

The religious problem which was basic for George was also his central problem in political economy. Stated in economic terms the problem was: how shall we account for poverty in the midst of plenty? And in its religious aspect the problem was: given a benevolent Creator active in human affairs, how can we account for the presence of want, suffering, and starvation? The urgency of the problem had been impressed upon George when as a youth he visited New York, where he was impressed by the contrast between the poverty of the East Side and the luxury of the West Side. The increase of man's capacity to satisfy human wants by harnessing power had the paradoxical effect, he was

[1] George, *Life*, p. 277.　　　　　　　　[2] *Ibid.*, p. 277.

puzzled to find, of making the struggle for existence more intense.

. . . human labor is becoming the cheapest of commodities. Beside glutted warehouses human beings grow faint with hunger and shiver with cold; under the shadow of churches festers the vice that is born of want.[3]

The problem which began to trouble George in the seventies and to the solution of which he spent his life, is stated in the first chapter of his classic, *Progress and Poverty*. A Franklin or a Priestley, he said, on being told of the technological advances of the next one hundred years would have inferred

that labor-saving inventions would lighten the toil and improve the condition of the laborer; that the enormous increase in the power of producing wealth would make poverty a thing of the past . . . he would have beheld these new forces elevating society from its very foundations, lifting the very poorest above the possibility of want, exempting the very lowest from anxiety for the material needs of life; he would have seen these slaves of the lamp of knowledge taking on themselves the traditional curse, these muscles of iron and sinews of steel making the poorest laborer's life a holiday, in which every high quality and noble impulse could have scope to grow . . . Now, however, we are coming into collision with facts which there can be no mistaking. From all parts of the civilized world come complaints of industrial depression; of labor condemned to involuntary idleness; of capital massed and wasting; of pecuniary distress among business men; of want and suffering and anxiety among working classes. All the dull, deadening pain, all the keen, maddening anguish, that to great masses of men are involved in the word "hard times," afflict the world to-day. This state of things, common to communities differing so widely in situation, in political institutions, in fiscal and financial systems, in density of population and in social organization, can hardly be accounted for by local causes . . . there is distress where protective tariffs stupidly and wastefully hamper trade, but there is also distress where trade is nearly free; there is distress where autocratic government yet prevails, but there is distress where political power is wholly in the hands of the people . . . evidently, beneath all such things as these we must infer a common cause . . . I propose to seek the law which associates poverty with progress, and increases want with advancing wealth . . .[4]

By a careful analysis of history George proved to his own

[3] George, *Moses* (pamphlet).   [4] George, *Progress and Poverty*, pp. 3-12.

satisfaction that poverty is the result of certain maladjustments within society which it is within the powers of society easily to remedy. He explained rationally why poverty is a function of progress and advanced a solution for the problem. There need be poverty only so long as society wills it. Involuntary poverty is unnecessary.

How a casual conversation with a teamster put George in possession of the "clew-end of the tangled skein of economic theory" is told in the *Life of Henry George* by his son. "Stopping for breath, I asked a passing teamster, for want of something better to say, what land was worth there. He pointed to some cows grazing off so far they looked like mice and said: 'I don't know exactly, but there is a man over there who will sell some land for a thousand dollars an acre.' Like a flash it came upon me that there was the reason of advancing poverty with advancing wealth. With the growth of population, land grows in value, and the men who work it must pay more for the privilege. I turned back, amidst quiet thought, to the perception that then came to me and has been with me ever since." [5]

The theory of George was set forth first in a pamphlet *Our Land and Land Policy*. Some ten years later it was expanded into book form under the title of *Progress and Poverty*, published in 1880. His thesis is based on the Ricardian definition of rent as the differential between the wealth which can be produced on a given piece of land and the wealth produced on land at the lowest subsistence level. The value of land may be regarded from two perspectives: the value it has because of its productive capacity and the value it has because of the density of population. All the value of land in excess of its "use" value is created by society at large; hence it is the part of reason and justice that society should benefit as a whole by the wealth which it collectively creates. George's proposal was that society should recapture these "social values" by confiscation. Society would take over the virtual ownership of the land by a tax equal to the rental value, and the revenue thus obtained would be applied to social services. Such a tax would be sufficient to finance the government. All other forms of taxation would be remitted. This program not only commends itself to reason but it is just, conforming to the eighteenth century principle of "rights" basic

[5] George, *Life*, p. 210.

in the philosophy of George. Property created by man's own labor remained in his possession; society only claimed that part of his income which represented unearned increment, to which the individual had made no contribution from his labor. Obviously this was not a theory which destroyed private property.

After he had demonstrated that poverty is the result of man's cupidity, to attribute it to God's providence smacked of high hypocrisy. It was to degrade religion; to treat it like a cloak with which to cover man's greed and brutality. ". . . though it may take the form of prayer, it is blasphemy." [6]

What sort of God is it that the Rev. Dr. Huntington worships and to whom the Episcopal collects and liturgy are addressed? Does the rector of Grace Church really think that the "most merciful Father," "Our Father which art in heaven," is really allowing bitter injustice and want to continue among His children in New York City and elsewhere simply because the Episcopal Church does not formally ask Him every Sunday "to suffer not the hire of the laborer to be kept back by fraud"? . . . Is the want and suffering that exist in the centers of our civilization to-day, the bitter struggle among human beings to live, and the vice and the crime and the greed that grow out of that struggle, because of God's neglect or because of man's? Is it in accordance with the will of God or is it because of man's violation of God's will? . . . Human laws disinherit God's children on their very entrance into the world . . . If he ignores this wrong and robbery, and yet prays to God to relieve injustice and want, his prayer is an insult to God and an injury to man. [7]

There is no scripture, said George, more abused than "The poor ye have always with you," used to support the view that the Most Merciful Father had decreed that a given number of His people should suffer want in order that another class might have the pleasure and virtue of doling out alms. Suppose, he said, that as a result of our importuning the Creator were to answer by making the earth more prolific; suppose that two blades were to grow in place of one; that the harvest were to increase a hundredfold. Would poverty disappear? No! "The classes that now monopolize the bounty of the Creator would monopolize all the new bounty." [8] And the increase in technology, in fact, by means of which the natural energies of coal, oil, gas, and

[6] George, *Progress and Poverty*, p. 546.
[7] George, in *The Standard*, January (1890), quoted by Geiger.
[8] George, *Progress and Poverty*, p. 547.

water power are utilized to increase material goods have had the
same effect upon the production of wealth that an increase in the
fertility of nature would have. "The effect has simply been to
make the few richer; the many more helpless!" [9]

Other writers in the field of political economy had a well-
defined religious interest. Frequently, however, in the work of
such men these two interests seemed to have little logical affinity.
Sometimes they stood in actual conflict. The distinguishing
mark of Henry George is his attempt to resolve the tension between the two fields of interest. As a result, George conceived
every problem in political economy as first a religious problem.
Ends toward which society should move were given by religion;
means of attaining these goals were given by economics and
politics. Through religious insights equality was established as
an ultimate social goal. Political and economic arrangements
must be directed toward this goal. "Though Christianity became
distorted and alloyed in percolating through a rotting civilization . . . yet her essential idea of the equality of men has never
wholly been destroyed." [10]

It can be demonstrated, thought George, that equality, which
he identified with justice, is not only a religious demand but also
essentially a prerequisite for the proper functioning of society.
This can be made clear by an examination of the nature of progress. Association and justice, he said, are the two essential factors
of progress. It is obvious that the advances of modern civilization in the sciences and industry are due to co-operative enterprise, and it would have been impossible to attain them by
mere individual effort. Also progress is a function of equality.
Inequality is followed inevitably by the enslavement of the
many in the interests of the few. The lives of the many, therefore, will be spent in the mere satisfaction of the demands of
the struggle for existence. The untapped cultural riches of
these industrial slaves is thus left as one of the undeveloped
cultural resources of society. "The mental power which can be
devoted to progress is only what is left after what is required for
non-progressive purposes." In the category of "non-progressive
purposes" were placed the energy spent in the struggle for the

[9] *Ibid.*, p. 548.   [10] *Ibid.*, p. 520.

satisfaction of desire at the expense of others, and in resistance
to such aggression, which drains off so much of the energy of
nonequalitarian societies. Justice or equality was thus raised to
the dignity of law, the supreme law of the universe.[11] Justice was
an essential concept, then, for the science of political economy;
and it was a deeply rooted religious idea. Thus religion and
political economy are in agreement, giving evidence of an ethical
principle operating in human affairs, affording new authority to
the Gospels.

. . . political science and social science cannot teach any lessons that
were not embraced in the simple truths taught to poor fishermen and
Jewish peasants by One who eighteen hundred years ago was crucified—the simple truths, which, beneath the warpings of selfishness
and the distortions of superstition, seem to underlie every religion
that has ever striven to formulate the spiritual yearnings of man.[12]

This urge toward justice in human affairs is given a metaphysical basis through the insights of religion. It becomes the
will of God operating in history, and it is available as a source
of inspiration to all reformers and prophets explaining in part
their ethical vigor.

From the depths of the unseen such characters (Moses) must draw
their strength; from fountains that flow only from the pure in heart
must come their wisdom. Of something more real than matter; of
something higher than the stars; of a light that will endure when
suns are dead and dark; of a purpose of which the physical universe
is but a passing phase, such lives tell.[13]

One result of this identification of religion and political
economy in the thought of George was that with the Hebrew
prophets he looked upon all history as the divine law in human
life. He boldly declared that an ethically unsound society cannot
be politically stable. It must be changed and made to conform to
more ethical standards or it must be destroyed. "This is the
lesson of the centuries. Unless its foundations be laid in justice
the social structure cannot stand." [14] The implications of this
thesis for the United States in the year of 1879 were clear.

Our primary social adjustment is a denial of justice. In allowing one
man to own the land on which and from which other men must live,

---

[11] *Ibid.*, p. 542.   [12] *Ibid.*, p. 523.
[13] George, *Moses.*   [14] George, *Progress and Poverty, p.* 545.

we have made them his bondsmen in a degree which increases as material progress goes on. This is the subtle alchemy that in ways they do not realize is extracting from the masses in every civilized country the fruits of their weary toil; that is instituting a harder and more hopeless slavery in place of that which has been destroyed; that is bringing political despotism out of political freedom, and must soon transmute democratic institutions into anarchy . . .

Toward the end of his work *Progress and Poverty* this catastrophic note is made more explicit. "It is the delusion which precedes destruction that sees in the popular unrest with which the civilized world is feverishly pulsing only the passing effect of ephemeral causes."

Can it be that the gifts of the Creator may be thus misappropriated with impunity? Is it a light thing that labor should be robbed of its earnings while greed rolls in wealth—that the many should want while the few are surfeited? Turn to history, and on every page may be read the lesson that such wrong never goes unpunished; that the Nemesis that follows injustice never falters nor sleeps! Look around to-day. Can this state of things continue? May we even say, "After us the deluge"? Nay, the pillars of the state are trembling even now, and the very foundations of society begin to quiver with pent-up forces that grow underneath. The struggle that must either rectify, or convulse in ruin, is near at hand, if it be not already begun.[15]

The final chapter of *Progress and Poverty* entitled "Conclusion, the Problem of Individual Life," is an epilogue on the subject of immortality. It has but little logical connection with the main body of his thought, indicated by the opening words, "My task is done." It is more in the nature of a confession of faith. That a treatise on political economy should end with a discourse on immortality is further evidence of the close relationship in his thought between practical problems and religion. Immortality seemed to be demanded as a capstone for his conception of the ethical character of the universe. It was a "metaphysical necessity." The struggle in this life to attain justice, to create beauty, to apprehend truth points toward a life beyond where such aspirations may be fulfilled or more fully realized. A belief in immortality, however, does not rest upon logical demonstration; the validity of such belief, said George, rests finally upon the validity of poetic insight.

[15] *Ibid.*, p. 548.

That the religious ideas of George did not have more influence
was due partly to the fact that he wrote as a layman, and
partly to the fact that he attacked vigorously the vested interests
of his day. His religious ideas suffered from the general disre-
pute into which his thought and action brought him in the bourgeois world. There was, of course, the additional contributing
factor that then, as now, religion was valued more as a consolation than as a spur to ethical action; more as an escape from
unpleasant facts than as an aid in creating new facts. Nevertheless, George did have a considerable following in religious circles. A number of influential clergymen in both the Catholic and
Protestant churches supported his reform work.[16] Also he found
some followers among those of Hebrew faith. Among the distinguished religious leaders in the New York area who openly
approved his ideas and lent their support with varying degrees
of enthusiasm to his work of reform were R. Heber Newton, of
All Souls' Episcopal Church; J. O. S. Huntington, son of
Bishop Huntington, of Syracuse, and head of the Episcopal
Order of the Holy Cross; Edward McGlynn, for twenty-five
years priest of St. Stephen's Church; Rabbi Gustave Gottheil;
Lyman Abbott, editor of the *Christian Union;* John W. Kram-
mer; Henry Ward Beecher, of the Plymouth Congregational
Church, Brooklyn; Richard L. Burtsell, of the Epiphany
Church; and Thomas A. Ducey, of St. Leo's Catholic Church.
A group of Swedenborgians formed the "New Churchmen's
Single Tax League" for the purpose of propagating his ideas.
Their journal, *The New Earth* (1889–90), was edited jointly by
John Filner, L. W. Wilmarth, A. J. Anchterlonie, and Alice
Thatcher.[17]

George's work as a reformer and lecturer took him on several
trips abroad, where he also received the support of clergymen.
The Reverend Hugh Gilmore, of Adelaide, South Australia, he
called a "Dr. McGlynn of South Australia." [18] In England he

---

[16] His theories were discussed in seminary classes in Christian Sociology (cf.
the Oberlin catalogue for 1894-95). An extended treatment of his ideas appeared
in the *Andover Review*, VI (1886), 421 ff. And President Andrews, lecturing at
Andover in 1889 on the subject "Some special bearings of political economy on
ethics" included a discussion of his work.

[17] Post, *The Prophet of San Francisco*, p. 50.

[18] George, *Life*, p. 533.

was assisted by the following clergymen: Stewart D. Headlam, Phillip A. Wickstead, J. E. Symes, J. M. Cruikshanks, M. Hastings, and others. Cardinal Manning, while not openly espousing his theory, was his friend. When the two met in London, Henry George said, "I loved the people, and that brought me to Christ as their best friend and teacher." "And I," said the Cardinal, "loved Christ, and so learned to love the people for whom he died." [19]

In 1885, urged by his boyhood friend, R. Heber Newton, Henry George addressed the ninth Congress of the Episcopal Church, at Detroit, on the subject, "Is Our Civilization Just to Workingmen?" To his emphatic "No" the conference responded with applause. But, for the most part, the Church at that time was scarcely aware that a labor problem existed or that religion has any responsibility for social matters. Individual clergymen who did advocate the economic ideas of George as a means of achieving social justice were apt to be subjected to the ecclesiastical discipline accorded to Edward McGlynn and Robert C. Bryant. The latter was pastor of the Floral Avenue Baptist Church, Binghamton, N. Y. He was advised to stop preaching the "single tax" or leave his pulpit. He left. Wealthy members of the church who had profited through real estate transactions objected when their pastor identified speculation in vacant lots with gambling. They refused to give financial support to the church. Bryant was notified that his

sermons on social questions were hurting the revenues of the church and that he would have to stop preaching along that line . . . It is said that there are four other preachers in this city who believe just as Mr. Bryant does, and they, too, have been warned against the preaching of "Georgism." [In his letter of resignation Bryant said] The labor problem must be settled upon a basis of right and justice before we can prosper as a nation. [His opponents are reported as saying that Bryant] has for some time been delivering sermons upon single tax instead of preaching the gospel, and they don't propose to get the socialistic, anarchistic or any other crazy theory instilled into the minds of their children before they learn to repeat the Lord's Prayer.[20]

[19] *Ibid.*, p. 438.
[20] The *New York Sun*, January 30 (1898), quoted in *The Kingdom*, February 10 (1898).

One of the stanchest supporters of George was the Catholic priest Edward McGlynn. In 1882 he had been disciplined by his ecclesiastical superiors because he seemed very much inclined "to favor the Irish Revolution." He had made himself suspect also by his advocacy of the American school system, of which he was himself a product.[21] Four years later, in the George-Hewitt mayoralty campaign, McGlynn was one of the key men in the George camp. George was the united-front candidate of a group of trade-unionists, Knights of Labor, socialists, intellectuals, and liberals. Opposing George was Abram S. Hewitt, son-in-law of Peter Cooper, and Congressman from New York. The Republicans nominated Theodore Roosevelt, but the real fight was between the first two candidates. The campaign, one of the most dramatic in the history of the American labor movement, helped to arouse a lethargic Protestant Church's interest in the struggle for social justice and precipitated a discussion within the Catholic Church which caused one priest to lose his chancel.

A mass meeting in Chickering Hall at the opening of the campaign was presided over by John W. Krammer. In his speech accepting the nomination, George said:

We have hordes of citizens living in want and in vice born of want, existing under conditions that would appall heathen. Is this the will of our Divine Creator? No, it is the fault of men; and as men and citizens on us devolves the duty of removing this wrong . . . Why should there be such abject poverty in this city? . . . because what the Creator intended for the habitation of the people whom he called into being is held at an enormous rent or at an enormous price . . . There is one great fact that stares in the face anyone who chooses to look at it. That fact is that the vast majority of men and women and children in New York have no legal right to live here at all. Most of us—ninety-nine percent, at least—must pay the other one percent by the week or month or quarter for the privilege of staying here and working like slaves . . . We are beginning a movement for the abolition of industrial slavery.[22]

Hewitt's letter of acceptance said:

The injurious effects arising from the conclusion that any considerable proportion of our people desire to substitute the ideas of anarchists,

---

[21] Post, *op. cit.*, p. 89.   [22] George, *Life*, pp. 469-70.

nihilists, communists, socialists, and mere theorists for the democratic principle of individual liberty, which involves the right of private property, would react with the greatest severity upon those who depend upon their labor for their daily bread, and who are looking forward to better conditions for themselves and their children by the accumulation of capital through abstinence and economy. The horrors of the French Revolution and the atrocities of the Commune offer conclusive proof of the dreadful consequences of doctrines which can only be enforced by revolution and bloodshed, even when reduced to practice by men of good intentions and blameless private life.[23]

Among the speakers were ministers and professors, including R. Heber Newton, Edward McGlynn, Daniel De Leon, of Columbia College, and Thomas Davidson, of the College of the City of New York. For participating in this meeting McGlynn was suspended from his office for two weeks.

About this time the authorities of the church also silenced Bishop Nulty of England who was using the theories of George to defend the cause of Irish tenants. In a famous pastoral letter to the clergy and laity of the Diocese of Meath he said:

The land, therefore, of every country is the common property of the people of that country, because its real owner, the Creator who made it, has transferred it as a voluntary gift to them . . . Now as every individual in that country is a creature and child of God, and as all His creatures are equal in His sight, any settlement of the land of a country that would exclude the humblest man in that country from his share in the common inheritance would be not only an injustice and a wrong to that man, but, moreover, would be an impious resistance to the benevolent intentions of his Creator.[24]

Ministers also took an active part in the campaign speeches.

One of the sensations I experienced in that campaign was caused by the sight, as I approached a large street meeting near Cooper Union, of a speaker in priestly robes addressing the crowd from a truck and raising it to a high pitch of enthusiasm by his advocacy of Henry George's election. He was the Reverend J. O. S. Huntington.[25]

Toward the close of the campaign Tammany, fearful of the influence of the popular priest, Edward McGlynn, had addressed a letter to Thomas S. Preston, vicar-general of the Diocese, asking if it were true that the Catholic Church approved of the

[23] Ibid., p. 473.   [24] Ibid., p. 363.   [25] Post, op. cit., p. 76.

doctrines of Henry George. In his reply the vicar-general condemned the principles of George as "unsound, unsafe and contrary to the teachings of the Church . . . if logically worked
out (they) would prove the ruin of the working men he professed to befriend." [26] This statement was distributed before
the Catholic churches of New York on the Sunday morning
preceding election.

The capitalist press, solidly against George, launched a
vicious attack against him. The "official" count gave Hewitt
90,552; George 68,110; and Roosevelt 60,435. It was before
the day of the Australian ballot, and George had no watchers at
the polls to check the count. John R. Commons states that there
is good ground for believing that George was counted out of
thousands of votes. A Democratic leader said before the election, "How can George win? He has no inspectors of election."
When the George movement was getting under way a Tammany
representative, William M. Ivins, Chamberlain of the City and
close friend of the Mayor, William R. Grace, called upon George
and promised him in return for his withdrawal a trip to Europe
and upon his return a seat in the House of Representatives.
There was not the slightest chance of George's being elected, he
said, no matter how many votes he received, for the "men who
voted knew nothing of the real forces that dominated New
York." "I said to him finally," said George, "Why, if I cannot
possibly get the office, do you want me to withdraw?" He replied,
"You cannot be elected, but your running will raise hell!" To
which George replied, "You have relieved me of embarrassment.
I do not want the responsibility and the work of the office of the
Mayor of New York, but I do want to raise hell! I am decided
and will run." [27]

Shortly after election day Bishop Corrigan issued a pastoral
letter attacking "certain unsound principles and theories which
assailed the rights of property." When McGlynn attempted to
defend the principles of George by showing that they were not
inconsistent with the teachings of the Church, he was suspended
for a year and ordered to Rome to defend himself. He refused

[26] George, *Life*, p. 477 ff.
[27] *Ibid.*

to go. Henry George, in the first issue of his paper, *The Standard*, defended him. McGlynn was punished, said George,

for taking the side of the working men against the system of injustice
and spoliation and the rotten rings which have made the government
of New York a by-word of corruption. In the last Presidential election Dr. McGlynn made some vigorous speeches in behalf of the
Democratic candidate (Cleveland) without a word of remonstrance.
His sin is in taking a side in politics which was opposed to the rings
that had the support of the Catholic hierarchy.[28]

In January, 1887, the Archbishop removed McGlynn from his
office at St. Stephen's, but this only increased the popularity of
the priest. His choir followed him and supplied the music for the
Sunday evening meetings of the Anti-Poverty Society. This
Society, organized by George and McGlynn as a semireligious
organization, attracted to its membership Catholic workers and
many representatives of other faiths.[29] In May McGlynn was
ordered to Rome for the second time and was threatened with
excommunication should he refuse. The threat was carried out
on July 2. A protest parade organized by the Anti-Poverty Society and consisting for the most part of Catholic workmen was
estimated by the *New York Herald* at 75,000. A small band of
priests known to be sympathetic to McGlynn were punished
also by a transfer to smaller posts. Two persons, devout Catholics who attended lectures by McGlynn at the Anti-Poverty
Society, were denied burial in a Catholic cemetery. Five years
later a change in the ecclesiastical authorities in New York resulted in McGlynn's being reinstated without restraints being
placed on his teaching, after he had appeared at Rome, on which
occasion there was little discussion between the Pope and
McGlynn concerning the relation of religion and social theory
and practice.

"Do you teach against private property?" asked his Holiness. "I do
not; I am staunch for private property," said the Doctor. "I thought
so," said his Holiness, and he conferred his blessing.[30]

[28] *Ibid.*

[29] The declaration of principle by the Anti-Poverty Society was brief. "The
time having come for an active warfare against the conditions that, in spite of
the advance in the powers of production, condemn so many to degrading poverty,
and foster vice, crime, and greed, the Anti-Poverty Society has been formed."—
Ibid.   [30] *Ibid.*

In 1897, although warned by his physician that the effort would probably prove fatal, George entered his second mayoralty campaign in New York. At that time he said, "How can I die better than serving humanity? So dying, will do more for the cause than anything I am likely to do for the rest of my life." [31] He died October 28 at the height of the campaign. As the body lay in state a moving mass of workers came to pay their last tribute. Nine thousand persons passed his bier in one hour. When the doors closed ten thousand persons were waiting to get in. Post closes his biography of George with a quotation from George's *Social Problems*, as a fitting epitaph for one who lived by the faith therein expressed.

What, when our time comes, does it matter, whether we have lived daintily or not, whether we shall have reaped honors or been despised, have been accounted learned or ignorant—as compared with how we may have used that talent which has been entrusted to us for the Master's service? What does it matter, when eyeballs glaze and ears grow dull, if out of the darkness may stretch a hand and into the silence may come a voice, "Well done, thou good and faithful servant; thou hast been faithful over a few things, I will make thee ruler over many things. Enter thou into the joy of thy Lord." [32]

The addresses at the funeral of Henry George also indicate something concerning the attitude of churchmen toward the person and ideas of the man. Among the speakers on this occasion were Lyman Abbott, Rabbi Gottheil, John S. Crosby, and Edward McGlynn. The latter said, "We can say of him as the Scriptures say, 'there was a man sent of God whose name was John,' and I believe that I mock not those sacred scriptures when I say, 'there was a man sent of God whose name was Henry George.' " [33]

[31] *Ibid.*, p. 173.
[32] George, *Social Problems*, quoted by Post, *op. cit.*, p. 328.
[33] Post, *op. cit.*, p. 185.

IV

RICHARD T. ELY; RELIGION AND ECONOMICS

PREVIOUS to 1890 probably no other man did more to turn the attention of organized religion in the United States to the ethical implications of the industrial revolution and to the religious obligations in the field of economics than Richard T. Ely. For more than twenty years his *Social Aspects of Christianity* and *Introduction to Political Economy* were read by every young minister who entered a Conference of the Methodist Episcopal Church. It was Harry F. Ward's reading of the *Social Aspects of Christianity,* when he was a young Methodist minister, that turned his attention to the field of social ethics. Ely's books were also on the required reading list of theological students in the church of the United Brethren in Christ and were used as texts in theological seminaries. His articles on the relation of religion and economics which in the early eighties began to appear in *The Christian Union, The Congregationalist,* and the *Andover Review,* were quoted widely by the religious and secular press.

Ely was one of the first American writers in the field of political economy to regard his subject from a distinctly religious viewpoint. He looked upon himself as an innovator in the United States of a new "historical" method in economics having for its distinguishing characteristic an ethical emphasis. Largely through his influence the American Economics Association was organized with a semireligious motivation. The purpose of the American Economics Association was to "study seriously the second of the great commandments on which hang all of the law and the prophets, in all its ramifications, and thus to bring science to the aid of Christianity." [1] The "platform" of the Association, prepared previous to its formal organization, stated:

[1] Ely, *Social Aspects of Christianity,* p. 25.

We hold that the doctrine of *laissez-faire* is unsafe in politics and unsound in morals; and that it suggests an inadequate explanation of the relations between the state and the citizens . . . We hold that the conflict of labor and capital has brought to the front a vast number of social problems whose solution is impossible without the united efforts of the church, state and science.

This statement from the Constitution was interpreted by Secretary Ely at the first conference of the Association held at Saratoga, September, 1885.

In other words [he said] we who have resolved to form an American Economics Association hope to do something toward the developing of a system of social ethics. We wish to accomplish certain practical results in the social and financial world, and believing that our work lies in the direction of practical Christianity, we appeal to the church, the chief of the social forces in this country, to help us, to support us, and to make our work a complete success, which it can by no possibility be without her assistance.[2]

Lyman Abbott and Washington Gladden were among the prominent ministers who supported the new Association. The former commended the program of the organization in an editorial in his magazine, *The Christian Union*. The first membership list of the Association included the names of twenty-three ministers.[3]

The source of Ely's ideas may be ascribed for the most part to his German professors. Shortly after his graduation from Columbia College, Ely went to Germany for two years of graduate study (1877–79). Reared in a Presbyterian rectory and having been early in life interested in religion, he found himself in sympathy with a school of German economists represented by Schmoller, Wagner, Held, and Brentano. These men brought to the study of economics certain ethical assumptions. They criticized the Manchester School for its "mammonism and self-interest." In place of the individualism of the classical school they proposed a system which provided for the advancement of the collective good as the goal of economic endeavor. Christian self-denial and self-sacrifice were emphasized.[4] While Ely was indebted chiefly to his professors in Germany for the formation

---

[2] *Publication of the American Economics Association,* I (1886), 2, 18.
[3] *Ibid.,* pp. 43-46.
[4] Ely, *French and German Socialism in Modern Times,* pp. 237, 244.

of his ideas, he was also influenced by English writers in the field of social Christianity, especially by Canon Fremantle's Bampton Lectures, *The World as the Subject of Redemption* (1885), for which he wrote the Introduction to the American edition.

Ely's chief contribution to religious thought was the impetus he gave to sociological studies, especially to industrial problems. A bourgeois world was inclined to look upon the Haymarket riot as the result of the activities of a few discontented trouble makers. Ely's sympathetic treatment of the labor movement helped such a world to see the event in its relation to the struggle for social justice. He represented the labor movement in such a light that the more sensitive religious minds who read his work came to understand it as "the struggle of the masses for existence." As a result of his work the ethical implications of the industrial life of the nation were more clearly revealed. Against the background of misery and suffering brought on by the depression of the post-Civil-War years, his writings on labor represented one of the few attempts to interpret to a comfortable and complacent religious world the aspirations and needs of the workers. On the educational value of the labor-unions which were then gaining a strong foothold and against which the secular and religious press were almost solidly hostile, he could write, "to-day the labor organizations of America are playing a rôle in the history of civilization, the importance of which can scarcely be overestimated; for they are among the foremost of our educational agencies, ranking next to our churches and public schools in their influence upon the culture of the masses." [5] And of the Knights of Labor, which in the eighties ranked in the American mind about the same as do the communists today, he wrote, they are a "grand society," although he admitted that individual Knights were guilty of "outrageous conduct." [6]

Christianity, for Ely, was summed up in the two commandments of Jesus which, he said, correspond to the two divisions of the Gospel: love of God and love of man. The first commandment gives us theology, and the second "when elaborated becomes social science or sociology." [7] Half the time of theological

[5] Ely, *The Labor Movement in America,* p. 121.
[6] *Ibid.,* p. vii.
[7] Ely, *Social Aspects of Christianity,* p. 4.

students, he suggested, should be spent on sociology, and the seminaries should be the intellectual centers for the study of sociology.[8]

Ely's ideas are important, for his books were read so widely that they tended to become the norm for all endeavor in the field of social Christianity. Wherever religion was concerned with social problems his work usually was used as a text. Of the thirteen branches of the Christian Social Union mentioned in an article in *The Dawn,* in 1892, six were studying one of Ely's books.

The "kingdom of righteousness" to be established by Christianity was not defined closely by Ely. In general it may be said to have resembled an aristocratic society tempered with charity. It came close to the Catholic conception of a hierarchical society within which the classes enjoyed unequal privileges but at the same time assumed definite obligations relative to their position. There was no absolute ethical standard for society as a whole, and there was little shifting from one class to another. But the medieval Catholic society was stable, fixed; Ely's world was pervaded with an underlying faith in progress and evolution. Gradually the entire social structure would lift itself to a higher plane of material and spiritual standards, wherein the condition of each class would be improved, but in which class lines would still prevail.

In his *Historical Materialism* Bukharin criticizes the idea of society as an organism. He notes cynically that the proletariat usually is pictured in the analogy as the back or hands and the ruling classes as the head. He charges the dominant ruling group and the Christian religion with having utilized this concept to justify existing class divisions, to inculcate acquiescence in the slave-master relationship. Society regarded as an organism in which the functioning of each part is essential to the whole obviously lends itself to a justification of the *status quo.* Such criticism would seem to be relevant to the work of Ely. Society, he said, is an "organism composed of parts performing functions necessary to the whole."[9] Practically, this was interpreted as meaning that the poor and servant classes were permanent and

[8] *Ibid.,* p. 18.
[9] Ely, *An Introduction to Political Economy,* p. 14.

essential factors in society. At least there was consolation, he stated, for these classes in the thought that society could not function without them. He advised the workers to reject all thoughts of equality and to avoid envy. "Cultivate an admiration for all genuine superiority . . . It is a grand thing for us that there are men with higher natures than ours." [10] Throughout his work there is the implication that "superiority" is in some way linked with economic status, as if one's economic rating and social position were an index of character. This is, of course, what every dominant economic and social group always assumes. Power appropriates for itself a moral base as further support for its efforts to perpetuate the class in which it rests, as illustrated in the history of such terms as villain, noble, and gentleman.

The notions of progress and evolution prominent in nineteenth-century thought figured conspicuously in the work of Ely and through his influence helped to confuse the religious mind of his day in its effort to grapple with the ethical implications of its new industrial setting. Progress was thought of as operating as a natural law in the social process. It was a primary function of economics to elicit such laws so as to "predict the general lines of future development" and to educate men in their use.[11] While these laws of progress were subject to human manipulation, there was a tendency to regard them as bringing justice and rationality out of exploitation and chaos either automatically or by some providential ordering of things.

Obviously this notion of necessary progress promoted social conservatism, or perhaps it was the natural conservative bias of Ely which accounted for his use of these ideas. The result was a program of mild reform rather than revolution, with emphasis on charity and benevolence rather than on social justice. "Love to God is piety . . . Love to man is philanthropy." [12] Every gift of a library or an opera house was regarded as evidence of an altruistic principle implicit within the social organism. He spoke of the "generosity of our philanthropists unparalleled in history, which gives rise to the trust that, as new evils arise, strength and

[10] Ely, *The Labor Movement in America*, Preface.
[11] Ely, *Social Aspects of Christianity*, p. 122.
[12] *Ibid.*, p. 86.

wisdom will be vouchsafed to us to conquer them, and that among us the idea of brotherhood of man will ever become more and more a living reality." [13] Also, when joined with this religious liberalism, the idea of evolution enabled him to regard every phase of contemporary society as an essential factor in the process, and if necessary, it must be good. Even competition received its halo.

Competition gives us a brave, strong, race of men, and the brave and the strong are merciful . . . Economic competition is an essential constituent of that social evolution which is producing the ideal man.[14]

Ely had become interested in socialist thought while he was a student in Germany. He attended a meeting of Christian Socialists in Berlin.[15] And on one occasion he said that if the term were restricted sufficiently he could be called a "Christian Socialist." During the height of the Bellamy Nationalist Movement, Ely made an address in Boston on the "Needs of the city."

We need two things, religion and nationalism. Put these together and we have religious nationalism. But is this not Christian Socialism? Yes, it is in a certain sense; and I rejoice in the growth here in Boston of Nationalism and Christian Socialism . . . I can only go part way with them, for I think they go too far . . . Christian Socialism— if you will take it in my conservative sense—is what I think we need; that is religion coupled with Nationalism.[16]

But even this guarded approval of socialist thought was an isolated instance. Ely repeatedly disavowed socialism and whenever he wrote on the subject he was careful to point out the divergence of his own point of view from the socialist philosophy. Nevertheless, he did give a sympathetic treatment of socialism in his book *French and German Socialism in Modern Times* (1883), which contains a chapter on "Christian Socialism," and socialists of that day credited him with having secured for their case a hearing in intellectual circles previously closed. At heart Ely was a reformer rather than a socialist. "What we need is a free and peaceful evolution of industrial institutions but not a

---

[13] Ely, *French and German Socialism in Modern Times*, p. 28.
[14] Ely, *Competition, Its Nature, Its Permanency, and Its Beneficence*, pp. 15, 16.
[15] Ely, *French and German Socialism*, p. 257.
[16] *The Dawn*, May (1890).

radical departure from fundamental institutions." [17] When he came to specific reform programs, he proposed little more than gentle tampering with the economic order. Such a mild reform measure as the eight-hour day he considered too radical for the churches to sponsor. "The church, as church, can scarcely take a position at the present time in regard to anything so definite and precise, and so uncertain in its results." [18] The duty of the Church, he said, is to advocate what amounts to paternalism, the sense of responsibility among the strong for the weaker brother. Within the church membership itself he advised:

. . . an entire absence of everything in dress which cultivates worldliness and awakens a desire for perishable riches must be enjoined . . . free pews, friendly intercourse between church members, and social courtesies to the lonesome and neglected, and an absence of all that fosters a caste spirit.[19]

With regard to the social obligations of the Church, he listed a number of reforms in which the Church should be active, such as child labor, women in industry, Sunday labor, playgrounds, public corruption, Saturday half-holidays, a juster distribution of wealth, and an attack on unjustified optimism.[20]

Through laws of inheritance and bequest he hoped to effect some modification of extreme inequalities of wealth. But equality was an unwelcome idea. Communism was not only "impracticable" but "undesireable." His social philosophy was derived from the humanitarianism of his day rather than from a realistic analysis of relevant historical material. His social ideal was defined vaguely as making the economic processes serve "the ends of humanity." [21] The new "historical" school of political economy, he wrote, "denotes a return to the grand principles of common sense and Christian precept. Love, generosity, nobility of character, self-sacrifice and all that is best and truest in our nature have their place in economic life." [22]

In his conclusions Ely denied the facts disclosed by his own analysis. His books on the labor movement and on social reform

[17] Ely, *An Introduction to Political Economy*, p. 245.
[18] Ely, *The Social Law of Service*, p. 270.
[19] Ely, *Social Aspects of Christianity*, p. 28.
[20] *Ibid.*, pp. 74-77.   [21] *Ibid.*, p. 127.
[22] Ely, *The Past and the Present of Political Economy*, p. 64.

show clearly the class-divided nature of American society; yet he did not recognize such facts in formulating a principle of social reform. He assumed that the basic factors in the American industrial struggle differed from those in Europe, where the reality of the class struggle was granted. If America repeats such class divisions "dire evils are in store for us," and the French Revolution was cited as a "terrible warning to those to whom much has been committed." [23] It was assumed that in America a mild emotional sentiment of benevolence and good will would be efficient to limit the deeply ingrained power of economic interests. Practically, he admitted that justice would not be achieved without a struggle; theoretically, he maintained that progress was inevitable. In defending the use of the strike and coercion he tacitly admitted that labor must fight for its rights.

The labor movement treats of the struggle of the masses for existence, and this phase is acquiring new meaning in our own times. A marvellous war is now being waged in the heart of modern civilization. Millions are engaged in it. The welfare of humanity depends on its issue.[24]

Yet he advocated a technique of reform based solely on good will, on the assumption that the controlling economic group would relinquish voluntarily its power, or at least could be radically moved by moral suasion.

It was charged by labor leaders and socialists in the time of Ely that religion was the servant of the dominant economic group and that Christianity had been used by the capitalists, as it had been used by masters in the days of slavery, to inculcate obedience and submission to authority by emphasizing meekness, acquiescence, and patience rather than rebellion against injustice. The work of Ely is interesting in this respect. While denying that economic interest conditioned religious views and insisting, on the other hand, that religion completely transcended interest, he developed a program for workingmen which stressed strongly just those qualities which served the interests of the bourgeois group to which he belonged and toned down those qualities that were essential to the interests of the workers.

[23] Ely, *French and German Socialism*, p. 11.
[24] Ely, *The Labor Movement in America*, p. v.

In his Preface to the *Labor Movement in America,* Ely gives a
"final word to workingmen."

Let every workingman try to make himself more indispensable in
his place, a better workman and a better man . . . There is no atom
of help to you or to any in drink . . . Beware of demagoguery, especially political partyism . . . Cast off the slavery of party politics, and with faith in the triumph of righteousness, ally yourselves
to every endeavor to elevate and purify public life . . . It cuts me
to the heart when laboring men are shot down in the streets. All
the wars have been at the expense of your blood. *Imitate no violence*
. . . Your triumph can come only by *peace* . . . With a full appreciation of all that is sad and disheartening in the condition of the
masses, I believe that, on the whole, the lot of mankind was never
a happier one than to-day . . . the past century has witnessed
an improvement in the position of the laboring classes in America
. . . This is not said to suggest to you that you fold your hands,
and lazily take things as they are, but to encourage the use of
conservative means for the attainment of your ends . . . Resist
wrong more strenuously than heretofore; strive for all that is good
more earnestly than you have ever done; but let all your endeavors
be *within the law* . . . The rich and powerful will always find protection . . . Law is often perverted, and fails to fulfill its function;
but even when it is worst administered, it affords some protection
. . . *Cast aside envy* . . . *Cultivate an admiration for all genuine
superiority* . . . nothing more disastrous to you could happen than
to live in a society in which all should be equal . . . It is well for
the small farmer to have a rich neighbor to take the lead in the use
of expensive machinery, the introduction of blooded stock, and in
other experiments, which, if disastrous, would ruin a poor man . . .
If your demands are right, if they are reasonable, then you will win
and hold your gain . . . The world will listen even to socialism,
if properly presented. If you keep to the right, the world will come
to you. *The right is bound to win. Educate, organize, wait.* Christ
and all Christly people are with you for the right. Never let go that
confidence. This is the sure guarantee of the successful issue of every
good cause, the righting of every wrong . . . You cannot proclaim
the wrongs under which you suffer with half the force with which
they are condemned in the Bible. But while the Bible is a good
armory from which you may draw weapons of attack, it at the same
time points out the right course for you to take, and furnishes you
with that comfort and hope which will enable you to continue your
efforts for righteousness, without the dangers of hate and bitterness
. . . even James follows his awful condemnation of the oppressor
with these wise words, *"Be ye also patient;* stablish your hearts;

for the coming of the Lord draweth nigh." No political economist could give you better advice. So when you are exhorted to faithful service, you are exhorted to a line of conduct quite in keeping with the teachings of science. And the *peace* and *contentment* which are promised good Christians have a high economic value, and in the brotherly love of those who have a common Father will you alone find that bond of union which can render your joint efforts completely successful.[25]

The dominant note of the statement is negative: "avoid," "beware," "cast off"; it implies more fear that conservative methods would be discarded than genuine concern for the achievement of justice. No social goal was proposed as an objective for which to fight. Economic equality was confused with biological differences and value judgments of character. Peace, contentment, respect for law and order were enjoined for all situations, for the "right is bound to win." All of the fallacies of liberalism that have made radical religion and the labor movement in this country so impotent for the past fifty years are exhibited in this "final word of advice," which unfortunately was taken to heart by the representatives of labor and social Christianity.

[25] *Ibid.*, pp. ix-xii (italics by the author).

V

THE SEMINARIES DISCOVER A SOCIAL PROBLEM

MUCH of the impetus of the Social-Gospel movement came from forward-looking professors in theological seminaries. Today most of the important theological seminaries in America offer courses in which sociology and economics are considered from the perspective of Christian ethics. This development in the seminaries dates from 1871, when, largely through the influence of Stephen Colwell, a chair of Christian ethics was founded at Princeton Theological Seminary. The purpose, as stated in the catalogue, was to discuss "Christian Ethics, theoretically, historically, and in living connection with various branches of the social sciences." [1]

Professor Charles A. Aiken, called to fill the new Chair of Christian Ethics and Apologetics, at Princeton, had been professor of Latin and at the time of his appointment was president of Union College. His interests inclined less to social ethics than to philology, a field to which he contributed distinguished scholarship. In the charge given at his inauguration, William D. Snodgrass maintained the position of Stephen Colwell that Christianity must be judged pragmatically in terms of its moral consequences in society. The standard of judgment should be "not what Christianity teaches in respect to doctrine and worship—what forms of faith, and modes of intercourse with God, it prescribes—but how it affects those who embrace it, as they appear in their ordinary intercourse with their fellowmen." [2] The inaugural address of Professor Aiken indicated, however, the relative interest which he felt in the two aspects of his department. Just before closing his historical discourse on "Christian Apologetics," he referred briefly to the subject of Christian

[1] Princeton Theological Seminary Catalogue (1872).
[2] *Inauguration of the Reverend Charles Augustus Aiken*, p. 7.

ethics. He would promote the interests, he stated, of the principal founder of the new chair "looking mainly to the exhibition here of a Christian Social Science—Christianity in its bearings on human society, on political economy, and the manifold civil and social relations on which Christianity has so deep and mighty and benignant a work to accomplish. What Christianity has done for man's secular welfare, and what lies in its purpose and power to do, will fall within the scope of this part of the course." [3]

A syllabus of Professor Aiken's course in "Christian Ethics and Apologetics," published by the Class of 1879 at Princeton, discloses no mention of "social science." Philosophical ethics was treated historically, and considerable attention was given to the ethics of the Old and New Testaments. There was one brief reference to labor. Classical philosophers, it stated, had degraded labor, but Christianity had given it a new dignity. "No redistribution of property could have been as valuable to the world as this exaltation of labor." Charity was regarded as the highest Christian ethic. Jesus had "ennobled poverty, for he was poor." The obligation to labor rests upon all Christians that they may have something to give. [4]

This new chair at Princeton may have influenced the faculty of Union Theological Seminary in 1877 when it requested George L. Prentiss to offer a course in Christian Ethics in the department of Pastoral Theology. Professor Prentiss had spent three years in Europe studying at Halle and Berlin. In England he had met Maurice, although there is no evidence that he was influenced by the social views of the latter. Professor Prentiss maintained a lively interest in current affairs. He wrote on the issues of the Civil War and published a book on the reform of the Civil Service. It is impossible to say how much of this material, if any, he introduced into his courses in ethics. In 1901 he wrote,

Thirty years ago Christian ethics, as an independent branch of Systematic Theology co-ordinate with dogmatics, was but little known in this country. Nearly all our ethics bore the name of "moral science"

[3] *Ibid.*, p. 30.
[4] C. A. Aiken, *Christian Ethics*, p. 51.

or "moral philosophy" and had little to do with Christianity. Manuals and elementary treatises then in general use, were based almost wholly upon the simple teaching of reason and conscience, irrespective of revelation or the Bible . . . neither in their ground, their motives, their means, or their ends, were they, strictly speaking, Christian. The term itself rarely occurred in them. Both Christian apology and Christian Ethics seem to me specially fitted to aid in the solution of some of the hardest present day problems concerning truth and duty, whether in the social, political or commercial sphere.[5]

The courses of Professors Aiken and Prentiss mark the beginning of a new interest in ethics, but these men gave little attention to social problems and their courses probably differed little from the traditional university treatment of philosophical ethics under the title "moral philosophy." [6]

Definite instruction in social ethics in the seminaries was begun after 1880 with the work of Francis G. Peabody, at Harvard, and William Jewett Tucker, at Andover.

There is some confusion as to who was the first person to teach a course in social ethics in a theological seminary. Historians have confused this point by crediting Professor Tucker with having inaugurated his sociological courses in 1879, the year he joined the Andover faculty. Thus Professor Rauschenbusch wrote:

So far as I know, Andover Seminary deserves the wreath of pioneer. In 1879 Professor W. J. Tucker, now president of Dartmouth College, annexed a perfunctory lectureship in pastoral theology and turned it into a sociological course. An outline of the course was published in the *Andover Review* and stimulated other professors to undertake a similar work.[7]

But the evidence in Professor Tucker's *My Generation* indicates that his sociological courses were not given during his first year at Andover but were developed later. The outline of his early

[5] George L. Prentiss, *The Bright Side of Life*, II, 395.
[6] According to Professor Bernard, the first course to separate the sociological material from philosophy was that of Robert Hamilton Bishop of Miami University in a course called the "Philosophy of Social Relations" (1834-36). Professor W. H. M'Guffey, professor of philosophy at the University of Virginia and a previous associate of Bishop's at Miami, gave a course in 1850 on the "Philosophy of Social Relations, or Ethics of Society"—L. L. Bernard, "The Social Sciences as Disciplines," *Encyclopedia of the Social Sciences*, I, pp. 321 ff.
[7] Walter Rauschenbusch, *Christianizing the Social Order*, p. 30.

lectures on pastoral theology include merely the briefest reference to the work of the Church in "Charities and Missions." This was expanded later to include the "new and enlarged functions of the church in modern society." Still later, elective courses in sociological subjects were added under the title "Social Economics." The evidence from the Andover catalogues points to the same conclusion. In 1879–80 the course is listed simply as "Lectures in Pastoral Theology." The following year this was altered to include "The Minister Among Men; Business and Social Relations; Responsibility for Those outside Church Influences; Attitude toward Public Interests." In 1885–86 the course included: "Applied Ethics: Charities of the Church; Temperance; Treatment of the Criminal Classes; and Study of Social and Economic Questions."

In 1879 Professor Rauschenbusch speaks of his course as having been published in the *Andover Review,* but an examination of the files shows that such material first appeared in 1889 as "The Outline of an Elective Course of Study." From this evidence it seems probable that Professor Peabody's course at Harvard in 1880 deserves to be credited as the first course in social ethics to be given in a theological seminary in the United States. Professor Peabody, however, modestly disavows such credit.[8]

The introduction of courses in social ethics at Andover was due largely to the emergence of a new liberal and humanitarian theology. Two seminaries, said Professor Tucker, were engaged in the progressive religious movement of the last two decades of the past century. Union sought to liberalize the doctrine of Christian Scripture and Andover attempted to "humanize theology." Courses in sociology endeavored to apply "theology to life" a constantly recurring phrase in the literature of the "new theology." The progressive movement at Andover showed three aspects: theological, critical, and humanitarian. In theology the concern was with the metaphysical problem of reconciling theology with natural science; in criticism, the problem was to establish the validity of the historical approach to the study of Scripture and early Christian literature; and in ethics, the individualistic basis of the Protestant religious philosophy and the

[8] Francis G. Peabody, in a letter to the author, February 23, 1933.

position of the creeds on the doctrine of human destiny were challenged.[9]

A succinct account of the theological position of the progressives is contained in "The New Theology," the Preface to *Freedom of Faith,* by Theodore T. Munger, a disciple of Horace Bushnell. From the standpoint of ethics four basic ideas are set forth: (1) humanitarianism—the dignity of man in contrast to the orthodox conception of total depravity; (2) the immanence of God—a concept by which the doctrine of evolution was circumvented and all sharp lines were destroyed between the secular and the religious; (3) the social base of personality and its corollary the solidarity of the race, opposed to the traditional Protestant individualism; it was considered impossible to save the individual apart from the salvation of society as a whole; (4) a new emphasis on the environment as a factor in character development.

The new theology seeks to replace an excessive individuality by a truer view of the solidarity of the race . . . It turns our attention to the corporate life of man here in this world,—an individual life, indeed, but springing from common roots, fed by a common life, watched over by one Father, inspired by one Spirit, and growing to one end; no man, no generation being "made perfect" by itself. Hence its ethical emphasis; hence its recognition of the nation, of the family, and of social and commercial life, as fields of the manifestation of God and of the operation of the Spirit; hence its readiness to ally itself with all movements for bettering the condition of mankind—holding that human society itself is to be redeemed, and that the world itself, in its corporate capacity, is being reconciled to God; hence also an apparently secular tone, which is, however, but a widening of the field of the divine and spiritual. . . . The New Theology accepts the phrase "a religion of humanity," but it holds that it is more than an adjustment of the facts of humanity. . . . The New Theology offers a contrast to the Old in claiming for itself a wider study of man. . . . The New Theology seeks to recover spiritual process from a magical to a moral conception . . . It regards faith as a moral act. . . . The New Theology emphasizes . . . "eternal" as a word of moral and spiritual import. . . . The word "Environment" has become a sort of key-word in modern thought.[10]

[9] William Jewett Tucker, *My Generation,* pp. 95-99.
[10] Theodore T. Munger, *Freedom of Faith,* pp. 25-37, 201.

The new theology created a favorable atmosphere for the discussion of social reform. Professor John Bascom,[11] of Williams, treated the relationship of religion to the social sciences as early as 1867 in a series of articles in the *Bibliotheca sacra*, published at Andover. The actual incorporation of courses in sociology into the curriculum was the work of William J. Tucker. A stray lectureship on Pastoral Theology had been shunted about from one department to another; finally at the suggestion of Professor Tucker it had been attached to his own Department of Sacred Rhetoric (homiletics). "It thus became the open door through which I had free access to those problems which were confronting the church." [12]

Professor Tucker's interest in social problems was derived from two sources. He had been influenced by Robertson,[13] Gladden, and the new theology, and he had been disturbed by what he had seen in the New England textile towns. After preaching in cities such as Providence, Lowell, and New Haven he returned to the classroom, he said, "not only quickened in spirit, but informed at certain points in regard to the social, industrial, and economic problems."

Of all these early teachers of social Christianity Professor Tucker had the most progressive social philosophy. However, since his autobiography was written forty years after the events under consideration, it is difficult to judge how accurately it represents his position in 1880 and how greatly intervening developments have unconsciously influenced his writing. He states that at the time he introduced his courses at Andover he had definitely rejected charity and missions as adequate Chris-

[11] John Bascom (1827-1911) a graduate of Andover, Professor at Williams and President of the University of Wisconsin, a prodigious writer on philosophy, religion, ethics and political economy. Like President Andrews of Brown, he exercised a liberal influence in New England. Washington Gladden said of him: "Of all the instructors, however, the one to whom I am most indebted was John Bascom."—Gladden, *Recollections*, p. 74.

[12] Tucker, *op. cit.*, p. 161.

[13] Rev. Frederick W. Robertson, of Brighton. His *Sermons*, and *Life and Letters* had a profound effect upon Tucker, while still a seminary student at Andover. "His (Robertson's) fundamental conception of Christianity as revealing the fact of human sonship, every man by nature a son of God, has been the conception which has most influenced me in my work in the pulpit and among men. It has given me a steady working faith in human nature. I have not been afraid of what may have seemed to others to be an overestimation of men."—*Ibid.*, p. 62.

tian ethics and had aimed at a more radical goal.[14] The vast army of unskilled labor, he said, who need charity the most, do not want it.

Their grievance changed the whole problem from that of charity to that of social justice. The idea running through these courses was that of the new obligations which society was assuming toward those who had received scant recognition or insufficient treatment as members of society. Broadly classified such were: (1) those who represented the demands of labor for a larger social hospitality; (2) those who through poverty and disease had lost social standing; (3) those who through crimes of various degrees had forfeited their right in society. These classes were asking in one way or another for a rehearing of their case. The coming question was not the familiar question of the protection of society and its interests, but the question of how to bring the untrained, the disheartened, the dangerous classes (criminals) into moral relations to society.[15]

An outline of Professor Tucker's course as given in 1889 follows:

The Social Evolution of Labor

A sympathetic approach to the study of the labor movement through the proper historical perspective.

1. The Transition from Slavery to Serfdom.
2. The Workman of the Free Cities.
3. The English Laborer at the Rise of Industrialism.
4. The Factory System.
5. Chartism and Trade Unionism.
6. English Labor Legislation.
7. The Political Relation of Democracy to the Laboring Classes.
8. Labor in the United States as affected by Slavery and Immigration.
9. Labor in the United States as affected by State Systems of Education.
10. Wages and Profits.
11. What Constitutes a Working-day; the Use of Leisure.
12. Socialism in the United States compared with Socialism in Germany and England.

[14] Yet his first course in Pastoral Theology made no mention of social relations other than those of "charity and missions."—*Andover Theological Seminary Catalogue* (1879-80).

[15] Tucker, *op. cit.*, pp. 172-73, 179. An outline and syllabus of Professor Tucker's elective course in *Social Economics* for the years 1889-91 were published in the *Andover Review*, II (1889), 85 ff. In 1889 the course was given under the title of "The Social Evolution of Labor"; in 1890, "The Treatment of Crime and the Criminal Classes"; in 1891, "The Treatment of Pauperism and Disease."

A selected bibliography,[16] "including those only which are easily obtained," was included in the *Review*. This outline and syllabus was used by the Department of Economics at Wellesley College and by ministerial and other discussion groups throughout the country.[17]

In the eighties few American intellectuals, if any, had grasped the cogency of a thesis which was usually labeled Marxian but which had been ably expounded by Alexander Hamilton—the supremacy of economic ideas over political ideas. Professor Tucker shared the prevailing confidence in the adequacy of the institution of universal suffrage to solve all political and economic problems and looked upon the democratic state as capable of acting impartially as the custodian of the welfare of all classes. He did say, however, that if economic power in the United States should ever dominate political power and have the power to manipulate government in the interest of capital, "one thing is sure . . . labor will demand its turn, and will get it." [18]

Professor Tucker probably gave the most liberal academic course in labor economics to be found in the United States in the eighties. Under a system of scholarships, seniors and fourth-year students in the Seminary were enabled to spend six weeks in the field gathering first-hand material on the labor movement—a new scheme of progressive education in the field of social science. Reports written on the basis of this field work were given permanent form in the *Theological Seminary Bulletin*, published by Andover, thus giving an additional incentive to scholarly work. Arley B. Shaw, a student in Professor Tucker's course, investigated "Labor Organizations in America" in 1885, visiting Boston, New Haven, Pittsburgh; interviewing labor leaders, economists, and workers; and attending a socialist meeting.[19]

[16] Sir Henry Maine on *Ancient Law* and on *Early History of Institutions;* Hallam, *Middle Ages;* Seebohm, *The English Village Community;* or Ashley, *English Economic History;* Herbert Spencer, *Descriptive Sociology, English and French;* Thorold Rogers, *Six Centuries of Work and Wages;* Karl Marx, *Capital,* 2 vols.; John Stuart Mill, *Principles of Political Economy;* Walker, *The Wages Question;* George, *Progress and Poverty;* Gunton, *Wealth and Progress;* Laveleye, *Socialism of To-Day;* or Ely, *French and German Socialism; Statesman's Year Book,* 1888; *Encyclopedia Britannica,* articles, "Political Economy," Ingram; "Slavery," Ingram; "Socialism," Kirkup. Reports of Bureau of Statistics in Massachusetts, 1874-1888.
[17] *Ibid.*   [18] *Ibid.,* p. 622.
[19] *Theological Seminary Bulletin* (1885), p. 21.

Herbert W. Boyd reported in 1888 on "The Wage System"; Christianity, he wrote, must overthrow the wage system, but must reject violence. Walter Shephard Upford, writing on "The Ethics of Socialism," said,

by means of the common ownership of the means of production and the equalizing of wealth, [Socialism] would promote justice, destroy class distinctions, remove much of the discontent of society which fundamentally is based on hunger and a sense of injustice and not on jealousy and envy as many have indicated;[20] it would substitute an ethical for an unmoral environment and develop a social ethical dynamic wanting under individualistic economy.[21]

Melvin J. Allen wrote a treatise on "Christianity and the Social Economy." The latter states: "The evolution of the social economy and the fuller understanding of the principles of Christianity are pointing toward a common ownership of the 'Instruments of Production.' " He recognized implicitly the principle of economic determinism as applied to theology. "The 'social evolution of labor' is modifying the old theology, which was wrought out under a different economic organization." He advocated three adjustments which should be made if the development of theology were to keep pace with the new needs of man under the changing forms of a new society.

(1) The doctrine of sin must be adjusted to the new conception of the social organism. Sin is not only disobedience to God, but social suicide. (2) The doctrine of man needs adjustment to the new relation of the individual to the race. He is a member of the social-economic organization. His character is affected by methods of production, distribution, and consumption of wealth. (3) The doctrine of redemption must be brought into relation to the present social order. A larger conception of the nature of "salvation" must be gained in order to put the church in touch with present social and economic movements. More emphasis must be placed on the present environment. The "storm centre" must be changed from the future to the present.[22]

[20] (vide Professor Sumner, of Yale, What Social Classes Owe to Each Other, 1883. . . . "to-day the next most vicious thing to vice is charity . . . The yearning after equality is the offspring of envy and covetousness, and there is no possible plan for satisfying that yearning which can do aught else than rob A to give to B."—William Graham Sumner, What Social Classes Owe to Each Other, pp. 157, 168.
[21] Theological Seminary Bulletin (1891), p. 31.
[22] Ibid., p. 13.

When Professor Peabody started his work at Harvard in 1880 he had no tradition to guide him in the selection of material. He was further handicapped by criticism from the right charging him with "bad economics" and from the left charging him with "sentimentalism."

Students indulged in good natured bantering over the new course, caricaturing it as "Drainage, Drunkenness, and Divorce" . . . "and a compositor at the University Press unconsciously reached the climax of criticism by sending to the office a galley-proof of the next year's offering which announced that my instruction was to be changed from a 'half Curse' to a 'whole Curse.' " [23]

The uncertainty concerning the proper classification of his courses was an indication of the pioneer character of his work. At first the course was called rather doubtfully "Philosophy 5"; then, "The Ethics of the Social Question"; finally William James suggested the title "Social Ethics," which was adopted as the permanent title of the department.

Professor Peabody states that his interest in social ethics grew out of his interest in the development of an inductive method in the study of ethics. In 1884 he wrote:

I was led to my subject by a somewhat different road from most of those who deal with it. As teacher of ethics I became aware of the chasm which exists between such abstract study and the practical application of moral ideals; and it seemed to me possible to approach the theory of ethics inductively, through the analysis of great moral movements, which could be easily characterized and from which principles could be deduced. I studied thus with my class the problems of Charity, Divorce, the Indians, the Labor Problem, Intemperance, with results of surprising interest. My class, under an elective method, grew from ten to fifty and was made up from five departments of the University. Each student made written reports of personal observation of some institution of charity or reform; and from these data thus collected I endeavored in each case to draw out the ethical principles involved The results of the examination showed that the students felt a living interest in the subjects treated; and I think they will be more public-spirited as citizens and more discreet as reformers by even this slight opportunity for research. There is in this department a new opportunity in university instruction. With us it has been quite without precedent. It summons the young men who have been imbued with the principles of political

[23] Peabody, *op. cit.*, p. 136.

economy and of philosophy to the practical application of those studies. It ought to do what college work rarely does—bring a young man's studies near to the problems of an American's life. What you say of the conflict with *laissez-faire* economics is precisely that which, under each head of my discussion I have tried to make clear; and it is refreshing to see that young men are quick to see the insufficiency of that school.[24]

But Professor Peabody used the inductive method not to analyze society for the purpose of isolating practical problems and their solutions but to elicit general moral principles. It is probably not unfair to say that he was more concerned with Christian apologetics than with social justice. As a result of his analysis he was able to substantiate the moral interpretation of the universe and to refute the pessimistic view of human nature implicit in the fiction of the "economic man." The hypothesis which he held to be valid as the result of his inductive studies were closely related to the prevailing concepts of evolution and philosophical idealism. All social facts, he stated, were a manifestation of a rational moral principle operating in the universe. A "central cosmic energy" endowed with moral qualities is the explanatory principle for all social reform. It is identical with the "power of the Christian life . . ." and further manifests itself as "a sense of responsibility toward the helpless, slowly expressing itself through economics and through legislation." [25] The practical import of this philosophy, with reference to social change, was identical with that which followed from the doctrines of Herbert Spencer and Professor Sumner. It led to an easy unwarranted optimism and to the support of the existing order.

Graham Taylor began his teaching at Hartford Theological Seminary in 1888 when he was called to the Chair of Pastoral Theology. His interest in social problems had been stimulated by his experience as pastor of the Fourth Congregational Church, Hartford, situated in the midst of a large industrial population. "Its spire arose above a district covering one quarter of the city's area into which three-fourths of its poor and delin-

[24] Sanborn, "The Social Sciences, Their Growth and Future," in *Journal of Social Science*, XXI (1886), pp. 7-8.
[25] Peabody, "The Philosophy of Social Reform."

quent people were densely crowded." [26] Also he had been influenced by Horace Bushnell, whose widow was an active supporter
of his church, and he had read the works of Fremantle, Seeley,
Kingsley, and Ely. After four years at Hartford he accepted a
call from Chicago Theological Seminary as Professor of Christian Sociology. In the fall of 1893 he entered upon his long
career in that institution in the same year that Professor Small
founded the Department of Sociology in the new University of
Chicago.

During the eighties there were in the seminaries a number of
special lecture courses on social problems. In 1885 A. J. F.
Behrends, pastor of the Central Congregational Church, Brooklyn, delivered a series of lectures at Hartford Theological Seminary on the subject "Some Social Problems of Our Times,"
published in 1886 under the title *Socialism and Christianity*.
President David J. Hill, of Bucknell University, lectured in 1887
at Newton Theological Institution on the subject "The Social
Influence of Christianity, with Special Reference to Contemporary Problems." In 1885 Francis A. Walker lectured at the Yale
Divinity School on "Socialism," and the following year Washington Gladden gave the Lyman Beecher Lectures on the subject
"The Relation of the Church and Ministry to Socialism."

After 1890 interest in social problems developed rapidly in
the seminaries. In 1892 seven seminaries inaugurated professor-
ships or lectureships in social ethics. The Divinity School of the
University of Chicago called Charles R. Henderson to fill the
Chair of Ecclesiastical Sociology; Graham Taylor was appointed Professor of Christian Sociology at the Chicago Theological Seminary; the Rand Chair of Applied Christianity was
founded at Iowa College for George D. Herron; Tufts introduced courses in sociology; Yale appointed Arthur Fairbanks
Lecturer on Social Science and Philosophy of Religion; Hamilton inaugurated a lectureship on Christian Sociology; and the
Adin Ballou Lectureship on Practical Christian Sociology was
founded at Meadville Theological School. In 1894 seminary
courses of a sociological nature were taught at General Theological Seminary, at Pacific Theological Seminary, and at Union

[26] Graham Taylor, *Pioneering on Social Frontiers*, p. 362.

Biblical Seminary. W. F. Blackman was called to Yale as Professor of Christian Ethics in 1894; and the following year Robert A. Woods, a protégé of Professor Tucker, was named Lecturer in Sociology at the Episcopal Theological School, in Cambridge. About this time summer schools were started for the study of the relation of social problems to religion. Iowa College held its first conference in the summer of 1894 under the leadership of Professor Herron. Oberlin held a conference the following summer under the direction of Professor John R. Commons. The Oberlin conference on the subject "Causes and Proposed Remedies for Poverty" was exceptional in inviting labor leaders and socialists to state their own cases. Speakers included Thomas J. Morgan, socialist leader of Chicago; Samuel Gompers, of the American Federation of Labor; N. O. Nelson; Professor J. B. Clark; and Washington Gladden. The conferences at Iowa College and Oberlin were sponsored by the American Institute of Christian Sociology, George D. Herron, President, and John R. Commons, Secretary. The Fourth Summer Session of the School of Applied Ethics was held at Plymouth, Mass., July, 1895. The Executive Committee was composed of H. C. Adams, Felix Adler, and C. H. Toy. Economics, ethics, education, and religion were studied with a faculty of thirty-five specialists.

Seminaries with university affiliations began to make arrangements for their students to attend the university lectures, or the university instructors gave lectures in the seminaries. In 1892 theological students at Oberlin College were listening to lectures on sociology by John R. Commons and Thomas N. Carver. After 1890 students at Union Theological Seminary were permitted to attend lectures at Columbia University. Of the 132 students registered at the Seminary in 1895, 78, or almost two-thirds, were attending lectures at Columbia, most of them studying the social sciences. The Seminary *Bulletin* for that year listed courses in Sociology by Franklin H. Giddings, Richard Mayo-Smith, and John B. Clark; also courses in philosophy and "practical ethics" by N. Murray Butler. Of forty-one graduate students listed in the School of Political Science at Columbia in 1893–94, nine were from Union Theological Seminary or

General Theological Seminary. A School of Sociology, organized in Hartford in 1894 under the Society of University Extension, held its sessions in the Seminary buildings and the Seminary president served as president of the School. [27] The Theological Seminary of Virginia introduced courses in sociology in 1898, and the following year Thomas C. Hall was called to fill the Chair of Christian Ethics at Union Theological Seminary.

Such is the story of the development of the teaching of social Christianity in the theological seminaries before 1900. It indicates that the subject first aroused interest in the seventies, that it received considerable attention in the eighties, and that it assumed the proportions of a movement in the early nineties.

[27] Curtis M. Geer, Hartford Theological Seminary, in a letter to the author, February 26, 1933.

VI

SOCIALISM IN AMERICA, 1870–1900

FOLLOWING the Utopian period when socialism was synonymous with colonizing schemes on the Owen or Fourrier
model, scientific socialism in America followed two important
lines. The first dates from July, 1876, in Philadelphia, where,
exactly one hundred years after the signing of the Declaration
of Independence, the Working-Men's Party of the United States
was formed by a convention of socialist groups. Delegates were
present representing the North American Federation of the
International Working-Men's Association; the Social Democratic Working-Men's Party of America; the Labor Party of
Illinois; and the Socio-Political Labor Union of Cincinnati. The
platform of the new party was based on Marxian socialism. At
the second convention, held in Newark, N. J., December, 1877,
the name was changed to the Socialist Labor Party of North
America. The *Socialist* and the *Sozial Demokrat,* the journals of
the Social Democratic Party, were taken over and changed to
the *Labor Standard* and the *Arbeiterstimme.* Later *The People,*
edited by Daniel De Leon, became the official organ. For twenty
years the Socialist Labor Party dominated the socialist world
in America. In the beginning of 1877 it had "sections" in twenty-
five states with a membership of ten thousand, but by the end
of that year it had dropped to between fifteen hundred and
thirty-five hundred. During the eighties the party waged a bitter
battle against the anarchists. The United Front campaign in the
Henry George mayoralty campaign, of 1886, was given party
support. Failing in an attempt to win over to socialism the
American Federation of Labor and the Knights of Labor, the
Socialist Labor Party launched a dual organization in 1896
called the Socialist Trade and Labor Alliance. In 1892 the S.L.P.
nominated its first presidential candidate, who won 21,512 votes

in six states. In 1898 the S.L.P. reached its zenith with a presidential vote of 82,204.[1] The following year a split occurred in the party ranks. Revolting against the leadership and policies of Daniel De Leon, an "opposition" headed by Morris Hillquit formed the Rochester group. Among the important points of difference was the policy on labor unions. The "opposition" objected to the dual organization policy of De Leon and renounced the Socialist Trade and Labor Alliance.

The second line in American socialism previous to 1900 centered in a mid-western group of liberals deeply tinged with Utopian socialism. J. A. Wayland, editor of the *Coming Nation* and the *Appeal to Reason*, was representative of the leadership of this group. Under his influence the Ruskin Commonwealth of Tennessee was organized. In 1896 the call went out from this group for a nation-wide convention of all socialists. As a result of that convention the Brotherhood of the Co-operative Commonwealth was organized in the fall of 1896. The threefold purpose of the Brotherhood was "To usher in—A union of socialists in the world, the Brotherhood of the Co-operative Commonwealth, Mutualism or the Kingdom of God Here and Now." Under the leadership of Myron W. Reed as President, and Eugene V. Debs as national organizer, the work of the Brotherhood was divided into departments for the teaching of socialism, the settlement of colonies, the establishment of industries by building and operating factories and mills, and for political action.[2]

In 1897 the remnants of the American Railway Union led by Eugene Debs joined with the Brotherhood of the Co-operative Commonwealth to form the Social Democracy of America. At the first convention, in June, 1898, the majority favored colonization as a means of achieving socialism. A minority opposed to this policy withdrew and under the leadership of Eugene V. Debs, Victor L. Berger, Seymour Stedman, and others organized the Social Democratic Party of America. At the convention of the latter group in 1900 a delegation from the Rochester group of the Socialist Labor Party was received. The two groups

---

[1] Harry Laidler, *Socialism in Thought and Action*, p. 501.
[2] Caro Lloyd, *Henry Demarest Lloyd*, II, 61.

worked together in the presidential campaign of that year. And at the Unity Convention, in Indianapolis, July 29, 1901, the two groups were merged under the name Socialist Party of America.

Thus in 1901 socialists in America were divided into two groups, the Socialist Party and the Socialist Labor Party, both of which have persisted to the present time. An examination of the platform of the two groups in 1901 discloses that the S.P. placed more emphasis on political action than the S.L.P. Both groups asserted their ultimate objective to be the capturing of the means of production for the workers and the building of a classless society free from exploitation. The S.P. platform had much in common with the parliamentary socialism of the English Labor Party, while the S.L.P. platform was more nearly like the position of the present Communist Party. The S.L.P. called upon the workers to put a "summary end" to the "barbarous struggle" under which the workers were exploited by the owners of the means of production. The S.P. declared its aim to be

. . . the organization of the working class and those in sympathy with it into a political party, with the object of conquering the powers of government and using them for the purpose of transforming the present system of private ownership of the means of production and distribution into collective ownership by the entire people.[3]

ᵏ Morris Hillquit, *History of Socialism in America*, pp. 349-53.

VII

THE CHRISTIAN LABOR UNION; AMERICAN
REVOLUTIONARY TRADITION MAINTAINED

ONE of the earliest efforts to bring organized religion into the class struggle on the side of the workers was that of the Christian Labor Union, organized in Boston in 1872. The leaders were Jesse H. Jones, a Congregational minister of North Abington, Mass.; Edward H. Rogers,[1] ship's carpenter and Methodist layman of Chelsea, Mass.; Henry T. Delano, Senior Deacon of the First Congregational Church, Charlestown, Mass.; and Judge T. Wharton Collens, of New Orleans, La., a member of the Roman Catholic Church. Other supporters were E. D. Linton, E. M. Chamberlain, George E. McNeill, Ira Steward, Thomas Little, W. G. H. Smart, Andrew, and James E. Bates. Reverend Jones was influenced by John Ruskin whom he called the "ablest writer on behalf of labor who has lived in modern times." [2] Judge Collens had been in his youth a disciple of Owen and Fourrier. Although the Christian Labor Union directed its attention chiefly to industrial problems, the leaders were interested in colonization schemes and commended to their members the work of Noyes and Nordhoff describing these early communist experiments. The writings of Josiah Warren [3] also influenced the leaders.

The work of the Christian Labor Union was largely educational. Two conventions were conducted in Boston and two publications were sponsored, *Equity* and *Labor-Balance*. *Equity*

---

[1] His photograph appears in John R. Commons's *Documentary History of American Industrial Society*, IX, 113.

[2] *Equity*, I, No. 1.

[3] Josiah Warren was a disciple of Robert Owen. He later rejected socialism for extreme anarchism. His chief economic doctrine was that price should be determined exclusively by labor-cost. He founded colonies and stores to demonstrate his theories whereby all profit was to be excluded and a system of labor exchanges substituted.—John R. Commons, *History of Labor in the United States*, p. 510.

described itself as "A Journal of Christian Labor Reform." The masthead carried the quotation from Proverbs "To receive the instruction of Wisdom, Justice, Judgment, and Equity." It was devoted to the discussion of

the Labor Question from the standpoint of the Bible. It takes the ground that Jesus Christ was the Supreme Reformer of all history, as well as the Saviour from sin; and that the reorganization of society into the Kingdom of Heaven is essential to the curing of men of sin, and the making them full "sons of God." For the current year it will be chiefly occupied with presenting practical steps which may be taken towards that end by any who love their fellow-men better than they love money.[4]

Leaders of the Union were also active in the Boston Eight-Hour League. At a joint convention of the two organizations held in Boston, May, 1874, a discussion was held on the subject "The Relation of Finance and of Christianity to the Labor Question." A resolution was passed commending the Christian Labor Union for its efforts to recall the Church to the fundamental principles of Christ "whose teachings were and are at variance with the system of industry and trade which prevails in our land." [5]

According to George E. McNeill, president of the Boston Eight-Hour League, the following questions were addressed to the religious world by the Christian Labor Union.

1. Do not the teachings, example and spirit of Jesus require of his churches to-day, that there should be mutual care in sickness, and such systematic provision for the help of those who have need, that the degrading sense of pauperism which now too often embitters their hard lot may be removed? 2. Do they not now require the church to establish labor partnerships and other industrial co-operative organizations, as a part of its Christian duty to its members? 3. Do they not also now require that the principles of labor service of each other as exemplified by the Master, in washing the feet of his disciples, should constitute the law of Industry and Exchange, and inasmuch as this requires concert of action, is it not the duty of the church to sustain those who abandon the present maxims of trade, and endeavor to act upon the principle which is inspired by Philosophy and Religion, that Cost is the Just limit of Price? [6]

---

[4] *Equity*, II (December, 1875).   [5] *Ibid.*, I (June, 1874).
[6] George E. McNeill, *The Labor Movement, the Problem of To-day*, pp. 140-47.

The editors of *Equity* criticized religious institutions for the attention given to the inner life of the individual, to the exclusion of any concern for the evils of the external world. The individual could not be adjusted to a world of brotherhood, said the editors, so long as he lived in a society based on conflict. The basic "antagonisms" in society such as that between the laborer and the capitalist must first be destroyed. As it was necessary to destroy the serf and the noble before attaining "equal citizens," so it will be necessary to eliminate the capitalist and the wage earner before we can have the "free artisan." Our present economic system, they said, precludes the practice of Christian virtues just as Czarism stood in the way of Christian freedom in Russia. "The system, the *system,* the SYSTEM is omnipotent," and until it is changed, to try to make good individuals is like dipping a cup into Niagara.[7]

Specific reforms were suggested, such as shorter hours, co-operative banks, workshops, and stores, reduction of the number of middlemen, a home for every worker, and the general raising of living standards; but the primary emphasis was upon the central task of changing the system. That system they sometimes called the profit system; sometimes, the private property system founded on the "love of money." They would follow the method of Christ and apply the axe to the root, a method, they said, against which his followers of today would rebel. There was no Protestant paper, much less a secular paper, which would permit in its columns a "thorough advocacy of the Bible political economy, and God's laws of property as written in that book."

The prevailing system of private property led to the concentration of wealth in the hands of a few individuals and corporations, to self-aggrandizement rather than service for the common good, and to the enslavement of the masses. The editors, although apparently unfamiliar with Marxian philosophy, expounded implicitly his doctrine of economic determinism and stated the case for the supremacy of economic ideas in the shaping of society. The dominant economic group, they wrote, will always bend all social institutions to conform to its interests and will.

[7] *Equity,* II (April, 1875).

All the vital interests of the nation are under their [the aristocracy of wealth] control, our means of livelihood, in the first place, our legislation, next our pulpits, our platforms, our press, our schools . . . They are to all intents and purposes our Masters.

If men are to be free they must control wealth. "If we wish to control society, we must deal with the power that always did and always will control all communities of men. That power is wealth." [8]

In place of the system of private property, involving private ownership of the means of production, they proposed a form of communism and stood for public ownership of machinery, transportation systems, the mediums of exchange and transfer, and the products of industry prior to their final distribution. Communism is the logical economic requirement of Christianity, wrote Judge Collens. It is the "outward evolution of the teachings of Moses and Jesus." [9] The editors of the *Labor-Balance* endorsed the platform of the Socialist Labor Party in 1878, described as "an attempt to establish Communism by political action." One section of the platform, which was printed in its entirety, stated:

We demand that the resources of life—the means of production, public transportation and communication, land, machinery, railroads, telegraph lines, canals, etc., become as fast as possible, the common property of the whole people through the government; to abolish the wages system, and substitute in its stead co-operative production with a just distribution of its rewards.[10]

In the first issue of *Equity* the editors gave a sympathetic interpretation of the organized labor movement in its historic position in the struggle for freedom and justice. Support was given to strikers. In the great Erie Railroad strike, when the workers demanded a regular pay day, the Company was named as the "sole cause of the trouble." It was the agent of Mammon that "oppressed the hireling in his wages." The American revolutionary tradition was cited as a precedent for revolutionary action.

[8] *Ibid.*, II (December, 1875).
[9] T. Wharton Collens, in *The Communist*, I (March, 1868).
[10] *Labor-Balance*, I (April, 1878).

Our fathers began the Revolution for less cause. Were their families in danger of being unhoused, or was their bread in peril? By no means. Only political rights, the right to vote taxes, were at stake. But the homes and bread of these men were imperiled. The Erie Railroad is the George III of the workingman's movement, the Government of Pennsylvania is but its parliament, and this event is the first gun of the new revolution. How significant the eager haste of Governor Hartrauft to call out the militia in defense of the company's property. Regiments to protect dead things, but not a soldier to secure the innermost right of living men. . . . Let no man misapprehend the meaning of this event. Orderly, industrious, sober citizens are driven by the injustice of a gigantic, unscrupulous corporation to a course of orderly violence . . . It foretokens that another Paul Revere's ride is coming steadily toward us out of the dim unknown. It is the beginning of the war between the corporations and the people . . . Is there yet wisdom in the land to forefend the swift approaching danger? [11]

The panic of 1873 caused considerable suffering during the winter months. On January 13 the unemployed of New York organized a demonstration to take place on Tompkins Square. They carried banners declaring themselves to be a "mass of starving workmen, assembled to proclaim their hunger in the ears of more prosperous and better fed Christians." The day before the demonstration the permit was canceled by the city authorities too late for the participants to be notified. There was no one at the square to warn the demonstrators of the city's action. Without warning the police fell upon the crowd. Mounted officers, charging them from front and rear, clubbed and rode down demonstrators and spectators. The editor's comment on the Tompkins Square "riot" read: "The truth of the matter is very brief. There was no riot . . . only the riot of the strong against the weak." [12]

A protest was sent to the Y M C A of New York City when that organization furnished "scabs" during a longshoremen's strike. The "Y" was criticized not only for its failure to take sides with the oppressed workers but for splitting the ranks of the workers. "All wage-laborers are the natural allies of each other against all capitalists, who, by their very functions, are

[11] *Equity*, I (April, 1875).   [12] *Ibid.*, I (June, 1874).

the natural oppressors of those whom they control." The protest quoted with approval the words of their revolutionary American fathers, "Resistance to Tyrants is obedience to God." The letter was signed by the Executive Committee of the Christian Labor Union, Jesse H. Jones, Henry T. Delano, and Edward H. Rogers. [13]

The workers were counseled to organize and fight for their freedom, for it would not be handed down from above.

As we the working-men of the land are the chief sufferers, so through us must be developed the power to redeem ourselves. No outside force will dash against society, break it in pieces, and set us free; but right in our own midst abide the influences which we must use to better ourselves, to inspire others, and to achieve an organization whereby we can seize the power which shall control the state and compel its ministrations to serve the interest of labor.[14]

The rising of the wage-workers to fight for their rights in the great strikes of 1877 was regarded as illustrating the words of Jesus, "I came not to send peace, but a sword." [15]

At other times the resort to coercion was seen as contrary to the Christian ethic and the workers were advised to trust in a benevolent providence which would automatically adjust injustice. In reply to a letter from a textile worker who asserted that the capitalists would never voluntarily give the workers justice but must be coerced, Jesse H. Jones said,

We cannot force them, and ought not to if we could. But if we are gentle under God's providence, even though He for a time permits us to be greatly abused by the rich, there will come a time when He will rise in His might and free us and the wage class forever, as He did the slave class . . . God is always on the side of the toiling poor, and always against the rich, for all the rich are oppressors.[16]

When a secular paper raised the question of civil rights occasioned by the denial to the Socialistic Labor Party of St. Louis of the right to carry the red flag, "the Emblem of freedom and standard of humanity," an editorial by Jesse H. Jones stated that the red flag properly had no such connotation and that the police were not infringing on real rights in suppressing its use.[17]

---

[13] *Ibid.*, II (March, 1875).　　　　[14] *Ibid.*, I (April, 1874).
[15] *Labor-Balance*, I (October, 1878).　　[16] *Equity*, I (August, 1874).
[17] *Labor-Balance*, I (April, 1878).

Christian communism relied upon more pacific methods than the "petroleum communism" of the Paris Commune and the Internationals. "Every one of the chief principles of the Internationals they hold," wrote Jones, "and can show chapter and verse for in the Bible; but in place of the spirit and method of the Internationals they put the spirit and method of Jesus." [18]

Equity struggled along for a little less than two years—April, 1874, to December, 1875. It suspended publication due to lack of funds, the Nemesis of all radical papers. Its financial difficulties were increased by its policy of refusing advertisements, which it considered the symbol of the profit system. The circulation never reached five hundred. It was thought, wrote Jesse H. Jones, in his epitaph for *Equity,* that when the program —"to offer a calm, deep, reverent, thorough discussion of the labor problem from the Christian standpoint"—became known, it would be welcomed in Christian circles.

[But] . . . except what two or three personal friends may have said, and a letter from a Negro minister in Arkansas, there has never come from a Christian brother one word of cheer. On the contrary, by silence or otherwise, the whole effort has been disapproved; and the editor, like Paul, is counted a "pestilent fellow," whom all would heartily rejoice to see silenced.

Those who could afford to help financially would not, and the poor workers could not. In contrast to the apathy of the bourgeois group was the support given by workers as illustrated by Mrs. Alice Agur, a widow with one child dependent upon her labor, who folded, wrapped, and looked after the mailing of the paper without pay.[19]

About the same group published *Labor-Balance* from October, 1877 to February, 1879. The last three numbers were issued in connection with the *Labor Standard* of Fall River, Mass. In 1878 the Christian Labor Union disbanded following the death of its chief patron, Judge T. Wharton Collens.

[18] *Ibid.,* I (October, 1877).
[19] *Equity,* II (December, 1875).

VIII

EDWARD BELLAMY; RELIGION IN UTOPIA

SOCIALISM in America received a tremendous impetus with the appearance in 1888 of Edward Bellamy's book, *Looking Backward 2000–1887*. Not since Julia Ward Howe's *Uncle Tom's Cabin* had a book received such widespread acclaim. Within ten years more than one million copies had been distributed. It was translated into German, French, Italian, Arabic, Bulgarian, and other languages. As one result of the sensational appeal of his book, Edward Bellamy, like Henry George, became the principal figure of a national reform movement, which took the name "Nationalism" from the central idea of his book, the nationalization of industry. Many clergymen were drawn into the movement. The influence of the book and of the Nationalist clubs was an important factor in developing a social consciousness in religion. The editor of *The Kingdom*, Herbert W. Gleason, said of Edward Bellamy's work, he awakened "public sentiment on the subject of social questions more than any other man of his generation." And W. D. Howells wrote in 1898 that Bellamy's work "revived throughout Christendom the faith in a millennium."

When he was about twenty years of age Edward Bellamy spent a year in Dresden, Germany, where he probably came into contact with the Marxian movement and literature. But the origins of his thought are to be found more in religious idealism than in Marxian socialism. He came from a family of clergymen. His father was a Baptist minister for thirty-five years in Chicopee Falls, Mass. Included in his paternal ancestry was Dr. Joseph Bellamy, a distinguished theologian of the revolutionary days, a preceptor of Aaron Burr, and friend of Jonathan Edwards. Edward Bellamy always maintained a keen interest in religion, especially in its ethical aspects. He was a diligent stu-

dent of the Bible. Mr. Bellamy's son, writing of his father's interest in religion, states:

I know that he had been an omnivorous reader of the Bible, because
all his life he referred to it in conversation and was wont to illustrate
points by reference to the Bible . . . My father was immersed in
his books during the whole period that I remember him, but he used
to emerge from his study on Sunday morning to read the Bible to me
and my sister, one year my junior. He used to discourse at length
about the social aspects of religion. The all-important thing to him
was treating your neighbor as yourself. I remember that he made
us repeat the Lord's prayer according to the version which appears
in Luke, in which is omitted the final phrase "for thine is the kingdom
and the power and the glory, forever and ever." He used to say that
he fancied the Lord did not care for adulation of this character.[1]

Early in life Mr. Bellamy manifested an unusual social interest, a dominant characteristic of his entire career. He dropped
out of Union College after his first year because he considered
that his father was making too many sacrifices to keep him in
school.[2] Travel and study abroad during his twentieth year
contributed to the development of this social interest.

I well remember those days of European travel, how much more
deeply that black background of misery impressed me than the pal-
aces and cathedrals in relief against it. It was in the great cities of
Europe and among the hovels of the peasantry that my eyes were
first opened to the extent of and consequences of "Man's inhumanity
to man." [3]

A further stimulation to the study of social questions was the
thought that no amount of diligent industry on his part could
place his children beyond the chance of want, and that all
parents must face the same possibility. Their children must ever
live under the specter of economic insecurity.[4] His first public
address, delivered while still in his teens, was on the subject of
social reform.[5] *The Duke of Stockbridge,* a story of Shay's
Rebellion, one of Mr. Bellamy's earliest works, also manifests
his concern for the cause of the oppressed.

[1] Paul Bellamy, in a letter to Herbert W. Schneider, March 2, 1933.
[2] *Ibid.*
[3] Edward Bellamy, quoted by W. D. Howells in the Preface to *Equality,* 1910
edition.
[4] Caroline Ticknor, *Glimpses of Authors,* p. 118.
[5] Bellamy, *Looking Backward,* p. ix.

The title of an unpublished essay written in his early twenties, *The Religion of Solidarity,* indicates his divergence from the extreme individualism of his day. The brief fragment quoted by W. D. Howells points to a dialectical approach to the problems of religion and of society, explaining the relation of activity and passivity in religion, the mystical union with a cosmic spirit and active ethical endeavor, and the relation between the individual and society. God is regarded as both transcendent and immanent. In his immanence he binds the universe together in unity and gives solidarity to the race. Men are one with each other through their oneness with God.[6]

Telescopic and microscopic are the two windows through which man looks out—the former opening on the infinite, the latter on the infinitesimal. Neither window should be obscured or ignored. Not the Buddhist in ecstatic contemplation seeking to merge himself in God in disregard of his actual status as individual; not the self-seeker in the vanity of individualism concentrating his being in microscopic activities (equally microscopic whether they concern fagots or empires since they are pursued in the spirit of individualism)—neither of these is the ideal man. But rather he whose spirit dwells among the stars and in all time, but whose hands are deft with the most menial tasks through which this soul of solidarity can find expression; who turns his hands with equal readiness to the founding of empires and to the washing of beggars' feet holding all tasks in equal honor, since with him the infinite motive overshadows the deed itself.[7]

An interesting note on this social aspect of Mr. Bellamy's thought is given in the *Memoirs* of Edward P. Mitchell. Describing a dinner given by Charles Scribner at the Union League Club, March 21, 1885, he notes:

All who sat at the dinner interested me keenly, but none more than Edward Bellamy. His *Dr. Heidenhoff's Process* and *Miss Ludington's Sister* had been published, though *Looking Backward,* by which he is now best remembered, was not to come for two or three years. When the party broke up into groups and the conversation became animated, Bellamy was the center of the largest special audience. He was developing with the eloquence of sincerity, his philosophy of the insignificance of the individual and the greatness of the commonweal. "When I die," he was saying to Charles Scribner and Stockton and

---

[6] Paul Bellamy, *op. cit.*
[7] Bellamy, *Religion of Solidarity,* unpublished ms., quoted by Howells, *op. cit.*

Stimson and Page and the rest, "I wish no burial place, no tomb-stone, no record of identity. I would have my friends carry my ashes to the top of Mount Tom on a bright windy day and scatter them by the handful wherever they might be blown farthest." [8]

Because of its literary excellence *Looking Backward* deserves to rank with the great classics of Utopian romance from Plato to Moore and Morris. The book combines poetic charm with a prophetic message. The attempt to unite the pagan ideal of the good life with the Hebraic concern for social justice gives the work a perennial and universal appeal.

In 1897 Mr. Bellamy published *Equality,* a sequel to *Looking Backward,* giving the political economy underlying the latter book a more detailed exposition. Julian West, the central char-acter, was a young Bostonian who suffered from insomnia. Un-known to anyone except a servant, the only other occupant of the house, West had built an underground chamber to his home, hoping to find rest at night. When that failed, as a last resort he had himself mesmerized. In the night his house burned to the ground. The servant perished in the flames. About one hundred years later, Dr. Leet, digging in his garden, came upon the un-derground chamber and discovered West. From then on the story contrasted the society Julian West had known in Boston in 1887 and the society of Dr. Leet in the year 2000. West described for his friend, the doctor, nineteenth-century society by the famous figure of the stagecoach to which the masses of humanity were harnessed. They dragged the coach painfully along a hilly and sandy road. The one object of all men was the desire to get up on top of the coach where the favored classes rode, and once there, to keep their seats. [9]

From the doctor, West received an account of how the new society was effected. Now, he was told, men divided the evolu-tion of democracy into two phases. The first, which included all the experiments in democracy up to the end of the twentieth cen-tury, was the negative phase wherein men merely looked for change and protested against previous forms of government; they deposed kings as drivers of the social chariot but permitted it to

[8] Edward P. Mitchell, *Memoirs of an Editor,* pp. 436-38. (I am indebted to Mr. John Bakeless for this reference.)
[9] Bellamy, *Looking Backward,* p. 10.

stay in the old ruts. In the second phase men awoke to the perception that their real objective was "the use of the collective social machinery for the indefinite promotion of the welfare of the people at large." [10] The first revolution had been political; the second one economic. Economic equality was the cornerstone of the new society, for it was only thus that life, liberty, and happiness could be attained by all the people. Only under the collective State could liberty be achieved.

How can men be free who must ask the right to labor and to live from their fellow-men and seek their bread from the hands of others? How else can any government guarantee liberty to men save by providing them a means of labor and of life coupled with independence; and how could that be done unless the government conducted the economic system upon which employment and maintenance depend? [11]

Thus it was that late in history men came to realize that the proper function of government was more than that of a police force.

"In my day," said West, "it was considered that the proper functions of government, strictly speaking, were limited to keeping the peace and defending the people against the public enemy, that is to the military and police powers."

"And in heaven's name, who are the public enemies?" asked Dr. Leet, "Are they France, England, Germany, or hunger, cold, and nakedness?" [12]

The argument turned upon the importance of giving the people ownership and control for their own use rather than to leave to an open free-for-all the means of producing wealth, in order that the material and cultural goods of life might be assured to all.

. . . no business is so essentially the public business as the industry and commerce on which the people's livelihood depends, that to entrust it to private persons to be managed for private profit is a folly similar in kind, though vastly greater in magnitude, to that of surrendering the functions of political government to kings and nobles to be conducted for their personal glorification. [13]

The book is tinged deeply with the faith of the enlightenment in the goodness of man.

[10] Bellamy, *Equality*, p. 19.   [11] *Ibid.*, p. 17.
[12] Bellamy, *Looking Backward*, p. 59.   [6] *Ibid.* (December, 1891).

Soon was fully revealed what the divines and philosophers of the old world never would have believed, that human nature in its essential qualities is good, not bad, that men by their natural intention and structure are generous, not selfish, pitiful, not cruel, sympathetic, not arrogant, godlike in aspiration, instinct with divinest impulses of tenderness and self-sacrifice, images of God indeed, not the travesties upon Him they had imagined.[14] [The new society was instituted not by a moral new birth of humanity but by the] . . . reaction of a changed environment upon human nature . . . It means merely that a form of society which was founded on the pseudo-self-interest of selfishness, and appealed solely to the anti-social and brutal side of human nature, has been replaced by institutions based on the true self-interest of a rational unselfishness, and appealing to the social and generous instincts of men.[15]

Mr. Bellamy's books made a strong appeal to the clergy and to social reformers, perhaps because the religious theme figures so prominently.[16] A minister of the new society explained to Julian West the difference between nineteenth-century religion and the religion of the new society. In the old Bostonian world that West had known in 1887, the gospel message of love had been defeated by the competitive and acquisitive business world. The minister himself was unable to bring his life into conformity with his words, for he also was a victim of the vicious system which compelled him to provide for his family by taking food out of the mouth of a weaker and less skillful rival.

While they warned their flocks against the love of money, regard for their families compelled them to keep an outlook for the pecuniary prizes of their calling. Poor fellows, theirs was indeed a trying business, preaching to men a generosity and unselfishness which they and everybody knew would, in the existing state of the world, reduce to poverty those who should practice them, laying down laws of conduct which the law of self-preservation compelled men to break. Looking on the inhuman spectacle of society these worthy men bitterly bemoaned the depravity of human nature; as if angelic nature would not have been debauched in such a devil's school! [17]

In the new society ecclesiastical religion with its denominations, vested interests, temples, and professional priests had

[14] *Ibid.*, pp. 287-88.   [15] *Ibid.*, p. 276.
[16] Thomas Dixon, Jr., pastor 23d St. Baptist Church, New York City, wrote, "I thank God for the book (*Looking Backward*) because it embodies the essence of Christianity."—*The Dawn*, February 12 (1891).
[17] Bellamy, *Looking Backward*, pp. 277-78.

been eliminated. Only the great religious teachers were retained, and their voices were made available to the masses by the use of a new electrical telephone device. The ritualistic and ceremonial aspects of religion were abolished. The religious teachers were prophets, not priests. The sanctions for their words were their inherent reasonableness. Their authority rested not in "human ordination or ecclesiastical *exequatur,* but, even as it was with the prophets of old, in such response as his words may have power to evoke from human hearts." [18] The disappearance of ecclesiastical machinery and denominational boards had not lessened the interest in religion. As the abolition of royalty had promoted good government and the elimination of private capitalists had permitted a rational ordering of economic life for the common good, so the disappearance of ecclesiastical capitalists would permit the flowering of a world-wide interest in religion. The great questions of human nature and human destiny, freed from the deadening influence of the finalities of religious dogmas and traditional theologies, would become matters of universal concern rather than the monopolies of a priestly class. The notions of priests that God was to be sought in the past, that the past was in some way more divine than the present, had been supplanted by the belief that men should look forward, not backward, for inspiration, and that man's conception of the soul and of God was progressive, enabling each age to have more certain and fuller knowledge in the sphere of religion.

Events had confirmed this belief. The emphasis immediately after the revolution had been upon material and economic production. That problem had been solved now for fifty years. The new cultural development, which had accompanied the economic changes, had resulted in the rise of simplified taste. Now the more goods they produced, since all needs were provided for, the less they seemed to want. Men were freed from engrossment with material concerns and were at liberty to explore the limitless cultural values. No more significant contribution had been made in the past fifty years to the happiness of the race, so everyone would tell him, than in the science of the soul and its relation to the Eternal and Infinite. What they now knew was

[18] Bellamy, *Equality,* p. 261.

only a step toward that greater body of truth which they expected to apprehend. But what they already knew was sufficient "to turn the shadow of death into a bow of promise and distill the saltness out of human tears." The tragic note had disappeared from their literature as a result of the new conception of life. This fuller knowledge of God was not merely a more secure conviction of the validity of traditional belief. It was a more profound insight into the nature of God made possible through the new forms of social relationships with its attendant social experience. The serpent of old had said "If you eat of the fruit of the tree of knowledge you shall be as gods." The story was obscure. Christ had said the same thing when he asserted that men might become the sons of God. And he showed them clearly what the tree and fruit was. It was the fruit of love, for universal love is at once the seed and fruit, cause and effect, of the highest knowledge.

It has only been since the great Revolution brought in the era of human brotherhood that mankind has been able to eat abundantly of this fruit of the true tree of knowledge and thereby grow more and more into the consciousness of the divine soul as the essential self and the true hiding of our lives.[19]

This had been the revelation which Christ came to impart but which the world had not been able to receive, with few exceptions, because the true prophet and revealer of God is love and the world had consistently crucified love.

The religion of Jesus, depending as it did upon the experience and intuitions of the unselfish enthusiasms, could not possibly be accepted or understood generally, by a world which tolerated a social system based upon fratricidal struggle as the condition of existence. Prophets, messiahs, seers and saints might indeed for themselves see God face to face, but it was impossible that there should be any general apprehension of God as Christ saw him until social justice had brought in brotherly love . . . "If we love one another God dwelleth in us" and mark how the words were made good in the way by which at last the race found God! It was not, remember, by directly, purposely, or consciously seeking God. The great enthusiasm of humanity which overthrew the old order and brought in the fraternal society was not primarily or consciously a Godward aspiration at all. It was essentially a humane movement. It was a melting

[19] *Ibid.*, p. 267.

and flowing forth of men's hearts toward one another, a rush of contrite, repentant tenderness, an impassioned impulse of mutual love and self-devotion to the commonweal. But "if we love one another, God dwelleth in us," and so men found it.[20]

In the last chapter of *Looking Backward* Julian West enters the home of his betrothed for the marriage supper. His heart is heavy with the suffering and misery of the city that pressed in upon him on his walk to the house. He cries out to the guests, "I have been in Golgotha. I have seen Humanity hanging on a cross!" Compelled to explain his words, he launches into an impassioned attempt to make them understand.

With fervency I spoke of that new world, blessed with plenty, purified by justice and sweetened by brotherly kindness, the world of which I had indeed but dreamed, but which might so easily be made real. But when I had expected now surely the faces around me to light up with emotions akin to mine, they grew ever more dark, angry, and scornful. Instead of enthusiasm, the ladies showed only aversion and dread, while the men interrupted me with shouts of reprobation and contempt. "Madman!" "Pestilent fellow!" "Fanatic!" "Enemy of society!" were some of their cries, and the one who had before taken his eye glass to me exclaimed, "He says we are to have no more poor. Ha! Ha!" "Put the fellow out!" exclaimed the father of my betrothed, and at the signal the men sprang from their chairs and advanced upon me.[21]

Although the author had no idea in writing *Looking Backward* of starting a movement of social reform,[22] the enormous popularity of his work and the seriousness with which people accepted his ideas, impelled Mr. Bellamy to devote himself to the task of giving them practical effect. The *Nationalist* (1889–91) was founded as the organ of the new movement. It was financed largely from the proceeds of the sale of his book. The first editor was Henry Austin who was succeeded by John Storer Cobb. After the failure of the *Nationalist*, Mr. Bellamy started the *New Nation*, which ran for two years and cost him

[20] *Ibid.*, p. 269.   [21] Bellamy, *Looking Backward*, p. 238.
[22] "In undertaking to write *Looking Backward* I had, at the outset, no idea of attempting a serious contribution to the movement of social reform. The idea was of a mere literary fantasy, a fairy tale of social felicity. There was no thought of contriving a house which practical men might live in, but merely of hanging in mid-air, far out of the reach of the sordid and material world of the present, a cloud-palace for an ideal community."—*The Nationalist*, I (May, 1889).

a third of his income. Nationalist clubs, inaugurated in Boston, soon spread throughout the country. In January, 1891, there were 162 such clubs in the United States. The Declaration of Principles stated:

The principle of Brotherhood is one of the eternal truths that govern the world's progress on lines which distinguish human nature from brute nature.

The principle of competition is simply the application of the brutal law of the survival of the strongest and most cunning. Therefore, so long as competition continues to be the ruling factor in our industrial system, the highest aims of humanity cannot be realized . . . We advocate no sudden or ill considered changes; we make no war upon individuals; we do not censure those who have accumulated immense fortunes simply by carrying out to a logical end the false principles on which business is now based . . . The combinations, trusts, and syndicates of which the people at present complain demonstrate the practicability of our basic principle of association. We merely wish to push this principle a little further and have all industries operated in the interest of all by the nation—the people organized.

The present industrial system proves itself wrong by the immense wrongs it produces . . . for the abolition of the slavery it has wrought and would perpetuate, we pledge our best efforts.[23]

The movement captured the imagination of the nation as quickly as the recent vogue of technocracy. In 1889 Professor Ely wrote: "We have in this country the American type of socialism, the New Nationalism, which has made so much noise in the world that it is difficult to realize that the first Nationalist Club has not yet held its second anniversary." [24] Organized labor was friendly to the movement. T. V. Powderly, head of the Knights of Labor, praised it; Samuel Gompers, president of the American Federation of Labor, wrote friendly letters, and P. J. McGuire, secretary of the A. F. of L., formed a Nationalist Club in Philadelphia.

From the first, ministers took an active part in the Nationalist movement. W. D. P. Bliss was on the organization committee of five appointed to select a name and a plan of organization for the Boston Nationalist Club, the first of its kind in the country.[25]

[23] *The Nationalist.*
[24] Ely, *Social Aspects of Christianity*, p. 143.
[25] *The Dawn*, I (September, 1889), 74.

The other members of the committee were Cyrus Field Willard, General A. F. Devereux, and Sylvester Baxter. Bliss lectured for the movement in New England and assisted in the formation of clubs. Among the other ministers in the Boston Club were Edward Everett Hale, Francis Bellamy, Frederick A. Hinckley, James Yeams, Philo W. Sprague, and Rabbi Solomon Schindler.

The New York club had the support of the following ministers: R. Heber Newton, James Huntington, H. H. Brown, S. G. Raymond, and De Costa. Other ministers who took an active part in forming clubs were Alexander Kent, president of the club in Washington, D. C.; F. E. Tower, Bristol, Conn.; W. E. Copeland, Tacoma, Wash.; George Cannon, Vineland, Calif.; D. McGurk, Tescott, Kans.; George P. Bethel, Columbus, Ohio; Silcox, Oakland, Calif.; Samuel Longden, Greencastle, Ind.; and many others. At least one theological seminary had a Nationalist club and Professor Graham Taylor, then at Hartford Theological Seminary, said "I suppose that in the broad meaning of the terms, Nationalism and Christianity are synonymous." [26]

The secular and religious press received the Nationalist movement with varied responses. In an editorial the *Christian Leader* explained that "Nationalism is a scheme to take, say, the tannery business, out of the hands of men trained to carry it on, and put it into the hands of politicians, secretaries and treasurers and committees, walking upon plush and sitting upon soft cushions." [27] The *Boston Post* commended editorially both the Nationalists and the Christian Socialists for carrying on their propaganda at the top, "not among the humble and the suffering where it would at best but foster a futile discontent, but among the favored classes." [28] "But more generally," said J. Foster Biscoe, editor of the *Nationalist*, "the religious press sees that Nationalism is the application to industrial life of the social ethics of Christianity." [29]

Thousands of people found in the Nationalist movement a medium for recording their dissatisfaction with the individualism and the acquisitive spirit of the age. The movement quickened the social conscience of multitudes within and without the

[26] *The Nationalist.*
[27] *The Boston Post*, quoted in *The Nationalist* (October, 1889).
[28] *Ibid.*　　　　　　　　[29] *Ibid.*

Church. It gave an impetus to the co-operative movement and provided the inspiration for the founding of many co-operative colonies. It was an important factor in the founding of the first Christian Socialist group in the United States.

It was at a meeting of Boston clergymen in February, 1889, most of them members of the Nationalist Club of Boston, called "to consider the subject of forming another organization, not hostile, but supplementary and auxiliary" that the Society of Christian Socialists was formed.[30]

[30] *Ibid.*

IX

W. D. P. BLISS; THE SOCIETY OF CHRISTIAN SOCIAL-
ISTS AND THE BROTHERHOOD OF THE KINGDOM

THE principal figure in the Society of Christian Socialists was a young Congregational minister who had played an important part in the Nationalist movement. W. D. P. Bliss had been impressed with the plight of the workers in his parish at South Natick, Mass. To identify himself more closely with them he joined the Knights of Labor in 1886, and the next year was sent as a delegate to the convention in Cincinnati. There have been more brilliant writers and speakers in the Christian Socialist movement, but no more devoted worker than Bliss. For more than forty years he continued to be active in the interests of labor. His chief contribution was made as an organizer, speaker, and editor. His lectures took him into the schools and churches of almost every state in the Union.

Although critical of the bourgeois tendencies of the Church, Bliss was a devoted churchman. "The large salaries, proud rectories, fashionable churches, and church clubs where, at expensive dinners, rich men discuss 'how to reach the masses' is not the way to bring in the Kingdom of Love." [1] Other radicals have used religion and the Church merely as a platform for their organizing, but not Bliss. He considered Professor Herron too critical of the Church which was to ignore the "social base of Christian Sociology." [2] After two short pastorates in the Congregational Church, Mr. Bliss entered the ministry of the Episcopal Church, giving as his reasons for the change a belief in a united church of "one body and one spirit." The implications of the organic view of society held by Christian Socialists implied Church unity rather than a number of competing denominations. Jesus Christ had established but one Church, and there could

[1] *The Dawn* (December, 1890), p. 8.   [2] *Ibid.*, VI (June, 1894).

be but one. And he regarded the Episcopal Church as the logical organization within which consolidation should take place, since it was the direct descendant of the universal Church. The Catholic Church stood for unity, not freedom; the Protestant Churches emphasized freedom without unity; and the Episcopal Church sought freedom in unity.[3] Under Phillips Brooks he served as founder and rector for four years of the Mission of the Carpenter in Boston. Vida Scudder has given us a note on that early labor church.

The writer's memory goes back to Mr. Bliss's Church of the Carpenter, to the little upper room in Boston where a handful of settlement pioneers, labor leaders and others gathered for worship; to the suppers recalling the primitive *agapé,* where we feasted on ham and pickles, and found intense relief in talking without reserve of the Christian Revolution. Many members of that old group have counted in our national life, some are counting still.[4]

During this early period of his ministry, Mr. Bliss also founded the Wendell Phillips Hall which he hoped would serve as the "Cooper Union of Boston." The Hall was supported and used as a center by the Central Labor Union, the Knights of Labor, the Amalgamated Building Trades Council, the Bricklayers' Union, and the Brotherhood of the Carpenter. The latter was a semireligious organization which met for supper and discussion and served as a supplementary group to the Mission of the Carpenter.[5] At such meetings concrete, practicable problems of the workers' world were dealt with from a religious standpoint. The stablemen of Boston were required to stand watch every fifth night as well as to work from five in the morning until eight at night. Mr. Bliss invited the men to a supper and encouraged them to organize in order to defend themselves against exploitation.[6]

With the exception of two years spent as an investigator for the United States Department of Labor and of the war years when he worked for the French and Belgian soldiers in Switzerland, Bliss devoted forty-four years to the work of the Church

[3] *Ibid.,* VII (January, 1895).
[4] Vida Scudder, in *The Commonwealth,* England (February, 1927); quoted by Reckitt, *Faith and Society,* pp. 190-91.
[5] *The Dawn* (November, 1891).
[13] *Ibid.,* p. 57.

and labor, as pastor and as executive officer of some denominational institution.[7]

Bliss was a charter member and suggested the plan of organization for the Church Association for the Advancement of the Interests of Labor (CAIL) founded in New York City in 1887.[8] Its principles were:

1. It is the essence of the teachings of Jesus Christ that God is the Father of all men, and that all men are brothers. 2. God is the sole possessor of the earth and its fulness; man is but the steward of God's bounties. 3. Labor being the exercise of body, mind and spirit in the broadening and elevating of human life, it is the duty of every man to labor diligently. 4. Labor, as thus defined, should be the standard of social worth. 5. When the divinely intended opportunity to labor is given to all men, one great cause of the present widespread suffering and destitution will be removed.

Membership was restricted to members of the Protestant Episcopal Church. Thirty-eight bishops of the American Church and four bishops of the Canadian Church were members. F. D. Huntington, Bishop of Central New York, was president.

Mr. Bliss also was a member of the Executive Committee and served as organizing secretary for the Church Social Union, organized in 1891 under the title Christian Social Union which was patterned after the English Christian Social Union. Robert A. Holland, of St. Louis, was most active in forming the original organization and served as vice-president. Other officers were: Bishop F. D. Huntington, president; Richard T. Ely, secretary; E. N. Potter, president of Hobart College; Everett P. Wheeler, New York, and W. Preston Johnson, president of Tulane University, New Orleans, vice-presidents; Henry A. Oakley, New York, treasurer. After about three years the Union almost ceased to function. It was reorganized November 17, 1894, in Boston, under the name Church Social Union, with a new constitution and placed on a distinctly churchly basis. Bishop Huntington continued to serve as president, and George Hodges,

---

[7] Other pastorates served by Mr. Bliss were: San Gabriel, California, 1898; Amityville, Long Island, 1902; West Orange, N. J., 1910-14; St. Martha's Church, New York City, 1921-25. He died October 8, 1926. The funeral service was conducted at the Cathedral of St. John the Divine.

[8] Spencer Miller, Jr., and Joseph F. Fletcher, *The Church and Industry*, p. 54.

Cambridge, as secretary. It was expected that the Union would unite with CAIL but the union of the two never transpired. Membership was restricted to the Protestant Episcopal Church. Membership of the Christian Social Union numbered about one thousand, and in 1895 the Church Social Union had about five hundred members. The objects of the Union were set forth by Mr. Bliss in 1892 as:

1. To claim for the Christian Law the ultimate authority to rule social practice. 2. To study in common how to apply the moral truths and principles of Christianity to the social and economic difficulties of the present time. 3. To present Christ in practical life as the Living Master and King, the enemy of wrong and selfishness, the power of righteousness and love.[9]

Mr. Bliss was associated with Dr. Josiah Strong in the American Institute of Social Service, organized in 1902 as an outgrowth of the League for Social Service, founded in 1898 by Josiah Strong and William H. Tolman.

The initial meeting to consider the organization of the first Society of Christian Socialists in the United States was held in the Baptist missionary rooms of the Tremont Temple, Boston, February 18, 1889, at the call of Bliss and Francis Bellamy, a cousin of Edward Bellamy. There were present nineteen people of "all churches and of no church." At a second meeting, one week later, a name was settled upon, and on April 15 a Declaration of Principles was adopted. They characterized capitalism as a dangerous plutocracy founded on economic individualism and advocated in its place a new order based on "a more equitable distribution of the benefits of society." The specific objectives were stated as twofold: "to show that the aim of Socialism is embraced in the aim of Christianity," and "to awaken members of Christian churches to the fact that the teachings of Jesus Christ lead directly to some specific form or forms of Socialism."[10]

Declaration of Principles of the Society of Christian Socialists: To exalt the principles that all rights and powers are gifts of God, not for the receiver's use only, but for the benefit of all; to magnify the

[9] *The Dawn* (January, 1892), and *Encyclopedia of Social Reform*, p. 275.
[10] *Ibid.*, II (May, 1890).

one-sidedness of the human family, and to lift mankind to the highest plane of privilege, we band ourselves together under the name of Christian Socialists.

We hold that God is the source and guide of all human progress, and we believe that all social, political and industrial relations should be based on the Fatherhood of God and the Brotherhood of Man, in the spirit and according to the teachings of Jesus Christ.

We hold that the present commercial and industrial system is not thus based, but rests rather on economic individualism, the results of which are: 1. That the natural resources of the earth and the mechanical inventions of man are made to accrue disproportionately to the advantage of the few instead of the many. 2. That production is without general plan, and commercial and industrial crises are thereby precipitated. 3. That the control of business is rapidly concentrating in the hands of a dangerous plutocracy, and the destinies of the masses of wage earners are becoming increasingly dependent on the will and resources of a narrowing number of wage-payers. 4. That large occasion is thus given for the moral evils of mammonism, recklessness, overcrowding, intemperance, prostitution, crime.

We hold that united Christianity must protest against a system so based, and productive of such results, and must demand a reconstructed social order, which, adopting some method of production and distribution that starts from organized society as a body and seeks to benefit society equitably in every one of its members, shall be based on the Christian principle that "We are members one of another."

While recognizing the present dangerous tendency of business towards combination and trusts, we yet believe that the economic circumstances which call them into being will necessarily result in the development of such a social order, which, with the equally necessary development of individual character, will be at once true Socialism and true Christianity.

Our objects, therefore, as Christian Socialists are: 1. To show that the aim of Socialism is embraced in the aim of Christianity. 2. To awaken members of Christian churches to the fact that the teachings of Jesus Christ lead directly to some specific form or forms of Socialism; that, therefore, the church has a definite duty upon this matter, and must, in simple obedience to Christ, apply itself to the realization of the social principles of Christianity.[11]

Officers of the society were elected May 7, and the first public meeting was held May 27.[12] Early in the following year a chap-

[11] *Ibid.*
[12] The officers were O. P. Gifford, president; Mrs. Mary A. Livermore, William Wilcox, W. P. Sprague, vice-presidents; Mr. Horace Dutton, treasurer; W. D. P.

ter was organized in New York City with R. Heber Newton, president.[13] With the exception of the metropolitan districts of Boston and New York, the Society of Christian Socialists did not find a very hearty response in the East. A more enthusiastic reception was accorded to the new movement in the more radical Western states. In May, 1890, at the Storrs Congregational Church, Cincinnati, an organization was formed for the state of Ohio. The officers were: H. M. Bacon, pastor Central Congregational Church of Toledo, president; Mrs. M. McClellan Brown, William C. Hopkins, and Mrs. Althea L. Lord, vice-presidents; E. P. Foster, secretary and treasurer; Miss A. McLean Marsh, financial secretary. The board of directors represented seven denominations. As a result of Mr. Foster's activities in the labor field, he was asked to resign from his church in Cincinnati. He continued to preach Christian Socialism from the pulpit of a labor church which he organized, and through the columns of a small paper which he published.[14] State organizations were formed in Kansas and Illinois also.[15]

There was a close connection between the Bellamy Nationalist clubs and the Society of Christian Socialists. Mr. Bliss and most of the more active members of the Boston group had been interested in both organizations. Joint meetings were often held by the two groups; for example, in New York they combined for a series of lectures by Lyman Abbott, De Costa, T. Wakeman, Leighton Williams, Walter Rauschenbusch, and others. On his lecture tours Mr. Bliss addressed meetings sponsored by joint committees of the two societies.

In the course of his lecture trips through the West, Mr. Bliss visited the Amana and Icaria communities. The colony idea

---

Bliss, secretary; Mrs. L. L. Norris, financial secretary; and Mr. F. E. H. Gary, clerk.—*Ibid.* (December, 1900).

[13] Other officers were: James M. Whiton, Leighton Williams, Miss A. A. Chevalier, Mrs. J. H. Elwell, vice-presidents; H. H. Brown, secretary; and C. B. Stover, treasurer.—*Ibid.* (May, 1890).

[14] *Ibid.* (May-October, 1890).

[15] The officers elected in Kansas were: H. C. Vrooman, president; Judge P. K. Leland, vice-president; Mrs. Bradford, vice-president; Professor Clarence Smith, secretary; and Deam Kimball, treasurer.

In Illinois the officers were: J. P. Brushingham, president; Lewis Saxby, secretary, and Miles M. Dawson, treasurer.—*Ibid.* (May, 1890).

interested him, as it did so many other socialists of that period. It appealed to him as a practical outlet for the need he felt for the union of manual and intellectual work. In 1892 he was working on the idea of a "union farm," or "fellowship of Christian Socialists." [16] He proposed to buy a farm near Boston where clergymen and others might live and devote a part of each day to manual labor. But he soon abandoned the notion of the colony as a significant method of reforming society. Although he consented to serve for a time as an associate editor of the *Social Gospel,* the journal of the Christian Commonwealth Colony, in Georgia, he wrote a critical article on colonies for *The Kingdom* under the title "Self-saving Colonies Condemned."

The radicalism of Mr. Bliss was derived from a variety of sources. As a member of the Class of 1882 at Hartford Theological Seminary he had heard some discussion of the relation of religion to social problems. His reading had been influenced by Henry George and articles in the *Christian Union,* probably those of Professor Ely. Later he was impressed by the work of Edward Bellamy, the English Christian Socialists, Maurice and Kingsley, and by the English Fabians. George E. McNeill,[17] was the one man living, wrote Mr. Bliss, from whom in spirit as well as in economic wisdom he had learned the most.[18] The firsthand contact with labor problems in his early parish work also was an important factor in shaping his ideas. As a pastor in New England mill towns, he had observed the operation of the industrial system. He was impressed with the effects upon men and family life of long hours, scanty food, and harsh

---

In Minnesota George D. Herron and Mr. J. T. Faxon, in June 1890, presented the cause of Christian Socialism to the Minnesota Congregational Club, composed of three hundred ministers and laymen.

[16] *Ibid.* (April, 1892).

[17] George E. McNeill (1836-1906). In 1869 he organized with others the Boston Eight-Hour League; with Wendell Phillips, Ira Stewart and others he organized the Massachusetts Labor Bureau, the first of its kind in the United States; he wrote the Rochester Labor Convention's declaration of principles adopted later by the Knights of Labor. Because of his support of the principle of trade unions, he broke with Mr. Powderly and was one of the active founders of the American Federation of Labor. Through the influence of Mr. Bliss he joined the Church of the Carpenter and served as Senior Warden.—*The Dawn* and *Encyclopedia of Social Reform.*

[18] *Ibid.,* VII (November, 1895).

surroundings. He became convinced that it was the duty of religion to direct its energies toward changing such conditions. Christianity, if it valued the individual, must turn its attention to society. The whole of society must be redeemed in order that the potentialities of life might be free to develop.

Long enough has the church tried to build the temple of God by polishing each stone without caring how the stones were laid together . . . Society moulds individuals as truly as individuals mould society. To forget this has been the cardinal mistake of the church . . . Sociology must be wedded to theology.[19]

For Mr. Bliss the implications of an immanent God and an organic society meant that every member of society—Mohammedan, Jew, or Agnostic—must be thought of as a child of God. To be a Christian was to be conscious of the relationship to God, as Father, and to men, as brothers. Such a theology required a radical change in the function of the Church. The Church did not exist to make men children of God; they were that already. The mission of the Church was to spread the "good news" of that relationship and to assist men to live in the light of such a world.[20]

Socialism was a necessary implication of Christianity. Behind the emphasis of Christianity on brotherhood and the basic socialist conception of the unity of society, he found the common idea of the "organic oneness of every man and woman." Likewise capitalism with its stress upon individualism was the antithesis of Christianity. Capitalism inevitably issued in a divisive society; Christianity implied a united co-operative society. The two were in direct conflict.[21]

Three practicable lines of action were laid down by Mr. Bliss as a general program for Christian Socialists: 1. Personal living: the Christian Socialist was to live simply, giving up time, money, and position if necessary for his convictions. 2. Social work: he was to educate, agitate, and organize; to distribute literature

---

[19] *The Dawn* (December, 1890).   [20] *Ibid.* (April, 1892).
[21] Mr. Bliss defined his views on Christian Socialism in *A Handbook of Socialism* (1895), and *What Is Christian Socialism* (a pamphlet reprinted from an article in *The Dawn* of January-February, 1890). His other important works were *Socialism, by John Stuart Mill,* editor (1891), *The Communism of John Ruskin,* editor (1891), an abridgement of Thorold Rogers' *Six Centuries of Work and Wages* (1896), Third volume *Social Progress* (1906), and *The Encyclopedia of Social Reform,* editor with W. H. Tolman (1897, rev. ed. 1908).

and speak whenever the opportunity arose; to promote labor organizations and to join a radical political party. 3. Work for reform legislation: by promoting such measures as the Australian ballot, single-tax measures, free technical education, free meals for school children, public ownership of utilities, and so forth. While it was pointed out that these measures were only first steps toward the ultimate economic revolution toward which they must work,[22] the tendency was for the dynamic of the Christian Socialist movement to be spent on petty reform measures. The revolutionary objective was obscured by the preoccupation with political reform.

On the whole Mr. Bliss and his followers had more in common with Henry George and Edward Bellamy than with Karl Marx. Like most of the Christian Socialists of his day, Bliss thought of socialism often in vague and sentimental terms, appropriating those elements of socialist philosophy congenial to general notions of brotherhood and ignoring the remainder. Bliss and his followers were too much the children of the nineteenth century fully to apprehend the significance of socialist theory, or to accept its radical notions when they were freely exhibited. These nineteenth-century Christian Socialists seemed unaware of the basic socialist doctrines of "surplus value," the class struggle, and economic determinism. Their socialism was built on the ideas of French Revolutionary Democracy more than on scientific socialism. George E. McNeill, Bliss's preceptor, was reported to have been more responsible than any other man for the opportunistic policy of early trade-unions. He kept labor from "declaring for extreme socialism." Socialism, he said, must arise from the people democratically, gradually. There was danger of anarchy and confusion, if it should come too fast.

There was a tendency to emphasize the method more than the goal in the writings of Bliss and his fellow theorist in the Society of Christian Socialists, W. P. Sprague.[23] Socialism be-

[22] "We get at the root of the matter only when we overthrow this system by political revolution. We must conspire at the ballot as Garibaldi, as Mazzini led their followers among the bullets."—*The Dawn* (November, 1891).

[23] Of Sprague's work *Christian Socialism,* Bliss wrote: "the first book to spring directly from the fruit of the Christian Socialist movement . . ." The work was based on the writing of Schaffle, Ely, and especially the English Fabians. Sidney Webb was quoted extensively.

came gradualism. Bliss defined socialism as "that sociologic principle which holds that the community (national, state, or local) should gradually, but more and more, own land and capital collectively and operate it co-operatively for the equitable good of all." [24] Often he equated socialism with a form of society slowly moving in the direction of co-operation. "Socialism is not an ideal state, but a mode of life which must gradually develop." [25] And Mr. Sprague wrote that the transition from private to collective ownership would be by "gradual means, without the least approach to confiscation or spoliation." [26] There was the implication that any social goal not to be attained gradually was not socialism.

The affinity of this line of thought with that of the Fabians is obvious. Bliss felt himself in close agreement with the English Fabian group. In 1895 he founded and edited for the first year the *American Fabian,* a venture in which he had the assistance of the contributing editors Edward Bellamy, Henry D. Lloyd, and Frank Parsons. The object of the *American Fabian* and of the American Fabian clubs which it represented "like that of the mother society is the diffusion of advanced ideas looking toward a more equitable social order than the present one." [27] The publication, like so many other liberal and radical journals of the period, was forced to suspend publication in 1900 due to financial difficulties.

In 1898 Mr. Bliss organized the Union Reform League modeled on the pattern of the English Fabian group. He thought of it as paralleling the work of the English order.[28] At first it functioned as a local organization in San Francisco, but later Bliss sought to enlarge its field to include progressives in all parts of the country. In the summer of 1899 the League sponsored a national conference in Buffalo. Although a reform organization with a fairly mild program of reform, to the enemy (the reactionaries) it sounded quite violent. Then as now the powerful vested interests of California were thrown into paroxysms of

[24] *The Dawn,* VI (May, 1894).
[25] *Ibid.,* VI (January, 1894).
[26] Sprague, *Christian Socialism,* pp. 182-83.
[27] *American Fabian,* II (January, 1897).
[28] *The Dawn* (June, 1899).

fear at the mention of red. When Bliss announced the red flag as the symbol of his new organization there was an immediate reaction in certain quarters which was not quieted by the fact that a white cross was superimposed on the red background.

The Union Reform League unfurls a new Banner to the breeze. Its ground work is red—symbol, not of anarchy, of destruction, but of society, of fraternity . . . yet on that crimson it would emblazon a white cross, symbol of peace, of life, of sacrifice. It would mean brotherhood realized through sacrifice, humanity made one in love.[29]

The Union Reform League, he stated in his address in San Francisco, was to "proclaim a revolution, and a revolution against what is at present the organized government of the land . . . (the) real governing power," he said was the Southern Pacific Railway. This brought forth from the organ of the Southern Pacific Railway an entire column of abuse, headed "A blatant son of thunder." The incident would indicate that the railway was not too popular at that time, for Bliss was invited to occupy for eight weeks the pulpit of the wealthiest and most conservative Episcopal church in San Francisco.[30]

THE BROTHERHOOD OF THE KINGDOM

The Brotherhood of the Kingdom was organized in December, 1892, at a conference of Baptist ministers in Philadelphia. The two moving spirits in the organization were Walter Rauschenbusch and Leighton Williams, of New York. It was through the exchange of ideas and fellowship of a small group of ministers, said Walter Rauschenbusch, that the notion of such an organization arose.

We saw the Church of Christ divided by selfishness; every denomination intent on its own progress, often at the expense of the progress of the Kingdom; churches and pastors absorbed in their own affairs and jealous of one another; external forms of worship and church polity magnified and the spirit neglected; the people estranged from the church and the church indifferent to the movements of the people; aberrations from creeds severely censured, and aberrations from the Christian spirit of self-sacrifice tolerated.[31]

[29] *American Fabian* (October, 1897).
[30] *Ibid.*
[31] Walter Rauschenbusch, *The Brotherhood of the Kingdom* (pamphlet).

The group saw these ills as due to two factors: first, the idea of the Kingdom of God had been abandoned as the key to the teaching and work of Christ; second, the notion of individual salvation had been substituted for the collective idea of the Kingdom of God on earth, thus "Christian men seek for the salvation of individuals and are comparatively indifferent to the spread of the spirit of Christ in the political, industrial, social, scientific, and artistic life of humanity . . ." [32] The purpose of the organization, therefore, was to make central in Christianity the idea of the Kingdom of God, "to reëstablish this idea in the thought of the church, and to assist in its practical realization in the world." [33] The methods for achieving that objective were:

1. Every member shall by his personal life exemplify obedience to the ethics of Jesus. 2. He shall propagate the thoughts of Jesus to the limits of his ability, in private conversation, by correspondence, and through pulpit, platform and press. 3. He shall lay special stress on the social aims of Christianity, and shall endeavor to make Christ's teaching concerning wealth operative in the church. 4. On the other hand, he shall take pains to keep in contact with the common people, and to infuse the religious spirit into the efforts for social amelioration. 5. The members shall seek to strengthen the bond of brotherhood by frequent meetings for prayer and discussion, by correspondence, exchange of articles written, etc. 6. Regular reports shall be made of the work done by members in such manner as the executive committee may appoint. 7. The members shall seek to procure for one another opportunities for public propaganda. 8. If necessary, they shall give their support to one another in the public defense of the truth, and shall jealously guard the freedom of discussion for any man who is impelled by love of the truth to utter his thoughts.[34]

For many years annual interdenominational conferences were held at Marlborough-on-Hudson. On the executive committee of the Brotherhood, in 1896, were: Mornay Williams, chairman; Samuel Z. Batten, recording secretary; Ernest Howard Crosby; Walter Rauschenbusch, corresponding secretary; William Howe Tolman; and Leighton Williams.[35]

[32] *Ibid.*   [33] *Ibid.*   [34] *Ibid.*
[35] A personal letter from Walter Rauschenbusch to John S. Billings, of the New York Public Library, April 2, 1896.

X

THE RADICAL RELIGIOUS PRESS; *THE KINGDOM* AND *THE DAWN*

THE DAWN, "a journal of revolution toward practical Christianity," was the official organ of the Society of Socialist Christians. It was edited by W. D. P. Bliss from May, 1889, to March, 1896, when it was discontinued. In December, 1890, Bliss acquired personal ownership of the magazine in order to make it a more thorough-going socialist paper and less a journal of liberal Christianity. At the time of the change the editor stated his new policy:

The Arena, Forum, Lend-a-Hand, The Statesman all publish articles on and by Christian Socialism of a general nature—*The Dawn* must now give more specific information on practical things to do in social, political and industrial life. . . . [Hereafter the paper will take a] more pronounced political stand.[1]

An editorial policy sympathetic toward organized labor was maintained and support given to the workers in strike situations. "It is time for war. The manufacturers all over the land are combining against their employees."[2] When workers lost their lives in the constant warfare going on in the industrial front in the coal fields of Pennsylvania, a four-inch box framed by heavy black rules announced:

SHOT

By hired tools of the capitalists

CHILDREN OF GOD

For such *The Dawn* mourns

"In as much as ye have done it unto one of
the least of these my brethren, ye have done
it unto me."—Matt. xxv. 40 [3]

[1] *The Dawn* (December, 1890). [2] *Ibid.* [3] *Ibid.* (June, 1891).

When a group of miners at Tracy City, Tenn., burned stockades and released three hundred prisoners, the editor commented upon the event:

[The miners] broke the laws of men, to obey the laws of justice . . . we honor them for it. We welcome this sign of returning manhood. They committed no violence to life. But where will it end, when workingmen begin to appeal to the propaganda of deed?—Where their brave deeds ended, who poured tea into Boston Harbor?—In a revolution? [4]

In politics *The Dawn* supported not only the socialists but all radical parties. Members of the Society of Christian Socialists were urged to join and support the People's Party and the Farmers' Alliance. A special campaign number was devoted to the People's Party in November, 1892. The Republican Party was accused of being the instrument of the "moneyed," behind which vested interests were entrenching themselves against a day of revolution.

Is the Republican Party preparing for revolution? Much evidence points this way. Strikes are becoming almost universal; the farmers are moving today as never before; markets are growing closer; manufacturers are combining against workmen and talking force; workingmen are less and less inclined to submit. It looks as if the Republican leaders believed that a crisis was at hand, and were preparing to inaugurate a strong policy in Congress, at the polls, in the Customs House, in the army, everywhere to defend the banks, railroads, corporations, and mortgage holders. The Republican Party is largely the Party of the moneyed; it looks as if it were preparing to defend that class at any cost. . . . Hereafter *The Dawn* will speak more plainly and to the purpose.[5]

Eighteen months after the appearance of the first issue of *The Dawn* the editor remarked that the principles and name of the magazine had "found their way into every church and denomination and into every state, into almost every community within our land." [6] And the *Nation,* characterized as "one of the strongest individualist papers of the land," was quoted as lamenting that "practically the whole church had gone over to a general Christian Socialism." [7]

[4] *Ibid.* (December, 1891).
[6] *Ibid.* (December, 1890).
[5] *Ibid.* (July, 1890).
[7] *Ibid.*

THE KINGDOM

The social movement in religion became coherent in the West during the era of the Populist revolt. Intellectual leadership for the group was supplied by a small nucleus of liberals at Iowa College, later Grinnell College, consisting of President George A. Gates, George D. Herron and Jesse Macy. *The Kingdom,* "a weekly exponent of applied Christianity," although serving primarily to co-ordinate the work of the Western group, exerted a stimulus upon the movement throughout the entire country. It was one of the earliest nondenominational religious papers to be devoted to the relation of religion to social problems.

The Kingdom was the successor of the *Northwestern Congregationalist.* The latter was founded in 1888 by Herbert W. Gleason, in Minneapolis. During 1893 Gleason published a number of articles on the social implications of Christianity, stimulated largely by the work of Professor Herron. The interest aroused by these articles moved the editor to publish in the issue of January 5, 1894, a symposium on "The Church and the Kingdom of God," consisting of an article by President Gates and a series of comments upon the article by some thirty ministers and educators representing various parts of the country.[8] Following up the national attention created by the symposium, a conference was called at Grinnell, Iowa, on March 12, 1894, of a group of people interested in the social aspects of religion. It

[8] The contributors to the symposium included most of the contemporary liberal and radical voices of organized religion: Washington Gladden, pastor First Congregational Church, Columbus, Ohio; Lyman Abbott, pastor Plymouth Church, Brooklyn; Samuel P. Capen, Boston; B. Fay Mills, evangelist; A. H. Bradford, pastor First Congregational Church, Montclair, N. J.; Professor John Bascom, Williams College; C. O. Brown, pastor First Congregational Church, San Francisco; Josiah Strong, secretary Evangelical Alliance, N. Y. City; John L. Scudder, pastor Jersey City Tabernacle and People's Palace, Jersey City; Judson Titsworth, pastor Plymouth Church, Milwaukee; George H. Wells, pastor Plymouth Church, Minneapolis; Joseph Cook, Boston; C. H. Edwards, pastor Central Church, Philadelphia; Dean W. S. Pattee, University of Minnesota; James Brand, pastor First Church, Oberlin, Ohio; Richard T. Ely, University of Wisconsin; Charles Beardsley, Burlington, Iowa; Nehemiah Boynton, pastor Union Church, Boston; Alex McKensie, pastor First Church, Cambridge; George D. Herron, Iowa College; N. G. Clark, Foreign Secretary, American Board, Boston; Nelson Millard, pastor First Presbyterian Church, Rochester; William E. Dodge, New York City; Wm. DeWitt Hyde, president Bowdoin College; George H. Gutterson, field secretary American Board; T. T. Munger, pastor United Church, New Haven; Sidney Strong, pastor Walnut Hills Church, Cincinnati; J. J. Blaisdell, Beloit College; Bishop John H. Vincent, Buffalo; J. H. Ecob, Albany, New York.

was decided by the group to take over the *Northwestern Con-gregationalist* as the official journal of the "new movement." The name *The Kingdom* was suggested by J. P. Coyle.[9] The new paper also received considerable support from a group which met for a conference at Iowa College in the summer of 1894 under the leadership of Professor Herron. Included in these groups were Robert A. Woods, B. Fay Mills, Thomas C. Hall, Graham Taylor, Jerry Macauley, Charles M. Sheldon, and J. P. Coyle.

Herbert W. Gleason, editor of the *Northwestern Congrega-tionalist,* continued as editor of *The Kingdom*. President George A. Gates [10] served as chief associate editor. Other associate editors were: Thomas C. Hall, pastor of a Presbyterian Church in Chicago and later the first professor of Christian Ethics at Union Theological Seminary; Lester W. West, pastor of the First Congregational Church, Winona, Minn.; Josiah Strong, secretary of the Evangelical Alliance; B. Fay Mills, evangelist; John P. Coyle, pastor First Congregational Church, North Adams, Mass.; George D. Black, pastor Park Avenue Congre-gational Church, Minneapolis; Professor John Bascom, Wil-liams College; James Brand, pastor First Church, Oberlin, Ohio; Professor John R. Commons, Oberlin College; Professor Charles Zeublin, University of Chicago; Robert A. Woods, South End House, Boston; Professor Jesse Macy and Professor George D. Herron, of Iowa College. The contributors included Richard T. Ely, Edward Everett Hale, Jane Addams, Ernest Howard Crosby, Graham Taylor, J. H. Canfield, William J. Tucker, Henry D. Lloyd, Frank Parsons, and E. Bemis.

While serving as a "family" religious newspaper, the chief function of the new journal was considered to be the promulga-tion of the gospel of social Christianity. In the first number it

---

[9] "B. Fay Mills was keen for the name of *God's World,* but I contested that title, for I could not bear to hear that name tossed about among the rough employees of the press room and composing room."—Herbert Gleason, in a letter to the author, December 8, 1932.

[10] President Gates was a native of Vermont. He was educated at Dartmouth College and Andover Theological Seminary. An ecclesiastical council, presided over by President Bartlett of Dartmouth, refused to ordain him because of his advanced views. Ten years later, however, President Bartlett squared the account by conferring upon him an honorary degree of Doctor of Divinity. Mr. Gates was president of Iowa College, Pomona College, and Fisk University.

was said *The Kingdom* "would rather fail in the attempt to preach the gospel of a social order redeemed in the name of Jesus than to succeed in anything else on earth." [11] Three years later, when the magazine was moved to Chicago, the purpose of the paper was explained as having for its first objective the "interpretation and application of Jesus's thought regarding the Kingdom of God—that order of society in which righteousness shall be supreme." It would seek to apply the principles taught and illustrated in the life of Jesus to every sphere of human relationships: "educational, political, commercial, literary, aesthetic, and religious." The paper served to destroy denominational controversy and promoted Church unity by uniting the representatives of many churches in a struggle for a common objective. While an exponent of Christianity, it would ally itself, said the editor, with those of every faith or of no faith who were working for human welfare.

The fundamental notion uniting the supporters of *The Kingdom* was a common emphasis upon the work of achieving the kingdom of God upon this earth. This was regarded as the essential function of Christianity. The founders of the paper, wrote Mr. Gleason, were "people who had caught a vision of the Kingdom of God as the chief object of Christian effort." [12] In the last issue of the *Northwestern Congregationalist* the editors, in announcing that the paper was to take the name of *The Kingdom,* said that they were following the new emphasis of contemporary Christianity which regarded the Kingdom of Jesus not merely as including the future state of the redeemed but as relating preëminently to the present world. The Kingdom of God meant the entire race of men when its social life had become filled with the spirit of Jesus Christ; it meant "a state in which the individual finds his salvation by losing himself for the good of others." [13]

The article by President Gates "The Church and the Kingdom of God" served as the manifesto of the new movement. It contained three propositions: 1. the Kingdom of heaven and the Kingdom of God does not refer to a life beyond the grave;

[11] *The Kingdom,* April 20, 1894.
[12] Gleason, in a letter to the author.
[13] *The Northwestern Congregationalist,* April 13, 1894.

2. the Kingdom of God does not mean the Church or any other institution; such an identification of the Kingdom with the Church, either concrete or invisible, being "one of the most dangerous of heresies"; 3. the Kingdom of God meant a society upon this earth in which all human affairs exhibit the nature and the spirit of God.

The concern of the editors was with social justice rather than with theology. They looked upon the preoccupation of religion with theology as one of the primary obstacles standing in the way of recognition of the social obligations of religion. There were occasional letters such as those of Professor Hall to President Gates treating some of the traditional themes of theology, but for the most part the paper concerned itself with the social problems of the day.

Under the impetus of the application of critical and historical methods to the study of the Scriptures, a new interest had developed in the teachings of Jesus, accompanied by a confidence that in them men would find the one solvent adequate for all social as well as personal problems.

Social justice [said George D. Black, an associate editor] as a dominant passion of religion, instead of theological and ecclesiastical questions, is peculiarly modern. [There is a conviction to-day shared by the editors that the] social question, the industrial problem, the race problem, the questions of international relations—in fact every question involved in the relation of man to man—must be brought into the school of Christ and answered there.[14]

The details of society under the rule of the Kingdom were not elaborated. In general it was regarded as involving a high degree of mutuality and a minimum of self-assertion. The new society was denominated variously the co-operative commonwealth, Christian Socialism, and the Kingdom of God. The fundamental sin of society was said to be selfishness and was identified with the profit motive of the competitive economic order. As self-seeking was the genius of capitalism, brotherhood and co-operation would be the foundation of the new order. Individualism and *laissez-faire* principles were criticized.

The curse of competition [said evangelist Mills] causes unemployment, waste, bitterness . . . men are crowded out of work by their

[14] *The Kingdom,* May 26, 1898.

own children, political corruption benefits the few at the expense of the many . . . To have political equality and industrial oligarchy is to store dynamite . . . Competition must go, and some form of co-operation must take its place.[15]

A liberal rather than socialist viewpoint on economic questions was maintained; the Populist movement was given some support; racial equality was defended in at least one issue; and a fairly sympathetic interpretation of the labor viewpoint in the great strikes of the nineties was presented. But it did not cover the labor news as thoroughly as did the *Social Gospel* or take as uncompromising a stand for the rights of organized labor as did *The Dawn*.

The column headed "General Church News" reads very much like the typical denominational paper of today with its major emphasis on the quantitive aspects of church life, and a close attention to finances. For example: "$90,000 has been given for work in China Inland Mission; $40,000 has been given for a church in Louisville; $100,000 for an American Church in Berlin; the Baptist Home Mission Society has received $379,129; the Board of Missions of the Presbyterian Church, South, closed the year without a deficit, the receipts were $146,000; the Witherspoon Building, Philadelphia, headquarters of the Presbyterian Church in this country, cost $1,000,000; Mrs. Andrew Carnegie has given $10,000 to place an organ in the Carnegie Library at Braddock, Pa.; the receipts of the American Board during the past seven months were $369,488, a gain of $77,613 over the corresponding time of last year"; etc., etc.[16]

But this financial emphasis should be judged against the background of the contemporary denominational magazines. *The Congregationalist,* presumably by age, tradition, and prestige the parent and preceptor of *The Kingdom,* was weighted down with the bourgeois attitude which estimated all situations in terms of money value. " . . . to ignore the sense of sin, the belief in its forgiveness and the personal profit—economic as well as otherwise—which has come to thousands who have had the assurance of forgiveness would be unscientific." [17]

[15] *Ibid.,* February 17, 1898.
[16] *Ibid.,* April 28, May 5, 1898.
[17] *The Congregationalist,* September 13, 1894.

A weekly column in *The Congregationalist* was scarcely to be distinguished from a Wall Street bulletin, and indicates the extent to which the Church was allied with financial interests, accepting uncritically the money point of view. It regarded industry and business enterprise solely from the perspective of uninterrupted profits, to the neglect of all human values. At the time of the Pullman strike it complained that in the West laborers were often more "independent" than the capitalist who had to bear contracts of "crushing weight." [18] And the sequence in the following comment betrays the prevailing scale of values. "Within the past week millions of dollars worth of property have been destroyed, great inconvenience and suffering caused, and several lives lost." [19] Stock market speculation was not only condoned but frankly encouraged. Two weeks before *The Northwestern Congregationalist* published its symposium on "The Church and the Kingdom of God" the *Congregationalist* was publishing this kind of material:

London has for some weeks been the theatre of a large and exciting speculation in gold shares . . . This mining speculation craze may likely extend to this country . . . The iron mills in Pennsylvania are in some instances running overtime . . . But the complaint is general that profits are small.[20]

And two weeks later it said:

The character of stock market speculation is low at the moment, legitimate dealing in securities of character being confined to a very few favorite bonds and shares. Perhaps in no direction is the outlook better than in the exploiting of new electric light, railway or power transmission enterprises. The growth of confidence of investors in bonds of such properties is very marked and soundly capitalized projects have a ready acceptance.[21]

The editorial policy of *The Kingdom* toward war was equivocal. A naïve editorial hailed the Russian Czar's disarmament proposal of 1898 as "the most significant event connected with the Kingdom of God on earth, which has transpired during the last quarter of a century." The avowed purpose of the Czar was to focus all efforts being made for peace and to "cement their agreement by a corporate consecration of the principles of equity

---

[18] *Ibid.*, May 3, 1894.   [19] *Ibid.*, July 12, 1894.
[20] *Ibid.*, December 19, 1894.   [21] *Ibid.*, December 27, 1894.

and right, whereon rest the security of states, and the welfare of peoples." [22] In the Hearst-sponsored Spanish-American War, as in the Great War almost twenty years later, the religious forces of the country were prostituted in the interest of imperialism under the guise of a "righteous war." Wavering at first when the war broke, *The Kingdom* did its part to promote for the Cubans a war of deliverance from the iron heel of the Spanish oppressor. In the incipient stages of the war a front-page box was devoted to a speech by Senator Hoar wherein America (the Archangel Michael) was pictured as striking down Spain (the demon of darkness), all in the spirit of love.[23] A sermon by Henry Van Dyke was quoted:

War is a sacrifice . . . To suffer for the benefit of others is heroic and Christlike. To bear the cross for the sake of delivering men is to be crucified with Christ . . . to put an end to a long record of robbery in peace and rapine in war; to deliver a fair portion of this continent from the incubus of the most obstinate barbarians who exist outside of Turkey; to bring liberty to captives, and let the oppressed go free; to secure permanent peace and righteous order to the remnant of a cruelly broken race; to uphold the honor of our country as an unselfish and powerful friend of the downtrodden; perhaps to bring the oppressor herself, through repentance, to a better mind, and send her forward in a new and nobler career—these are high, generous, Christian aims.[24]

Ernest Howard Crosby,[25] a disciple of Tolstoy and an associate editor of the *Social Gospel,* wrote to the editor of *The Kingdom* deploring the pro-war policy and holding up the example of secular papers opposing the war, naming *The Coming Nation,* the socialist journal of the Ruskin Colony, "that has neither church nor chapel"; Gene Debs's *Social Democracy; Justice,* the paper of the Wilmington "single-taxers"; *Common-*

[22] *The Kingdom,* September, 1898.
[23] "When I enter this war I want to enter it with the sanction of international law, with the approval of our consciences, and with a certainty of the applauding judgment of history. I confess I do not like to think of the genius of America angry, snarling, shouting, screaming, kicking, clawing with her nails. I like rather to think of her august and serene beauty, inspired by a sentiment even toward her enemies not of hate, but of love, perhaps a little pale in the cheek, and a dangerous light in her eye, unerring, invincible as was the Archangel Michael, when he struck down and trampled upon the Demon of Darkness."—*Ibid.,* May 12, 1898.
[24] *The Kingdom,* May 19, 1898.
[25] See biographical note on pp. 161-62.

wealth, another socialist paper; (but) "I do not know of one nominally Christian (paper) which does not approve of this war."

While the dominant editorial policy of *The Kingdom* was decidedly favorable to the war, the militaristic trend of the government was criticized at times, and the policy of the paper was qualified by the signed editorials of President Gates in which he pointed out that war was being used to divert attention from the urgent need of meeting the economic questions of our own country. He quoted with approval the words of Charles Sumner, "there is no dishonorable peace; there is no honorable war." He confessed to the relevancy of Puck's ironic thrust.

We cannot expect [that paper said] the ministers of the church to preach the unbending peace gospel of their Master in time of war, any more than we can expect them to preach the Sermon on the Mount in time of peace.

He pointed out the hypocrisy of a nation in making heroic pretensions of sacrificing itself for the Cubans when it did nothing to end the rule of sweatshops and child labor within its own borders.

The real difficulty is not a quarrel with Spain but it is in ourselves. The one and a half million reconcentrados involved in our sweatshop system, crowding a quarter of a million children under fourteen years of age into that murderous toil, furnishes an appeal to sympathy immeasurably beyond that of the suffering Cubans . . . our infamous industrial system, many parts of which know no law but profit . . . logically heads up into the sweatshop horrors and child labor of our great cities and factories. To end these wrongs a war must yet be, either of mind or a physical war which may have many analogies to that of France one hundred years ago. Some of us resolutely decline to have our sympathies and interests withdrawn from the immeasurably greater needs lying at our doors.

But following this straightforward statement, President Gates concluded that since we were in the war, "now we must win it." [26]

There seems to have been little sympathy in the contemporary religious press for the social emphasis of *The Kingdom,* hence it was ignored or mentioned disparagingly in other religious

[26] *Ibid.,* May 26, 1898.

journals. On the occasion of the appearance of the prospectus announcing the forthcoming magazine, an unfortunate typographical error was seized upon by the editor of the *Congregationalist*. The announcement had stated that the *Kingdom* would advocate certain causes "without impartiality." The editor of the *Congregationalist* said that he had taken this extraordinary remark as a typographical error but that examination of an article on the first page of the initial issue of *The Kingdom* criticizing a prominent Congregationalist layman, led to the conclusion that this statement was intended to stand as printed. "If the new paper is to condemn what is called the competitive system of conducting business, we hope it will yet preserve impartiality toward those engaged in it." [27]

In 1896 an editorial in *The Kingdom* stated that "Luxury is a crime." The editorial was based on the remarks of Bishop Potter, on the occasion of his consecration of Grace Chapel, when he had been critical of the distribution of wealth.

The growth of wealth and of luxury, wicked, wasteful and wanton, as before God I declare that luxury to be, has been matched step by step by a deepening and deadening poverty which has left whole neighborhoods of people practically without hope and without aspiration. At such a time, for the church of God to sit still and be content with theories of its duty outlawed by time and long ago demonstrated to be grotesquely inadequate to the demands of a living situation; this is to deserve the scorn of men and the curse of God.

The *Churchman* replied to the *Kingdom* in a long editorial taking the latter to task for its radical views on property, wealth, and its "meaningless tirade on luxury." The capitalistic bias and aristocratic flavor of the prevailing religious press is exhibited in this delicious bit of casuistry in which the *Churchman* interpreted the Bishop's remarks. It is really those, whom

. . . we denominate the poor [who are given to the] indulgence of appetite and the most extravagant expenditures (in proportion to means) for mere bodily comforts. Look at the output of beer, of whiskey, and tobacco in this country in the course of a year! . . . Who consume it? The poor. And so habituated have they become to the use of these absolutely "wasteful and wanton" (to quote Bishop

[27] It should be noted, however, that in the next issue there appeared a sympathetic account of the founding of the Chair of Applied Christianity for Professor George D. Herron.—*The Congregationalist*, April 12, 19, 1894.

Potter's words) luxuries that we are now told that these things are necessaries of life . . . no candid observer can shut his eyes to the fact that in these days wealth is being poured out—squandered, one might almost say—in aid of poverty, to a degree almost incredible. Three-fourths of the current talk about the "iniquity of wealth" and the "crime of luxury" is born of envy, hatred, malice and all uncharitableness.[28]

The Kingdom used this controversy to good advantage. A symposium was conducted on the subject of luxury. Contributions were solicited from religious liberals and economists, such as Richard T. Ely and Henry D. Lloyd.

In 1896 President Gates read a paper before the college section of the Southeastern Iowa Teachers' Association. His object was "to acquaint the public with certain notorious facts relating to the unscrupulous methods of a well-known schoolbook monopoly in introducing its textbooks into the public schools." The address was indorsed by the Association. A year later it was published by the Kingdom Publishing Company under the title *A Foe to American Schools*. The publishing company under attack had previously sent out a circular stating "We ask our patrons and correspondents to look around them and view the business transactions of this company and its agents. We invite such a test." But when this was done in the study of President Gates, the Company asked for an injunction to restrain its publication. The injunction was refused. The Company then brought suit for $100,000 damages against President Gates personally and another suit for the same amount against the publishing company. Clarence Darrow assisted in the defense. In the case against President Gates, fourteen of the fifteen counts were dismissed, which practically threw the case out of court; but in the case against the Kingdom Publishing Company the judge ordered a verdict in favor of the plaintiff on a technicality. A witness stated that owing to the judge's instruction, the evidence in the case was not considered at all. Although the case involved a man of national reputation and one of the largest publishing houses in the country and was front-page news during the trial, not a line of the evidence appeared in Associated Press dispatches. With this judgment hanging over it *The Kingdom* was

[28] *The Churchman*, quoted in *The Kingdom*, June 5, 1896.

forced to suspend publication, and the final number was published April 20, 1899. Unfilled subscriptions were filled by Graham Taylor's paper *The Commons* and by *The Social Gospel*, published by the Christian Commonwealth, Georgia.

Viewed against the background of its time the magazine deserves high praise for its courage in the support it gave to unpopular causes, to the defense of the oppressed, and to the attack upon evil in high places. The words of one of its friends, however, a "prominent minister," writing in 1903, probably need qualification. He wrote, "the little paper, while it lasted, struck the highest and truest note of any publication in America before or since." [29]

[29] Isabel Gates, *The Life of George Augustus Gates*, p. 20.

XI

HENRY DEMAREST LLOYD: THE NEW CONSCIENCE

THE treasurer of the defense fund set up to assist the Kingdom Publishing Company in its legal battle with the American Book Company was Henry D. Lloyd, of Chicago, one of the leaders in the mid-western group interested in the new movement of social Christianity. Like Professor Ely and Edward Bellamy, his interest in religion originated in the rectory. His father, minister of a Dutch Reformed church in New York City, regulated his household with a solemnity and gravity becoming to an orthodox Calvinist. Daily family prayers were omitted not more than three times in Lloyd's youth. Partly under the influence of Henry Ward Beecher, Lloyd early in life abandoned the irksome discipline of the orthodox faith in which he had been reared, but he continued to maintain an active interest in religion. His commencement oration at Columbia College in 1867 prefigured the dominant interests of a lifetime: religion and social reform. The theme of the discourse was the exploitation of Africa by soap manufacturers and the connection between missions and commercial gain. For the next thirty-five years Lloyd was busy with the task of analyzing the unethical basis of contemporary business practice and exploring the relation of religion to social justice. As a successful newspaper editor in Chicago, he was in a strategic position to render service, through a sympathetic interpretation of the labor movement, to a middle-class audience.

Although Henry Lloyd was identified most closely with the radical group in Chicago, he corresponded with ministers and laymen in all parts of the country, and his influence was considerable in arousing an interest in social problems in church groups.

No one and no message [wrote William Thurston Brown] ever made me so glad to live as yourself and your message . . . your splendid faith—faith which I have not found in Israel was a revelation to me . . . no voice from a pulpit ever strengthened my faith in man as did your words and yourself, and I am glad to acknowledge the debt.[1]

The story of the development of Henry Lloyd's social philosophy is an epitome of socialist history from 1880 to 1890. Starting as a liberal democratic reformer, he moved on to Utopian socialism, and finally adopted Marxian views.

As an author and journalist Henry Lloyd regarded his work as that of a scientist gathering with Darwinian patience factual material from the economic world with which to confound the abstractions of the champions of the *status quo*. He was one of the earliest competent critics of *laissez-faire* economics. In 1882 he published his article "The Political Economy of $73,000,-000," in which the inside story of *Black Friday* and the career of Jay Gould were used to illustrate what could be done by "scientific devotion to the principles of competition." His editorials and magazine articles were among the first formidable attacks upon the individualism of classical economic theories in the United States. His proof of the inadequacy of the prevailing economic theory on purely rational grounds was useful material for moralists who wished to discredit the system on ethical grounds. Henry Lloyd at times did both.

Lloyd first attracted national attention by an article in the *Atlantic Monthly*, March, 1881, "The Story of the Great Monopoly," which exposed the tactics of the Standard Oil Company with regard to their treatment of competitors and their manipulation of governmental agencies. The article created a sensation. Seven editions of the magazine were required to supply the demand. For most Americans who read it, this was an introduction to the subject of concentration in American industry and their first inkling of the enormous power wielded by that new phenomenon in American life, the trust.

In 1894 Lloyd expanded this story of the Standard Oil into book form and published it under the title *"Wealth against Commonwealth."* It consisted largely of a "transcript of the record" taken from legislative proceedings. The book was a

[1] Caro Lloyd, *Henry Demarest Lloyd*, II, 52.

devastating account of the ruthless tactics employed in the formation of one great trust. Of more importance, however, than the dissection of the economic body of a great financial institution was the description of the ability of the economic power of concentrated capital to manipulate "democratic" machinery. Standard Oil did everything to the Pennsylvania legislature, wrote Lloyd in one of his cryptic sentences, except "to refine it." The implications of this fact he regarded as ominous for the future of democracy.

His book was used widely by ministers and others concerned with a new social movement in religion. "There is no class," wrote Lloyd to his friend Winfield Gaylord, "that has taken more to heart the message of the facts I gave . . . and no class which has made more sacrifice than the ministers in doing their duty as the guardians of the people against the sinners of wealth." [2] Lloyd wrote to Washington Gladden for the names of several hundred ministers to whom he might send free copies of the book. Gladden wrote of the book: "I wonder that Lloyd's book has not caused more excitement. I hope that and trust that it is doing its work silently; but it surprises me that it does not cause insurrection. We must wait; the day of judgment will come." [3] B. Fay Mills, an associate editor of *The Kingdom*, and one of the most successful evangelists of the day, who was shifting the emphasis of his preaching from the personal to the social note, wished to make use of the material in Lloyd's book. But he first called on officials of the Standard Oil in order to hear their side.

I told them [wrote Mills to Lloyd] that I had come to ask Mr. Rockefeller what his theory was of life by which he seemed in his private life so estimable and in his public life to be so wicked. I was received with . . . great courtesy and spent six or eight hours with his private manager and with Colonel Dodd . . . I went through *Wealth against Commonwealth*.[4] [Lloyd replied] I was very glad to get your frank and kind letter . . . and was intensely interested in what you say of your interview with the Oil Trust people. The question that you wanted to ask Mr. Rockefeller is one which has been constantly on my mind. The apparent contradiction between his personal and his commercial life is very baffling unless one takes

---

[2] *Ibid.*   [3] *Ibid.*, I, 200.   [4] *Ibid.*, p. 212.

the ground that a man's commercial character is also a part of his personal character. (Winnetka, Ill. May 12, 1896.)[5]

Mills was told that the company would welcome an investigation by a committee of ministers and economists. Mills then wrote to Edward Everett Hale and about a dozen other ministers and professional men asking them to serve on the committee. The conference failed to materialize when the company refused to consent to the presence of Henry Lloyd, upon which several members of the committee insisted.

In the eighties and nineties of the past century the socialist movement in the West was concerned largely with colonization schemes. Lloyd took an active part in such plans. The project of writing a history of the colony movement came to his mind, and he even considered joining one of these groups. He visited the Shakers at Mount Lebanon, New York, and was acquainted with Alfred Kinsley who founded the Topolobampo Colony in 1886. He wrote letters of encouragement to George Howard Gibson when the latter was considering founding a colony; he had friends in the Colorado Co-operative Colony, and in July, 1897, he made an address at the Ruskin Colony at Cave Mills, Tennessee, on the occasion of the laying of the cornerstone of Ruskin College. He looked upon these struggling experiments as the natural accompaniment of social theory—action arising from theory. The sight of these people, who were suffering privation and hardship to demonstrate that there was a higher way of life possible than that offered in the competitive business world, excited his admiration. As the capitalist press noted with satisfaction the failure of these colonies one after another, Lloyd noted a victory in their apparent failure. He wrote in his notebook:

Always failures? Only within these communities has there been seen in the wide borders of the United States, a social life where hunger and cold, prostitution, intemperance, poverty, slavery, crime, premature old age, and unnecessary mortality, panic, and industrial terror have been abolished. If they had done this only for a year, they would deserve to be called the only successful "society" on this continent, and some of them are generations old. They are little

[5] *Ibid.*

oases of people in our desert of persons. All this has not been done by saints in heaven, but on earth by average men and women.[6]

That the colonies were not able to survive economically was not a discredit to the philosophy of co-operation on which they were founded. It merely proved that socialism was not to be achieved piecemeal. The social problem had to be "solved in the womb of society by all" and not in isolated units.[7]

On the petition for a national convention of all socialists which resulted in the organization of the Brotherhood of the Co-operative Commonwealth, 1896, Lloyd's name was third on the list, following that of Debs. Although he was elected president by almost unanimous choice in the referendum vote, Lloyd declined to serve.

Lloyd considered his social philosophy to have been derived from what he conceived to be the true spirit of Christian philosophy. Economic freedom was but a corollary of spiritual freedom; and the demand of the worker for a fuller life was consistent with a principle of the religious equality of all men before God. Thus the new religion of labor was but an extension of the principles of Christian brotherhood. First had come religious freedom for the worshipper; then freedom for the citizen through universal suffrage; now men were approaching the final step in their emancipation in the fight for economic freedom. Economic democracy might be looked upon as the "first-born son of the liberty that came with Christ." The new religion would extend the sphere of the "Kingdom of God unto the unevangelized territory of trade, commerce, and industry." [8] Religion, like art, had been too long confined to churches and museums; it must now be made regnant in every human relationship.

In that day when we shall live our religion and our art . . . we shall have no exclusive temple of holiness and beauty, but every building like every deed, will be dedicated to the good and the beautiful, not for worship, as something beyond us, but for use in this or that daily expression of the productive energies of the common people.[9]

In the new religion there would be but one form of worship—work; but one form of prayer—aspiration. He clothed the ideals

[6] *Ibid.*, pp. 66-67.   [7] *Ibid.*
[8] *Ibid.*, p. 260.   [9] *Ibid.*, pp. 270-71.

of labor with the highest religious sanctions. He saw not merely
the cry of the hungry for bread, the revolt against oppression;
he regarded the unrest of the workers as part of the heroic
tradition of mankind, the modern phase of the age-old struggle
for a higher freedom and liberty for all men. It was the
"still, small voice" working for the emancipation of man from
tyranny.[10]

The criticism of the Church and of the traditional forms of
religious practice by men like Henry D. Lloyd and Henry
George, themselves deeply religious, was a thorn in the flesh of
a complacent institution. Lloyd had not joined the Church, he
wrote to a ministerial friend, not because he was irreligious, but
because he felt that the Church had lost the true spirit of religion as manifested by its callousness to the appeal of those
suffering from the injustice of the economic order. Institutional
religion, he wrote, tends to restrict itself to intermittent moods
of emotional fervor embellished with occasional charities and
surrounded by the accessories of song and stained-glass windows. It had accepted rented pews and preachers dependent
upon men of wealth. Thus genuine religion, founded on the
practice of the brotherhood of man and the apprehension of the
fatherhood of God, which is the outcome of a common struggle
for a high ideal, was developing outside the Church. A "new
conscience" or religion was welling up in the hearts of men,
irrespective of Church affiliations or religious conviction, which
revolted against "having one brother live in the slums, and another on the boulevard, one under a death-rate twice that of the
other." The heaviest indictment of the Church was that both
clergy and laymen ignored in silence the things that were done
daily in industry—to women in sewing rooms, to miners in
Spring Valley. While preaching "thou shalt not steal" it with-
held its anathemas from those who robbed wholesale, depriving
whole classes of people of home, life, liberty, and time for salvation.

. . . to consider it worshipping God to sing, pray, and listen to sermons, while all about them from the world without the church-

[10] Lloyd, *Man the Social Creator*, p. 118.

windows rise the cries of those who are being murdered, plundered, betrayed, seems to me, in truth atheism, not piety.

Mazzini and Emerson, to whom Lloyd refers as his masters, led up to, he wrote, but did not reach the concept of man as his own redeemer. It is this latter thought that is the central idea of his work, *Man the Social Creator,* which comes close to the humanism of Comte.

All the beauties and helps of the old-fashioned trust in God will some day reappear in a trust in man. Each of us will recognize that it is humanity which is the representation of the God he has been wor- shipping, praying to, loving, and trusting, and will transfer his loy- alties and hopes to the "really living God," man, having eyes to see that this is he who will make him walk in green pastures, to lie down by still waters . . .[11]

But in another instance he said that man is not truly God; he is better described as the "priesthood of God." God is the "sum total of our ideas," the immanent creative spirit in the universe transforming "matter into life and life into God." Such a con- cept of God required a new interpretation of the function of the Church. As God is immanent in all of mankind, so the Church must be co-extensive with the human race.

To a religious world preoccupied with the salvation of indi- viduals, Lloyd counseled the changing of institutions rather than individuals. The problem of building a better world was pri- marily an economic problem, not the moral problem of making bad people good. The task was one not merely of changing a few individuals but of destroying an entire economic system and the philosophy supporting it. A deeper cause than the de- pravity of individuals must account for the most dangerous factors of our social condition. Monopolists must be controlled, but they cannot be overcome until the political and industrial philosophy under which they have been permitted to grow has been cleared away.[12]

He pointed out how a dominant class makes the institutions of society subserve its own class interest; how in religion a bourgeois group selects for emphasis those traits which give

[11] Caro Lloyd, *op. cit.,* II, 8.   [12] *Ibid.*

security and permanence to the social order, while it disparages those qualities in the Christian tradition which made for change and rebellion. The new religion, however, would have for its strongest words, not "submission," "repentance," "trust"; but "unite," "create," "rise," "progress." [13]

. . . Resistance to tyrants, wrote Lloyd, is obedience to God, everywhere, in industry just as much as in politics, in the factories, or mines, just as much as in the state house. The Christ that will be, revolted by the torture of the flesh of the weak by the strong, shall teach the highest care of the body, the temple of the spirit.[14]

In 1886 when the Haymarket riot had set Chicago in a turmoil, and passions were aroused by the inflamed press, Henry Lloyd demonstrated how the new religion would function in a conflict.

On May 3, 1886, a fight occurred between some workers and scabs in front of the McCormick reaper works. Police arrived and fired indiscriminately upon the crowd of men, women, and children. Six were killed and many wounded. The next day a mass meeting of about two thousand people was held at the Haymarket for the purpose of "branding the murder of our fellow-workers." Mayor Carlton of Chicago, fearing trouble, attended. At about ten o'clock when the meeting was almost over, he left. In his own words:

I went back to the station and reported to Bonfield that I thought the speeches were about over; that nothing had occurred yet or was likely to occur to require interference, and I thought he had better issue orders to his reserves at the other stations to go home.

In the meantime a storm was gathering, and the crowd at the meeting had thinned out to a few hundred. Suddenly one hundred and seventy-six policemen marched upon the crowd and commanded it to disperse. At this juncture a bomb exploded in the midst of the police, killing one of their number and wounding others. Firing broke out on both sides. Seven policemen and four workers were killed and about sixty policemen and fifty workers were wounded. The leading anarchists of the city who had called the mass meeting and the editors and the staff of their paper were indicted. The eight men indicted included Samuel

[13] *Ibid.*, p. 127.   [14] *Ibid.*, p. 13.

Fielding, formerly a Methodist lay preacher. The eight men were charged not with having thrown the bomb but with having incited people to violence through their writing and speaking. The trial was conductetd in an irregular and partial manner. Judge Gary appointed a special bailiff to summon a jury of his own selection. Out of a panel of one thousand, only five were workers, and these were immediately excused by the state. In vain did the defense show that four of the eight were not even at the meeting and that the state's case rested on perjured testimony. The men were tried not for murder but for their political views. All were found guilty. One committed suicide in his cell; three were given life imprisonment; and four were hanged on November 11, 1887.[15]

On the Sunday following the execution Lloyd addressed the Chicago Society for Ethical Culture. His address, *The New Conscience*, was the occasion for an elaboration of his ideas on religion and labor. It attracted international attention.[16] The situation was tense. Judge Gary had recently addressed the Bar Association on the "tyranny" of labor. "The monopolies of capital are a mischief which calls for a remedy, but the burden from them upon the individual is so light as to be scarcely felt. Corruption in office adds temporary burden to taxes, frauds at elections put the wrong men in office. But none of these evils, unless in very rare instances, deprives anybody of the necessities of life. The tyranny of labor under which labor groans stops industry and takes bread from the mouths of hungry women and children. *What can we do to break it down?*"[17]

Lloyd did not mince his words. To a city still trembling from

[15] Six years later, in granting a pardon to the three imprisoned men, Governor John T. Altgeld reviewed the entire case. His denunciation of the partial manner in which Judge Gary had conducted the case ended for the governor what had promised to be a brilliant public career.—Morris Hillquit, *History of Socialism in the United States*, pp. 243-52.

[16] The address was published in the *North American Review*, September, 1888. Mr. Lloyd read it in London before the Fellowship of the New Life, afterwards the New Fellowship, parent of the Fabian Society, by whom it was published in pamphlet form. Governor Altgeld wrote to Lloyd: ". . . I would rather be the author of one such article than to hold any office in the gift of the American people. It will do more for the cause of humanity and will bring a greater meed of fame to its author than would a lifetime of the average high office-holding . . ."—*Ibid.*, p. 115.

[17] *Ibid.*, p. 101.

the fear of revolution he stated that the organization of labor was not revolution but the remedy for revolution. The revolution had occurred years before. It had "whirled the peasant and his children from his cottage loom and his village shop and non-competitive brotherhood, and herded them into tenement houses and factories." [18] The revolution had come with the entrance of high finance which chained people to an interlocking system of contracts, franchises, monopolies, stocks, charters, pyramiding directorates, and stifling debts. There are those, he said, who have cautioned us to avoid haste in dealing with this problem, as Lyman Beecher did on the slavery question, "but there has always been one thing that put God and man in a hurry—injustice." [19]

In dealing with the industrial problem, said Lloyd, the new religion of labor will retain the virtues of duty and tenderness, but it will do more than practice "the personal virtues of goodness; it can express its energies of righteousness only by public co-operation in the public welfare." [20] The Christian virtue of love also will be enjoined. It still is to be regarded as an effective instrument of social change.

The heart of man can not withstand the gentle force of love. Let the apostles of the new love like those of the old love, taking no thought of the morrow, having no stones and no slings, go forth among mankind to found the new church of love—the church of deed not of doctrine . . . It will conquer not by the blows it gives but by those it takes. The love it bears to the weak and lowly and oppressed will shake the new tyrants of the industrial world out of their vested rights as surely as the gentle words of Jesus and Socrates drove the lords of the political world out of their divine rights.[21]

While love is to be appealed to as one means for establishing social justice, Lloyd was too near to the industrial struggle and viewed such situations as that in which the city was then enmeshed too realistically not to appreciate that some measure of coercion would be necessary to bring justice to the workers. The value of peace and nonresistance, he stated, must not be elected to a higher place in the scale of values than that of social

[18] Lloyd, *Man the Social Creator*, p. 118.
[19] Caro Lloyd, *op. cit.*, p. 115.
[20] *Ibid.*, p. 127.   [21] *Ibid.*, p. 109.

justice. "There is but one evil greater than reform by force—
the perpetuation, the permanence of injustice." [22]

Lloyd voted the Socialist ticket in 1896 and 1900 and in the
last years of his life regarded himself as a thorough-going socialist. He was on the point of openly identifying himself with the
Socialist Party when he died suddenly in 1903. His notebook
written during that year indicated the dominant part Socialism
played in his thinking at that time and that he regarded it as the
symbol for a spiritual rebirth in human relationships. "Christianity," he wrote in his last notebook, "is the religion that was,
socialism is the religion that is to be." [23] Politics under the two
old parties is merely politics. "Our old politics, Democratic and
Republican, rest on habit, the persistence of organization, on
the bribes of money, on power, on selfish self-interest, but there
is no heart-beat in them, no hope or love." But socialism is true
democracy.

[It] strikes from the poor and the weak the many shackles of poverty, ignorance, monopoly, and opens to every man the closed door
of opportunity to be all that he may be, which proclaims that everything is the property of everybody, that each is the steward for his
brother and his neighbor of all that he is and has, that without money
and without price, by just being born into the ruling family of all
the people each one can have this salvation.[24]

[22] *Ibid.*, p. 112.   [23] *Ibid.*, p. 258.   [24] *Ibid.*, p. 268.

XII

CHRISTIAN COMMONWEALTH COLONY;
CHRISTIAN COMMUNISM IN GEORGIA

A COLONY unique in the history of American communities was that of the Christian Commonwealth, at Commonwealth, Georgia. The colonists sought to realize in practice the kind of society envisaged in the theories of such men as Herron, Bliss, and Bellamy. Started by a Congregational minister in 1896, it attracted to its midst during the four years of its existence between 350 and 400 people and through its magazine enlisted the support of religious radicals in all parts of the United States. The *Social Gospel*, founded as the organ of the colony but covering the entire field of social Christianity in America, had on its staff or among the contributors most of the leaders in this "new movement" to which the name of the magazine had been given. Following a series of disasters brought to a climax by an epidemic of typhoid fever, the colony disbanded in 1900.

The object of the founders, Ralph Albertson, George Howard Gibson, William C. Damon, and John Chipman, was to "organize an educational and religious society whose purpose is to obey the teachings of Jesus Christ in all matters of life, and labor and in the use of property." [1] The important word in the quotation is "property." All things were to be owned in common, and all who came were to be welcomed. No one was to be turned away. The tramp was to be received on an equal basis with the college professor. "Scientific Socialism" was criticized as "selfish" because it would restrict its gifts. In the Kingdom of God the injunction of Jesus to "turn not away from him that asketh" was to be taken seriously. And Christianity, instead of a dogma, was to be taken as a way of life equally valid for social as well as for personal relationships. From the Sermon on the Mount would be elicited an economic and political code. The resultant

[1] *Social Gospel*, February, 1898.

philosophy was a curious mixture of ideas drawn from Karl Marx, St. Francis, and Jesus.

The founders were disillusioned completely with the system of capitalism, the competitive world in which man must make his living at the expense of his brother. In the colony they would establish a co-operative society where men might share even their labor, where everyone might be the servant of the rest, even in their economic arrangements. They would set up an island of love and co-operation in the center of selfish capitalism, but not with any idea of escaping from their obligations to society, for they would maintain an open door that all who would, might enter. From the pulpit, from the college professor's chair, from the shops and farms, these idealists came, seeking a better way of life than they had known. Dissatisfied with the separation of theory and practice in institutional religion, fretting under the discrepancies between the protestations of brotherhood made from the pulpit and the ruthlessness of industrial life, they were resolved to follow an absolute love ethic of complete sharing. Their success would be a vindication of the efficacy of Christianity for solving social problems; their failure would be the failure of love. The social equation they set for themselves was: to prove by demonstration that Communism plus a passionate loyalty to Christian brotherhood equals the Kingdom of God. They underestimated the brutality and refractory quality of the type of human nature bequeathed to them by an individualistic society, but their heroic attempt to incarnate their ideal in a concrete situation is an absorbing chapter in the history of social Christianity in America.

In 1893 Ralph Albertson, a young theological student from Oberlin College, was pastor of the Lagonda Avenue Congregational Church in the industrial section of Springfield, Ohio. He had been impressed by the writings of George, Bellamy, and Tolstoy. While an undergraduate he had gone to Columbus to talk with Washington Gladden. Faced with the problems of an industrial parish, he was disturbed by the plight of the workers. What was his responsibility as a Christian minister? Did Christianity offer a solution to the problems of society as well as to the problems of the individual? He invited Professor Herron to deliver a course of lectures at the new institutional church which the workers of his congregation had just completed. In the passionate attacks which Herron made upon the capitalist system Albertson found some support for his own radical tendencies, but he must have action. In 1894 he went to Chicago. It was the year of the great Pullman strike. Albertson talked with Lucy Parsons, Altgeld, Florence Kelley, Bayard Holmes, Louis Post, Debs, Darrow, Comings, and Ernest Crosby. He spoke at the Forum conducted by Graham Taylor in The Commons, and visited Jane Addams at Hull House. In little group meetings which he attended possible tactics for meeting the revolutionary times were discussed. There were those who favored the colony idea. Albertson returned to Springfield with his mind and heart aroused by the violence and suffering attending that industrial struggle in Chicago. Then a strike broke out in the factories surrounding his own church. He addressed the men and spoke from his own pulpit on the issues of the strike. While all his sympathies were with the workers in their struggle for justice, he could not reconcile the strike instrument with the principle of non-resistance which seemed to be implied in the Christian ethic of love. He recognized before his eyes the class struggle but could not reconcile with his religion the solution proposed by Marx, the organization of the oppressed class to assert their rights against their enemies. The way of Christ had been the cross. Society as individuals must be redeemed by vicarious suffering. The colony idea became more important in his thinking. He finally resigned his pulpit and went to Andrews, N. C. A small colony had been founded there by William C. Damon. The latter, after teaching the classics for twenty years in a Methodist College at Napa, Calif., sought a better environment than that offered by the capitalist society in which to educate his children. An option had been acquired on one thousand acres of valuable timber land. Under the influence of Damon the colony was strictly prohibitionist in sentiment and was called the Willard Co-operative Colony. Together Damon and Albertson worked out plans for "The People's University" which was to be the center of the reorganized colony. An advance circular headed "The People's University" read in part:

Members will be admitted upon Fellowships and Scholarships . . . Fellowships will be held by persons who have given and surrendered all their property, real and personal, to the University. We own all things in common. Distribution is made "according as each hath need."

We believe that the political economy taught and lived by Jesus Christ is practicable, that the love and brotherhood of the Kingdom of Heaven may be realized on earth. We believe in the possibility of unselfishness, and we want to provide for the education of young people in an atmosphere free from greed. We pray "Thy Kingdom come" and we propose to live in that Kingdom on Earth ourselves and teach others so.

Scholarship members included those who paid to the University $100 for an individual and $250 for a family. The University was to be a "Labor Exchange Branch."

In the summer of 1896 Ralph Albertson contributed a series of articles to *The Kingdom* setting forth his ideas on socialism, property, and the relation of Christianity to social problems. He received a number of letters from people interested in pushing the ideas therein expressed in the direction of practical experimentation. Among his correspondents were John Chipman, of Florida,[2] and George Howard Gibson, of Lincoln, Neb. These two men had some previous correspondence as a result of which they had decided to found "The Christian Commonwealth Colony." A circular printed sometime between January and September, 1896, stated that there were twenty-five families ready to locate, with more ready to join. The circular read: "We have accepted the law of love, the standard of Christ, the teaching of the same Spirit that led Christ and his disciples to have 'all things in common.' It is the one way out of selfishness." Admittance to the colony was to be open to all "and never denied to any who give their devotion to Him." The colony would be started within sixty days probably in Northern Florida or Western Georgia where the land had been investigated and found satisfactory. "We plan for the visible kingdom of God on earth, for a holy land, to be redeemed by purchase out of the hands of the selfish and given to the meek."

Gibson and Chipman probably formed their contacts through

[2] A grandson of Daniel Chipman, the first Senator from Vermont, and a great-great-grandson of General Israel Putnam, of Connecticut.

the columns of *The Kingdom,* and, also through this medium, eventually joined Albertson and Damon. The articles in *The Kingdom* which gave rise to the founding of the Christian Commonwealth Colony were:

Nov. 25, 1895. "A Proposition," by John Chipman (Wade, Fla.) It was proposed to found a colony deeded to Jesus Christ. The fourth chapter of Acts was quoted and other Scripture referred to as authority for the Communist colony as the proper Christian method for solving the economic problem. The article brought forth a number of replies.

Dec. 13, 1895. "Is Communism Practicable?" by the Reverend C. S. Jobes (Menomonee, Wis.) Common property involves too great a surrender of individualism to be in accord with the best interests of the Kingdom of God. The New Testament words may point to an ideal not yet practicable.

Dec. 17, 1895. A reply to the above, by John Chipman.

Dec. 27, 1895. "Is It Practicable?" by J. H. Arnold (Redfield, S. D.) The answer is "no," as is proven by the drab picture of the Amana colony, Iowa.

Jan. 10, 1896. "Communistic Societies Unwise," by W. Harper (Americus, Georgia). The colony idea is un-Christian because it takes people out of society.

Jan. 17, 1896. "Communism Again," by George Howard Gibson (Lincoln, Neb.). Communism demanded by the Christian life. His family had been organized for ten years as a Christian Commune under the name of the Christian Corporation. Earlier colonies in America had failed, for example, the Brook Farm, because they were imperfectly Christian. "We reach·out glad, loving fraternal hands to Mr. Chipman whose proposition was printed Nov. 29th, and will locate with him in the best place to serve one another and the world."

Feb. 21, 1896. "A Reply From Mr. Chipman," by John Chipman. All objections answered.

Sept. 18, 1896. "Communism as a Remedy," by Henry Preserved Smith. All who complain of the evils of the social order were "Romanticists" belonging to the tradition of the back-to-nature movement. The social problem, he said, is a "problem of theology. For if there be a just and benevolent Ruler of the Universe, justice and love must be manifest in the constitution of human society as well as in the order of lower nature."

Albertson's articles during this period were: July 24, 1896, "Selfish Socialism"; Sept. 11, 1896, "Common Property"; Oct. 16, 1896, "The Social Incarnation"; Nov. 27, 1896, "New Evangelism"; April 2, 1897, "The Christian Commonwealth." These five articles were published later in pamphlet form under the title "The Social Incarnation."

It was agreed between them to launch a new colony. Albertson would have preferred to remain in North Carolina, but Chipman held to a location farther south. After a prospecting trip of three hundred miles on foot in October, 1896, Albertson, McKenzie, and Chipman decided on a site. On November 1 they purchased an old plantation of about one thousand acres, one-half upland, the rest swamp, situated about twelve miles east of Columbus, Ga. The high land was mostly worn-out cotton land. Chipman advanced $1,000 to make the first payment, and a mortgage for $3,000 was given on the balance.

The first contingent of colonists including the Damons, Albertsons, and others from Andrews, N. C., arrived the day before Thanksgiving, 1896. The Gibsons, Browns, and others from Lincoln, Neb., arrived the day before Christmas. A third group consisting of twenty-six persons, also organized by Gibson in Nebraska, arrived the following summer, August 27. They made the three-month trip from Lincoln in prairie schooners. Some of the dangers and hardships of the earlier westward trek of pioneers were repeated in this turning of the tide upon itself. One child died on the journey.

Through the personal contacts of members of the colony and through the colony magazine, the *Social Gospel*, many religious progressives and social workers became interested in the colony. "Golden Rule" Jones, Mayor of Toledo, who with N. O. Nelson and Ernest Hammond presented the colonists with a power plant, wrote:

I am a socialist. I believe in Brotherhood and can only find peace in advocating those principles that will lead men to live brotherly . . . What is called "success in business" to-day will be commonly understood to be only another form of exploitation or plunder long before the twentieth century is half over . . . Profit getting according to present-day methods is very largely robbery pure and simple; legal and respectable, I know, but so would highway robbery and gambling be both legal and respectable, if the highway robbers and gamblers made the laws as the profit getters do.[3]

[3] *Social Gospel*, May, 1901.

Jane Addams was a visitor at the colony. Edward Everett Hale offered them three hundred dollars to build a cottage for invalids, and Luther Burbank sent flowers and fruits from his home in Santa Rosa, Calif. Tolstoy was interested in the colony and corresponded with members. At one time he thought of sending the Doukhobors there. In a letter to Ernest Crosby, Tolstoy wrote:

I thank you for the information you give me, but must say that I feel especially concerned about all that goes on in The Christian Commonwealth. I read all their journal with deep interest and never cease to rejoice at the firmness of their views and beautiful expression of their thoughts. I should like to get as many details concerning their life as possible.[4]

Others who evinced an interest in the colony by letters or contributions included Bishop E. N. Potter, Charles Sheldon, Vida D. Scudder, Graham Taylor, John P. Gavit, Mary McDowell, E. T. Keyes, Henry D. Lloyd, Josiah Strong, Aylmer Maude, Keir Hardie, Frank Parsons, Tom Johnson, Ernest Howard Crosby, Bolton Hall, Wilbur E. Copeland, Hiram Vrooman, Emily Balch, Robert Blatchford, Alonzo Wardell, B. O. Flower, Herbert W. Gleason, Myron T. Reed, J. Stitt Wilson, Eltweed Pomeroy, Sam Walter Foss, B. Fay Mills, President George A. Gates, George D. Herron, William T. Brown, and hundreds of others.

SOCIAL PHILOSOPHY OF THE COLONY

To understand the motivation behind the colony one must bear in mind the strong negative attitude toward the existing economic order.

We believe that the competitive system of individualistic warfare, bearing the fruits of bitterness and oppression, is a great evil from which all who love must free the world and themselves as far as they may be able.[5]

Behind the individualism of the competitive business life they saw selfishness written large as the basic fact of that society. Accepting as they did the Christian assumption of the mutual responsibility for one another, and conceiving the Kingdom of

---

[4] *Ibid.*, October, 1899.   [5] *Commonwealth Details*, p. 3.

God as a society of brothers, they looked upon the job of revo-
lutionizing society as a primary task of their religion. Professor
Herron had said, "The worst charge that can be made against a
Christian is that he attempts to justify the existing social order." [6] They were impressed with the incongruity of teaching
children to love one another, then turning them loose in a world
where, if they lived at all, it was on the antithesis of that principle; a world dominated by the law of the jungle. The environment must be revolutionized so as to promote habits of mutuality. Selfishness was the commanding evil of the business world,
and private property was its stronghold; thus they reasoned that
if they could rid the world of that incubus they would release
men from the major incentive to sin.

While we do not hold that all sin is necessarily the product of property-selfishness, we do hold that property-selfishness is fundamentally
and directly responsible for the prevailing conditions in human life
in which are cultivated the deepest and darkest passions of all men,
both rich and poor, putting every man at necessary warfare with all
other competitors for life crushing down tens of thousands of weak
ones while the "fittest survive." [7]

The social philosophy of the colonists was centered in their
socialized and secularized notion of the Kingdom of God conceived as a society of brothers capable of realization on this
earth.

We have been drawn together by a common passion for individual
and social righteousness and for what we conceive to be the Kingdom
of God. It is the purpose of our lives as individuals and our life as an
organization to join ourselves to one another and to Christ in bearing
away the sins of the world. We make straight the way for the surely
coming reform of the twentieth-century which will be a reform of
propertyism and industrialism.

The incarnation is the gospel message of the New Testament. It is
the coming of God into human flesh and human life . . . Not only
are they who receive him individually to become the children of God,
but they receiving him into their social life, are to become the
Kingdom of God.[8]

As selfishness was the central fact of the capitalistic world,
so love was to be the foundation stone in the new society of the

[6] *Social Gospel*, March, 1898.
[7] Albertson, *Social Incarnation*, pp. 40-41.　　　　[8] *Ibid.*

colony. The injunction of Jesus "love thy neighbor as thyself" was to be the formal constitution of their life, and was known by them as the Law of Love. There was to be no creed but repentance for selfishness and obedience to the Law of Love, enlarged to apply to all social relationships. "The purpose common to us all was to demonstrate the practicability of the law of love in industrial life." [9]

There was no consciousness of fanaticism among the colonists. On the contrary they looked upon their plan as moving in the direction of rationality as well as justice. It was the world at large that was irrational in its social life, however sane its individual members might be, moving haphazardly without a plan and so destructive to human life. The way of Jesus based on the way of love combined justice and expediency.

The message of Commonwealth is not a message of fanaticism; it is a message of courage and good cheer to those who are capable of an earnest and faithful and cool-headed obedience to a high social ideal . . . The message that humanity needs to hear is the Kingdom of God is at hand. We hope to convince men of the truth of these oft repeated words. We attempt to portray this truth and to show that the truth is workable and livable and rational and feasible and possible of realization to common men and women. [10]

Professor Herron had emphasized the importance of the cross as the symbol of vicarious suffering in personal and social life, declaring that there is no other solution for social problems. This thought appears constantly in the writing of the editors of the *Social Gospel*. In a co-operative community such as the Christian Commonwealth where everyone shared responsibility, where all economic and other relationships were a common concern, they believed that love could be made to prove the solvent for all difficulties. Love was redemptive. By the demonstration of their willingness to share their all with a new member, they would arouse in him a corresponding spirit of good will. Thus they expected that even the indigent and the criminal, who would be received into their fold on an equal basis with all members, would be won over to their way of life by the sheer power

[9] Albertson, *The Christian Commonwealth,* an unpublished MS.
[10] *Social Gospel,* February, 1900.

of example. With the Marxians they sought to establish a class-less society, but their method was to be renunciation rather than coercion. "The meaning of the cross to the industrial and commercial world is the crucifixion of selfishness, which means the renunciation of private property, which is the way we must take who would 'bear away' the social sins of the world." [11] This technique of social change was consistent with the counsel of Jesus to overcome evil with good. This demonstration on the part of the poorer members of society would have its effect upon the more powerful members of society who would be moved, they believed, to voluntarily relinquish their power and change society into a co-operative venture. It was in part the method employed by Gandhi in his prison fast. The colonists would expect to suffer.

The body of men and women so given up to the passion for social righteousness that they would gladly die for it, must pass through the passion week of social reconstruction and suffer on the cross of commercial hatred, before the Kingdom in largeness can come.

They confidently expected that their way of life could be made operative throughout all of society.

The greatest need of the world is its need of love applied to its economic life. We need social reforms, but primarily we need social regeneration. Logically and necessarily redemption will precede reformation and love is the only redemptive force to count on . . . there are some, perhaps many . . . who seek the way of salvation for the purpose of walking in it, who are not scared by names of things, and who, when reason and revelation both call, will lovingly lay all upon the altar of the new social sacrifice which shall awaken social conscience in a disorganized humanity and lay the foundation of the divine social system of brotherhood and love—the Kingdom of God." [12]

Philanthropy which had masqueraded as the Christian ethic must be attacked, the colonists said, as the enemy of justice, the good standing in the way of the better. Individual and social vicarious living would pour out its all in an equalitarian society.

The pagan charities of a Croesus or a Vanderbilt and the cold blooded, clean skirted beneficence of a Lady Bountiful may represent

[11] *The Kingdom,* September 11, 1896.
[12] Albertson, *The Social Incarnation,* pp. 4, 11.

the activities of the Church, but they are by no means distinctively Christian . . . The call of Christ is a call to live the vicarious life— the life that pours out itself for other life—the life that is lovingly immersed in the life of the world—the life that is individually lost and socially found.[13]

The most important principle in the social philosophy of the colony was its insistence on the common ownership of property, for it was thought that the institution of private property had given rise to the preying of one man upon another in order to provide for himself and his family, to the accumulation of the material basis for the good life in the hands of the few with all of its attendant ills of a personal and social nature: the excitation of covetousness and avarice, exploitation, the elevation of ruthlessness and cunning into prime qualities for survival in the business world. "The root of social wrong is selfishness and the chief bulwark of selfishness is private property." [14] ". . . it sets man against man as an aggressor to get from, and a defender to keep from others all that is possible." [15] Money and property, like all other personal endowments, were to have in the colony no other function than to serve the common good. Communism seemed to them to follow naturally from their initial assumption of the obligation resting upon all Christians to follow literally the law of love.

Personal wearing apparel was privately owned but it as well as the houses we had to live in, was freely given to anybody who needed it, regardless of any theory of communism. I must say that through the entire history of the enterprise, there was the most unselfishness exhibited that I have ever known or heard about.[16]

This feature of complete communism was the aspect which most appealed to the writer in the Socialist paper, *The Coming Nation,* who described the colony:

If any man becomes a member of the colony he must add what he can to the commonwealth of the place, whether it be much or little. If it be much, it gives him no higher standing than if it is little, for it is for the common good and he reaps the benefit either way. The common interest is the concern of all and is shared alike by all.[17]

[13] *Social Gospel,* June, 1901.
[14] Albertson, *The Kingdom,* September 11, 1896.
[15] Albertson, "Christianizing Property," *Twentieth Century,* May 27, 1897.
[16] *Ibid.*
[17] Albertson, *The Christian Commonwealth.*

In the letters of inquiry from prospective colonists questions were frequently received concerning this problem of equality. "Suppose I should want to take a trip to Europe, or go home to see mother, or want to dress better than my neighbors, or want to send my daughter to Europe to study art in Paris; how should I get the money to do it with?" The answer of the colony was that it would provide all legitimate needs to the best of its capacity, that socialism envisaged a society where luxuries as well as necessities were free for all but that

at present the call of Christ was to give up needless luxuries and worldliness and mammonism and selfishness and bear the cross of social redemption. Commonwealth should not attract people whose first thought is about a trip to Europe for themselves. It is an organ of social sacrifice wherein the disciples of Jesus find abundant life—with tribulations.[48]

Mr. and Mrs. Marchand, the former an ex-president of the Icaria Community, Iowa, were living in Columbus and took an active interest in the colony. They lived with their daughter and son-in-law, Mr. and Mrs. William Ross, who frequently visited Commonwealth and maintained a close contact with its members. Mr. and Mrs. Ross had also been members of the Icaria colony, and the latter had been the editor of their French journal. Mrs. Marchand spoke of Commonwealth as being in the same category as the "peaceful French and English Communists" whose work was now "bearing fruit." Referring to Mrs. Marchand, the editor of the *Social Gospel* wrote: ". . . her memory of the revolution of 1848 is very distinct, and it is refreshing to mark how deeply imbedded in her soul are the truths that separate her girlhood from the force methods of her co-patriot French communists." [19] Keir Hardie was a friend of the colony. Another link with European thought was through Mr. and Mrs. Franks, two English Christian Socialists who had heard of the colony in London and had joined the Commonwealth group.

While the colonists lived in the simplest manner, it was a poverty self-imposed, not because of a belief in the virtue of asceticism *per se,* but because of a belief in the absolute nature of an equalitarian ethic.

[18] *Commonwealth Details,* p. 11.   [19] *Social Gospel,* June, 1898.

. . . all beauty and every luxury belong in the Kingdom of God—but so does every child of God belong in that Kingdom—so does economic justice . . . therefore no one child of God can live in a palace while another lives in a hovel.[20]

We have more in common with St. Francis, Albertson said, than with Marx.[21] In the joyous self-giving of the Franciscan brothers and in their voluntary poverty they found a bond of unity and of sympathy with their own way of life.

We have [he said] this advantage over Francis of Assisi. We live in an industrial age. We have machinery. We have group production, organization, modern science. And our objective is primarily social. Otherwise his faith and his life are for us to follow. To preach a social gospel, however, we must have land and industrial equipment.[22]

When Albertson wished to pay the highest compliment to three of the founders of the colony he said of them: "Damon and Chipman and Gibson were prepared to live up to their most radical convictions; they were of St. Francis metal." [23] Sabatier's life of St. Francis was a popular volume in the colony. The diary of Sue Fay Hinckley, teacher of the Commonwealth school, contains several quotations from that work.

The Bishop of Assisi said to Francis one day: "Your way of living without owning anything seems to me very harsh and difficult." "My Lord," replied he, "if we possessed property we should have need of arms for its defense, for it is the source of quarrels and law suits, and the love of God and of one's neighbor usually finds many obstacles therein: this is why we do not desire temporal goods.[24]

At the beginning of the colony it was decided that an open-door policy would be maintained, according to all who entered the colony full voting and owning membership regardless of their economic standing. This principle was considered of central importance by the colonists. It was a distinguishing characteristic of Commonwealth which defined for them "Christian" communism as compared with the type of communism practiced in other communities. It was a necessary corollary to their law of love.

[20] *Ibid, June,* 1901.   [21] *Ibid,* September, 1899.
[22] Albertson, *The Christian Commonwealth.*
[23] *Ibid.*   [24] Sue Fay Hinckley, *Diary.*

We cannot turn aside, nor exclude, the least of his brethren. To our feast we must call the halt, the maimed, the lame and blind, the prejudiced, the ignorant, the criminal and the poor. As Christ called them and loved them, so must we.[25]

When Jane Addams visited the colony and found this open-door policy in operation, she asked in amazement why they were not besieged with applications from the poor and destitute of the countryside. Her comment on that occasion is of interest as giving a first-hand description of a fundamental aspect of the colony life by a discerning and sympathetic mind.

The visit Miss Smith and I made a year or two later to a colony in one of the Southern States, portrayed for us most vividly both the weakness and the strange august dignity of the Tolstoy position. The colonists at Commonwealth held but a short creed. They claimed in fact that the difficulty is not to state truth but to make moral conviction operative upon actual life, and they announced their intention to "obey the teachings of Jesus in all matters of labor and the use of property." They would then transfer the vindication of creed from the church to the open field, from dogma to experience.

The day Miss Smith and I visited the Commonwealth colony of three score souls, they were erecting a house for the family of a one-legged man, consisting of a wife and nine children who had arrived the week before in a forlorn prairie-schooner from Arkansas. As this was the largest family the little colony contained, the new house was to be the largest yet erected. Upon our surprise at this liberal giving "to him that asketh," we inquired if the policy of extending food and shelter to all who applied, without test of creed or ability, might not result in the migration of all the neighboring poor house population into the colony. We were told that this actually had happened during the winter until the colony fare of corn meal and cow peas had proved so unattractive that the paupers had gone back, for even the poorest of the Southern poor-houses occasionally supplied bacon with the pone if only to prevent scurvy from which the colonists themselves had suffered.[26] The difficulty of the poor house people had thus settled itself by the sheer poverty of the situation, a poverty so biting that the only ones willing to face it were those sustained by a conviction of its righteousness.[27]

[25] Albertson, *Social Incarnation*, pp. 8, 44.
[26] Mrs. G. H. Gibson states that she cannot remember a one-legged man with nine children, or any cases of scurvy, or any migration from poorhouses.—*Personal letter to the author.*
[27] Jane Addams, *Twenty Years at Hull House*, pp. 277-79.

It was this complete sharing and universal gesture of brother-hood that vindicated the colony against the criticism that it was merely saving its soul by withdrawing from society, instead of remaining in the world to accomplish its salvation. Among the men who criticized the colony on this ground were Herbert W. Gleason, editor of *The Kingdom,* and W. D. P. Bliss, the latter an associate editor of the *Social Gospel* for a brief period. Replying to Bliss's article "Self-saving colonies condemned," [28] Gibson wrote "A defense of the Commonwealth Colony." [29]

By giving up private property [wrote Gibson] and its pursuit, and making ourselves brothers to all men we have for all time joined our-selves to the world, instead of having separated ourselves from it . . . We have solved the problem of getting men to live together as brothers . . . We have brought into brotherhood relation here pro-fessional men and common laborers, the highly cultivated and the unrefined . . . We have made real brothers of men who belong to the various orthodox churches and to no church. In politics we have blended Republicans, Democrats, Populists, Prohibitionists, and Tol-stoyan non-resistants. We have welcomed people who came to Com-monwealth in Pullman coaches, in box cars, and on foot. Not a tramp has been turned away from our doors. We have all lived for months and months on less than three cents each per meal, in order to divide with the world's destitute ones.

The colonists also counted on their poverty to protect them from members in too great numbers who came for selfish reasons. "A brotherhood cannot function in any other way, for if it prospers and becomes exclusive, it attracts only selfish folk." The oppo-site policy was responsible for the failure of other colonies, "Money, not manhood; entrance fees, not love; they trusted." [30] "The leading inducement to enter a society of brothers must be made nothing material to get or to tempt the selfish beyond to-day's bread and this must be labored for when strength to labor is possessed." [31]

The drive for perfection, the passion for incarnating man's dreams of social justice in sticks and stones is a universal note of all social creative endeavor. Aesthetics and ethics coincide at this point. The artist and the savior would reshape the physical

[28] *The Kingdom,* April, 1899.
[30] *Social Gospel,* June, 1900.
[29] *Ibid,* April 6, 1899.
[31] *Ibid,* January, 1900.

stuff of life until it more nearly conforms to their ideas of beauty or of justice, or of both in the case of these Utopian socialists following Bellamy, Morris, and Ruskin. The obstinacy of his material plus faith that his abstract ideal will inevitably become concrete lead the prophet to look for a complete overthrow of the existing order. This is usually dependent upon one strategic factor which must be destroyed before the new era may be ushered in. For the colonists this factor had a double aspect of human selfishness and the institution of private property. Each one in a way impregnated the other; but by destroying the one, they hoped to be able to control the other. Thus they would prepare the ground for the final flowering of that spirit of mutuality which lies within nature as the incarnation of Deity. The good life, the ultimate goal of the highest intellectual and ethical argosies seemed not at all a far off event, rather it appeared to be almost within reach to this little group of colonists as they started on their high adventure on the day before Thanksgiving, 1896.

While various groups and individuals began arriving in Commonwealth during October, the formal organization of the colony was not perfected until January, 1897, when about one hundred people from Ohio, Florida, Nebraska, Washington, Massachusetts, California, and other states formed what they were pleased to call an "educational and religious society whose purpose it is to obey the teachings of Jesus in all matters of life and labor and the use of property."

Members were asked, but not required, to sign a covenant:

I accept as the Law of my Life Christ's Law that I shall love my neighbor as myself. I will use, hold or dispose of all my property, my labor and my income, according to the dictates of love, for the happiness of all who need. I will not withhold for any selfish ends aught that I have for the fullest service that love inspired. As quickly as I may be able to, I will withdraw myself to the co-operative life and labor of a local Christian Commonwealth. As a member of this organization, I will work according to my ability in labor together with God, for the production of goods for human happiness.

The government of the colony was loose and democratic. There was an elected president to preside at business meetings and an executive committee composed of the superintendents of the various departments of labor, but most of the important business of the colony and all important policies were transacted by a meeting of the membership of the entire colony. William C. Damon served as president during most of the life of the colony. Gibson was president for one year. Although Albertson was the most influential member and the natural leader of the group, he refused to be elected president because of a desire to set the example of humility.

It was not until two years after the founding of the colony, when internal difficulties threatened disruption, that the colony was incorporated. This was looked upon as the first important compromise with their absolute standard of love and nonresistance, the first concession to expediency, for it meant that the forces of the State were invoked to protect their property.

The charter was granted by the Muscogee County Courts November 14, 1898, and the first election under the new articles of incorporation was held December 3 in the new schoolhouse. William C. Damon was elected president; Sue Fay Hinckley, vice-president; Jule Talmadge, secretary; Jacob Troth, treasurer; and a long list of minor officials were named. Under the new charter all newcomers were required to apply for membership within three months after their arrival. During that time they were to be on probation. Nonmembers were asked to sign a contract stipulating what had been previously only verbally understood, that they were not to receive wages other than board.

During the first year of the colony most of the effort of the members was devoted to clearing the ground, erecting cottages and work houses, and to laying the foundation for future development. In 1898 their physical equipment included about twenty-six buildings: a sawmill, barns, blacksmith shop, dining room, print shop, school, bachelors' hall, cotton mill, farm buildings, fourteen cottages, and the plantation house.

A cotton mill was opened in January, 1899, for the manufacturing of towels. A sum of $250 for this purpose was donated by Mrs. Burleigh Curtis, of Paris, France. The colonists could not escape from the capitalist system, for the products of their mill had to be sold on the competitive market. An advertisement in the *Social Gospel* read, "We can undersell the each-for-himself world if we will."

By 1898 when the first issue of the *Social Gospel* appeared, a large nursery and a thirty-five acre orchard had been planted, three hundred acres had been fenced for pastures, and two hundred acres were under cultivation. They raised oats and rye, and some wheat and barley. The principal crops were corn, sweet potatoes, and garden vegetables. Their most ambitious project was an orchard of ten thousand Japanese plum and peach trees, and a young nursery of 50,000 stock. The farm stock was small, consisting of eight cows, six mules, two horses, twenty pigs, a small flock of poultry, about 50 hares, and a few beehives.

Machinery included a twenty-five horsepower sawmill, grist-mill, shingle machine, looms, three boilers, and engines, steam washing machine, steam sawmill, cane mill, feed mill, printing equipment including a cylinder press, and a blacksmith shop. Each morning Mr. Hinckley, the superintendent of labor, assigned the work for the day, after consultation with the superintendents of the various departments which included farming, sawmill, printing, orchard, head housekeeper, cotton mill, school, head of the commissary, buildings, and so forth.

One major problem in a communist society is how to secure industrial efficiency without economic rewards and how to treat the lazy members of the community. In the Soviet world the principle of graduated economic rewards is still maintained in a modified manner, although profit has been eliminated as a basic goal. "Socialist competition" and differential of incomes is used to stimulate production. But in Commonwealth there was absolute equality. ". . . all who brought property and money, literally and legally had not a whit more than the tramp who had crawled out of a freight car for a drink of water, and found himself an equal owner in this Kingdom of God." [32]

A time chart of labor was kept showing each person's contribution, but it was never used as a basis for rewards. Under the pure communism practiced in the colony the only incentive was that of the common need. The problem of efficiency, said Albertson,

[32] Albertson, *The Christian Commonwealth.*

was never solved, but "we came nearer to it than the outside world . . . We uncovered motives that have not been discovered in New York . . . Everybody, men, women and children found in the common good the only reward they wanted and in the displeasure of the community the greatest punishment possible . . . In general we followed the principle of 'from each according to his ability' and so far as the community was able to furnish it, 'to each according to his need.' "[33]

Through all of the heat and the even more disastrous killing frosts of Georgia seasons, wrestling with a stubborn run-down plantation soil, attacked by the malaria which awaits the Northerner in most Southern states, these pioneers went forth joyously to tackle every problem, finding their satisfaction in the struggle for a common end and rewarded with an exhilaration of spirit out of all proportion to the results of their labors.

There was a pleasure about this rare condition that nothing else in all the experience of my life can parallel. I can't describe it very well. I think it amounts simply to a feeling of nearness to other people . . . I am inclined to think that it is only in life organized something like ours was that a true, keen happiness can come from contact with people one does not like. And as for those one does like, there is something indescribably beautiful that comes among such as the direct result of the abolition of private property. . . . We plunged into the woods with axes and into ditches with spades and into fields and hedges and wherever labor was needed and worked ourselves into unutterable weariness day after day, and month after month, in that exquisite new joy of comradeship and the hope of an honest world.[34]

In their family relationships the arrangements of homes, dress, and the care of children, the colonists followed conventional lines. Homes were provided for families as fast as they could be built. Fourteen such cottages were erected, and five families lived in the "big house."[35] The homes were simple structures, but were decorated and made homelike by the hands of love. Flowers were used to cover up the rough lumber and

---

[33] *Ibid.*   [34] *Ibid.*

[35] Cottages were occupied by the Comingses, Gibsons, Cooks, Damons, McDermotts, Albertsons, Loiselles, Henrys, and in the big house were the Peases, Croyles, Carmans, Halls, and Staiffs.

relieve the severity of the home-cut boards. Sue Fay Hinckley described her own cottage thus:

April 13th, 1900. Oh this South! Its blossoms are something to live always in one's memory. Lou just rode past with her arms as full as they could be of great pink azaleas, Wonderful just to see. Such a mass of soft pinks! A great handful came to me and is on our little stand. Just behind it is a branch, ceiling-high, of dogwood with its great snowy blooms. On my dresser is a vine of fragrant yellow jasmine . . . And in a vase is such a cluster of honeysuckle as it would seem wicked to pick from a vine in the North . . . A wonderful South! [36]

At first meals were prepared by each family; later a common dining room was built and most of the members made use of it, although four families still preferred to eat at home. The food necessarily was meager and plain. The one unfailing staple was corn meal prepared in every conceivable fashion. A bit of doggerel sung by the children while "doing the dishes" was eloquent testimony of their feelings.

> Corn bread for breakfast,
> Corn bread for dinner,
> Corn bread for supper,
> Way down on the colony farm.
> We won't go North any more.[37]

The diet included great quantities of sweet potatoes; pork bought in limited amount; a few eggs; a pitiful supply of milk and butter. Cottonseed oil was used in place of lard. They manufactured their own cereal coffee and peanut butter. During their lowest period they lived on three cents per individual meal. Some idea of the variety and quantity of the food may be had from a typical weekly ration list. Rations for March, 1899. For 100 people: adults 64, children 36 (23 single men, 10 single women) 600 pounds corn meal, 100 pounds wheat flour, 150 pounds wheat middlings, 100 pounds pearl grits, 7 gallons cottonseed oil, 30 gallons milk, 5 dozen eggs, some pork, fish, and minor concomitants.[38]

Distribution of expenses for six months (Jan. 1st to July 1st, 1899). Total expense, $2473.00: agricultural supplies, $512,

[36] Hinckley, *Diary*.   [37] *Social Gospel*, April, 1898.   [38] *Ibid*, April, 1899.

mechanical, $217, cotton mill, $276, food, $405, clothing, $66.[39]
But on the whole they continued healthy and happy and carried on their principle of sharing, which they applied to the
smaller items of life as well as the larger and more important
matters.

. . . here on my desk is a cup of sugar, from Ida McDermott. Mine
was all gone and they are out at the house—but Ida uses hers so
carefully that it never seems to give out; then she gives it out. Bless
her! [40]

The making of beds was done by the single women, something of
a chore because of the large number of bachelors. One pastor in
the North on hearing of this situation had the brilliant idea of
using the colony to relieve his congregation of all its "old maids."
He wrote asking if he could not "colonize all his Christian single
ladies." [41]

Although in the South during the incipient stages of the colony there was some suspicion that the sex relations of the members were irregular, an erroneous assumption generally made by
the public with reference to almost all colonies, this phase of
social life was not open to experiment. When one member with
an opposing viewpoint appeared at a meeting he was voted down
immediately. At no time was an unconventional attitude toward
sex tolerated. Several marriages among members of the colony
took place and the celebrations attending such ceremonies were
among the happiest social gatherings of the colony. The only
serious rupture in the amicable and peaceful life of the colony
was precipitated by the advent in the colony, via the "rails," of
a person who advocated considerable more freedom in sex relations. He seems, however, to have been chiefly interested in discrediting the colony in the eyes of Southern neighbors. He was
expelled because of his evident intent to disrupt the colony.
Another single member of the colony was expelled because he
had concealed the fact of his marriage.

Clothes were private property, each family having a special
mark for their garments. But some restraint was placed upon

[39] Albertson, *The Christian Commonwealth*.
[40] Hinckley, *Diary*.   [41] *Social Gospel*, February, 1898.

members in the matter of wearing apparel in an effort to preserve the standard of equality. Sue Fay Hinckley describes in her diary a "spring opening of hats." Each woman was entitled to two.

The colony school was accredited by the Muscogee County School Association, and Sue Fay Hinckley, teacher of the school, was a member of the county teachers' association. A few children from the countryside were permitted to enter the Commonwealth school. The curriculum differed but little from the curricula of the county schools except that the children were indoctrinated with the communist philosophy and were taught the merits of an economy founded on productive service for the common good. That this early training was not without results may be judged from an amusing incident that transpired after the dissolution of Commonwealth. A group of ex-colonists had moved to Long Island. In the town where they had taken up their residence the local hotel proprietor offered to employ some of the women. When one of the children heard of this, she exclaimed, "Well, I never! Does Mr. Brown need our ladies to help him when he has a dozen ladies sitting around all day on his front porch doing nothing?" And another family of former colonists had made arrangements to rent an apartment. This was explained to the daughter who said, "Rent, what's that? Do you mean that we must pay Mr. Jones for using his rooms when he has a whole house that he never uses?" [42] The colony children were described as the "best co-operators we had." A letter written by sixteen-year-old Ruth Damon reveals the extent to which the youth of the colony shared the ideals of the Commonwealth.

. . . there are about eighty of us in the colony now, and we are all of us happy and contented. We have a post-office (of which George Damon is the postmaster), a saw-mill, a blacksmith shop, a printing-office . . . Everything here is classed as ours, not yours or mine. Nearly everything is held in common. To make a long story short, we are one big family, and this is the most unselfish way to live. We are nearly always happy. Every individual looks out for the other's needs and wants, and by that way none are left to suffer.

[42] Sue Fay Hinckley, in a conversation with the author.

Our motto is: "From each according to his ability; to each according to his need." I would not exchange this life for any sum of money. I think it is the only way this wicked world can be awakened to righteousness and Christianity.

There is an abundance of material in this world that is needed so much, but it is going to waste. The rich people take the best, and the poor people go without, while the rest is destroyed.

If everyone lived as we are living here at Commonwealth, there would be no rich and poor. Everyone would fare alike, as everyone should. The outside world's motto is "Every man for himself." Now which do you think is the best? Our motto or the above?

I most sincerely believe nothing could induce me to give up this grand, noble work, which I am convinced meets with God's approval. I realize more and more of what little use I have been, and how utterly small and insignificant I am, but I *will* become something more than a mere self-seeker who breathes, eats, sleeps and works a little and cares only for worldly pleasures . . . Think of these hard headed business men who glory over their gains and live off the poor, while the poor are dying from cold and starvation, and even the ground they are buried on, sometimes, is all but denied them. Some men are rich in money, but poor as Job's turkey in God's blessings. Think of John D. Rockefeller, what he is making off the poor and needy! It's an awful sin, and the older I get the wiser I become on such things, and the less I love riches . . .[43]

Many different denominations were represented in the colony, including Episcopalians, Congregationalists, Presbyterians, Methodists, and Quakers. Albertson was a Congregational minister; John Chipman was an Episcopalian and spent his life in the Southern states as an Episcopalian rector; Jacob Troth was a Quaker and president of the Virginia Peace Society; William Damon had taught for twenty years in a Methodist college in California. While some retained their denominational affiliations, there was a general feeling of discontent with the Church for its failure to take a stand on the industrial problem and its acceptance of the gifts of the capitalist world without scrutinizing the sources from which they came. Their only solution of modern social problems is in the

altruism of Jesus and this solution is strictly the business of the church. The church cannot be free of blood-guiltiness if she stands aside while the weak are oppressed and the innocent suffer . . . If

[43] Ruth Damon, in a letter quoted by the *Social Gospel*, December, 1898.

the existing church cannot or will not take upon herself the promotion of righteousness and the conservation of the common good in economic affairs, then we shall see a new church, an organization of the people of God . . . The church which should stand in the majesty of its commission and bid it (the warfare of business) cease, takes it, rather, for granted that might is right, that shrewdness should crush weakness, and plays the charity part of a Red Cross society while the horrid butchery goes on. Worse, she takes tribute of the victors!

Beauty and art and magnificence have taken the place of love and justice and truth. There is a place for them in our lives, but we may not enjoy them before our fellows have health, justice, cleanliness, fellowship . . . That which is built upon silk-cushions and cut glass, gold plated service and mahogany furniture and pipe organs, and high salaried ministers, while the poor suffer and the sick die of neglect, and all this money is wrung from the hands of poorly paid labor—is built upon sands.[44]

Religious services were held twice on Sundays with considerable experimentation in the order of service. Damon preached expository sermons and liked to discuss theology, "so that his preaching was less popular than he himself"; Chipman conducted a high-church Episcopalian service but with so little response that he "gave us up for lost." Troth led a Quaker meeting. Most of the Sunday speaking was done by Albertson whose faith in Commonwealth and in the life they were leading and whose capacity for calling out the best in each member were among the important bonds that held the colony together, making their hardships appear less irksome and lending a deeper significance to the enterprise than was apparent because of its physical aspects. Morning prayers were held daily after breakfast but attendance was optional. A Bible-study group met just before the Sunday-morning service. A mid-week service corresponding to the "prayer-meeting" was held on Thursday evenings when readings were given from favorite authors and from the Bible. An outline of a series of Sunday-morning studies in the Old Testament was printed in the *Social Gospel*.

The political economy of the Hebrew Theocracy; law regarding usury; the fact and reasons for the year of jubilee; the rejection of God as King and of Brotherhood and Equality, with consequent oppression and final national destruction; and the brave work of the

[44] *Social Gospel*, June, 1901.

prophets who by preaching brotherhood and righteousness to one people spoke the truth for all people of all times . . .[45]

There was something of missionary ardor in the early organization of the colony. Those who signed the covenant but did not join the colony were "to preach the gospel" and gather about them "a band of converts . . . with whom they can join hands, hearts, and property in the uplifting redemptive work of our leader, Christ." [46]

The life of the colony, which never advanced in its physical aspects very far beyond the pioneer stage, was marked by hard, sweating labor, but that only made the evening fellowship around the open hearth the sweeter. Study groups were formed for the discussion of literary, philosophical, and scientific subjects. Adult education classes met three evenings a week. The library numbered about 1,400 volumes. The women's society studied Morris, Emerson, and a special class met for the study of Shakespeare. Mrs. Albertson gave piano lessons to the children. There were peanut roasts, hiking in the woods, and parties to celebrate anniversaries when the slender provisions were augmented in what must have seemed an extravagant manner. Afternoon teas were also a part of co-operative life. That not all the members attained to the high personal standards marked out by the leaders may be gathered from this rather human bit of feminine by-play.

Went to call on Mrs. Colette this afternoon. She is an odd little woman full of prim ways and little preciseNesses—giving me information about Karl Marx, Christine Nihilson, Emerson and the school of transcendentalists, as if every school girl didn't know perfectly well the facts she imparted. She also took me to task for not sufficiently softening a "C" in a French name. She carefully noted meanwhile, so that I could not help but be aware of it, the cut of my dress, taking pains to get around where she could see the back of it. It is the only place in Commonwealth where the dress would not have been frankly questioned about if any interest were felt.[47]

While the general impression given by the colony life is that it was too rigorously tied down to the stern tasks of wresting a living from a none-too-congenial soil to permit of much light-

[45] *Ibid*, February, 1898.
[46] *Ibid*.   [47] Hinckley, *Diary*.

heartedness; still, one episode at least would indicate that life was not too depressed by preoccupation with weighty matters, for one member of the colony took his departure because of the alleged frivolity of colony life.

As Mr. Maginnis departed, he did us much good by saying that his objection to Commonwealth was that there was too much frivolity and not enough serious conversation. Now we have been accused of almost every failing under the sun save this one . . . too sober, grave, sedate—even extremely dull—and under the weight of daily burdens our consciences seemed to say "amen" . . . But frivolous! We had such a laugh over it that our dinners digested rapidly. Sure proof that the criticism was true.[48]

The Social Gospel

About eighteen months after the founding of the colony, the question of a journal to relate the colony more closely to the world at large was proposed. At first there was some opposition, allayed when Albertson agreed to take full responsibility for it and to turn it over to the colony when it became self-supporting. It was said that the colony should meet the primary physical needs of life before further obligations were assumed. But as it turned out, the magazine, which was given the name *Social Gospel*, became one of the principal means of support of Commonwealth for the next two years. A thirty-six-page monthly publication, it undertook to cover the entire field of social Christianity and to interpret through one or two pages of colony notes the life of the colony for the benefit of friends throughout the county. There were editorial and feature articles on the subject of Christian Socialism, book reviews and a summary of national and international events with editorial comment on its ethical significance. Labor news was given special attention. When *The Kingdom* was forced to suspend publication, unexpired subscriptions were filled by copies of the *Social Gospel* and by Graham Taylor's publication *The Commons*. The circulation of the *Social Gospel* numbered about two thousand which were distributed in America and Europe.

While the colonists did not approve of coercion, a sympathetic attitude was maintained toward the efforts of labor to organize

[48] *Ibid.*

and improve its position. Industrial conflicts were described as "industrial warfare between the opposing forces of profit extorting capital and organized labor." The class struggle was recognized, at least implicitly, as it was by almost no other religious journal of that period. Some effort was made to arouse a social consciousness by pointing out the solidarity of mankind, that all members of the upper- and middle-economic groups by reason of their receiving a living from such a class-divided society were implicated in its sins and must share social responsibility for its injustice. The incident of the trial of Sheriff Martin, of Wilkes-Barre, Pa., for the shooting of striking miners in the fall of 1897, when eighteen miners were killed and forty wounded, was used to illustrate how all members of a society which permitted conditions to arise which would inevitably bring on such a tragedy must be judged guilty of having taken human life. "The miners, their condition, the strike, their death are the products of your selfish greed and the system you uphold for the sake of it." [49] The story of New England manufacturers who beat down the wages of their operators for the alleged reason of meeting the competition of the South, where overhead was much lower, was used to indicate the futility of trying to improve society by piecemeal reform. Only a thoroughgoing change in the entire system would avail finally to solve the problem. Often the mere recital of the bald facts of an industrial struggle, omitting any moral judgment, was impressive; for example, the case of the Chicago-Virden Coal Company, Virden, Ill. Ignoring the State Arbitration Board, the company locked out the miners and, when the Governor refused to call out state troops for the protection of hired strike breakers, armed a force of private gunmen to protect a trainload of Negroes imported from Alabama to break the strike. The workers attempted to keep them out. Twenty lives were lost and fifty men wounded. In September, 1899, the *Social Gospel* reported that sixty-five strikes were in progress, with troops under arms in four states. While the sympathies of the editors were with the workers, they were prevented from actively participating in the struggle with the workers in the interests of justice because of their principle

[49] *Social Gospel*, 1898.

of absolute nonresistance, according to which they looked upon strikes as instruments of coercion and inimical to the principle of love. The qualification of their pacifism on the occasion of the law suit, did not seem to have materially affected their philosophy of social change.

The editorial policy toward war wavered. It neither supported nor attacked the government for its conduct in the Spanish-American War, but maintained on the whole a mildly critical position. To have been consistent, of course, with its principle of nonresistance and absolute love it should have been plain-spoken in its criticism of the government for its use of force in the settlement of international disputes. The editors did, however, point out the incongruity of holding high Mass on the "Vermont" in the Brooklyn Navy Yard while at the same time the "Mayflower" was flying the red flag indicating that powder was being loaded in its magazines, and of playing of Easter music by the navy band and the singing of anthems by the choir while hammers and drills played a chorus to the god of war. Such contrasts between theory and practice were said to be an indication that the Church and State had "entombed" the teaching of Jesus. "Christ is not risen. He is crucified by their fighting." [50] But if the editors hesitated to take a clear-cut position of pacifism, at least one associate editor left no doubt where he stood on the question. Ernest Howard Crosby was thorough-going and forthright in his absolute renunciation of all wars, and of this one in particular.

There should be no "buts" and "ifs" for Christians in this matter of war. War means hate: Christianity means love, and there can be no truce between them. . . . No argument whatever is admissible in its behalf, and only on the plea of some kind of insanity can the lips that defend it be recognized as other than savage and pagan. We must prick the bubble of this monstrous illusion which makes a by-word of the pretensions of the followers of the Prince of Peace. [51]

Ernest Howard Crosby, Henry C. Potter, William Dean Howells, Bolton Hall, and Charles Francis Adams signed a manifesto directed to the workers of America disavowing the war. The Maine question should have been arbitrated, they said,

[50] *Ibid.*   [51] *Ibid.*, July, 1898.

and Spain was no more cruel than the United States; the war was merely a device for speculators to sell shoddy supplies to the government. The editor of the *American Fabian* characterized this manifesto as the "most notable perversity that has come to our attention . . . social reformers, above all men, should be the first to see the altruistic significance of this war." [52]

A stronger position was taken by the editors on the question of imperialism. After the war they pointed out the inconsistencies of the idealistic, unselfish protestations with which America entered the war and the imperialistic actions thereafter. "We have lied to all the world about territorial expansion . . . In remembering the Maine, we have forgotten Christ."

An evaluation was placed by the editors of the *Social Gospel* upon missions which confined themselves to personal evangelism while ignoring social conditions.

The churches will spend thousands of dollars in an effort to teach Christian Cuba the falsity of certain Roman dogmas. The government may spend more money to relieve famine and distress. But these are little things. The Cubans need free land and seeds and tools and education, a fair opportunity as men to provide for themselves. Charity will do them but little good and may even do harm. Industrial democracy would be their salvation, and neither the superstitions of Romanism nor the wage-slavery of Protestantism could stand before it.[53]

Commenting on the report that 1,363 Student Volunteers had sailed for foreign fields, two hundred within the year, it noted:

What a pity they have gone to organize their converts for commercial warfare and pit them against each other for all the work and in all the interests of this life.[54]

The list of authors reviewed in the pages of the *Social Gospel* gives some insight into the interests of the readers and members of the colony. It included Richard T. Ely, Vida D. Scudder, Werner Sombart, Albion W. Small, George C. Lorimer, John R. Commons, Hauptmann, Washington Gladden, Frank Parsons, Edward Carpenter, Bolton Hall, John Fiske, Walter Wykcoff, and John Wolman.

[52] *American Fabian,* May, 1898.
[53] *Social Gospel,* May, 1899.
[54] *Ibid,* August, 1899.

Gibson and Albertson did the editorial work of the magazine with a board of associate editors composed of George D. Herron, William T. Brown, James P. Kelley, S. H. Comings, John Chipman, W. D. P. Bliss, B. Fay Mills, Thomas E. Will, and Ernest Howard Crosby. The last named was one of the most interesting men on the board. A graduate of the Columbia Law School and of the College of the City of New York, the successor of Theodore Roosevelt in the New York State Legislature, Crosby was appointed in 1889 by President Harrison as Judge of the International Tribunals in Egypt. He is said to have written his decisions in French and Italian. After serving on the Tribunal for five years he resigned, and on the return trip he visited Tolstoy in Russia. As a result of the latter's influence, he gave up a public career and devoted himself to farming, writing, and lecturing on social subjects. His *Plain Talk in Psalm and Parable* was published in 1899.

Crosby tried to adapt Tolstoy's doctrines to a program of revolution. He had considerable influence with the colonists and upon the religious and social thought of his day. In a series of articles in *The Kingdom* on William Lloyd Garrison, he set down a seven-point program for a revolutionary movement, including nonviolent resistance. Like Marx he insisted that such a movement must have a working-class basis, although intellectuals might make some contribution. It must originate among humble, not among "respectable" people. It will be charged with "stirring up the people," if it is effective, he said, and also with turning the world upside down.

Any movement which has its source and its chief support among the great and wealthy and learned, which is never accused of rousing the passions of the oppressed, or of running counter to the prevailing religion of the day, which finds church and state friendly and complacent . . . which hesitates to denounce when denunciation is deserved . . . will be found wanting in the elements inherent in a great cause.[55]

A member of one of New York's aristocratic families, he was made to feel the lash that awaits those who try to cross class lines and whose ways of life become a reproach to the conscience

[55] *The Kingdom.*

of a privileged class. He made an effort, at least intellectually, to identify himself with the working class, whose battles he thought of himself as waging. "I take my place in the lower classes. I renounce the title of gentleman because it has become intolerable to me." [56] As has been indicated Crosby was one of the few public men in America to disavow the Spanish-American War. All his life he was a courageous champion of social justice. No mere philanthropic gestures, nothing short of a complete revolution, he said, could wipe out the profit-seeking system and so approach the ideal implied in the Kingdom of God on earth.

William T. Brown, another associate editor of the *Social Gospel*, was a Yale graduate who was condemned for heresy by the Congregational Church. He later became a Unitarian minister in Boston and was the author of three books on social Christianity.[57]

James P. Kelley, a Phi Beta Kappa member of the Class of 1877 at Brown, was a teacher for many years in New England preparatory schools. He made an extended visit to the colony and served as associate editor during the publication of the *Social Gospel* at Commonwealth. After the dissolution of the colony when the magazine was moved to Jamesport, L. I., he was a coeditor with Albertson. He published *The Law of Service* in 1894.

Thomas E. Will, graduated from Harvard College in the class of 1890 and a Fellow in Political Economy in 1891, was appointed president of Kansas State Agricultural College in 1897. Two years later, about the time he became an associate editor of the *Social Gospel*, a Republican governor came into office in Kansas. Among the early acts of the latter was the appointment of two Republican regents in the place of two Populists, which

[56] Ernest Howard Crosby, *Plain Talk in Psalm and Parable*, quoted in *The Kingdom*, March, 1898.
[57] *After Capitalism What?*, *The Real Religion of Today*, and *The Axe at the Root*. "It must be apparent," he wrote, "to most of us that what was true of slavery is now true in respect to the wage system and indeed the entire economic order . . . One cannot conform to the existing system and preach a gospel which is in any sense good tidings to the poor . . . people are asking for bread, and what are we giving them? Words, words, words!"—*The Kingdom*, March 10, 1898.

enabled the Board of Regents to make a clean sweep of the liberals on the faculty of the college. President Will and four professors: Ward of New York, Bemis of Chicago, Parsons of Boston, and Emch—were released in June, 1899, although all of them had contracts until June, 1901. President Will had incurred the displeasure of the conservatives in the State when he invited William Jennings Bryan and Professor Herron to make the college commencement orations in 1898 and 1899. The *Kansas City Journal* said on the occasion of Herron's address: "Rather burn your colleges to the ground than to let such doctrines go out." The ministers of Manhattan, Kans., the college seat, called upon the State Board of Regents and demanded the removal of Ward, Parsons, Emch, Will, and others on the ground that the men did not believe in the divinity of Jesus. The *Social Gospel* in commenting upon the event said that their real offense was "opposition to the selfishness which dethrones Jesus, opposition to the rule of economic might, and insistence that the law of love and of equal right has some claim and is a higher wisdom." Under these men, it continued,

there was free, fearless, severe search for truth along economic lines, which search is dangerous to established error and injustice. But the party in power now proposes to change the course of study by cutting out much if not all study of sociology and political economy, as branches not needed by the sons and daughters of farmers and mechanics.[58]

The disciplining of Will and his colleagues was typical of the treatment accorded almost all of the professors in the nineties who evinced radical tendencies in their social philosophies. Whether in the field of religion or of political economy, they were made to feel the displeasure of economic power which had been irritated by criticism of business practice. Other similar instances included the case of H. C. Adams, in 1886, at Cornell, who incurred the dislike of Henry Sage by his remarks on the Gould Strike; E. W. Bemis, in 1895, at the University of Chicago, who was dismissed by President Harper as a result of pressure brought to bear by important business interests; and the cases of E. Benjamin Andrews, at Brown, Richard T. Ely, at Wis-

[58] *Social Gospel*, July, 1899.

consin, George D. Herron, at Iowa College, and E. A. Ross, at Stanford.[59]

Benjamin Fay Mills provided an interesting example of the transition between the personal evangelistic emphasis of Christianity in the nineties and the emerging interest in a social message. Mr. Mills, one of the most successful evangelists of his day, was requested in 1898 by fifty Boston ministers to conduct a series of meetings in that city. His liberal tendencies are indicated by his choice of a Polish Jew as an assistant. When he began to treat economic issues in his Boston meetings some of the wealthier patrons of the lecture series withdrew their official support. His "Sociological Section Meeting," a feature of the Boston meetings, was something of an innovation in evangelistic services. Mr. Mills was associate editor of both the *Social Gospel* and *The Kingdom*. He also served on the faculty of the Summer School of Applied Christianity, at Iowa College.

In February, 1899, a three-inch snowfall and a heavy freeze had done serious damage to the crops and fruit trees with disastrous effects upon the already meager food supply. Owing primarily to slim rations there were dissension and difficulties in the spring of that year, which almost caused the break-up of the colony and which left a permanent scar. A member of the colony had written a book in which Commonwealth was represented as a "free love" colony. The explicit purpose of the author was to discredit the colony in the eyes of Southern and Northern friends. He was expelled, but returned some weeks later vowing to effect the dissolution of Commonwealth with the aid of an inside accomplice. The latter turned out to be a fairly bad customer with a record of gun play in Texas, rather refractory material for the Kingdom of God; yet viewed from another angle, an excellent touchstone on which to assay the potentialities of the love ethic. A sheriff was called to take the men into custody. These two men with the aid of about ten others sought to throw the colony into bankruptcy, hoping to benefit through the subsequent liquidation and distribution of the assets. The schism among the members of the colony over the principle of coercion and force implicit in the handling of this affair created

[59] Bernard, *op. cit.*

a crisis. At a meeting of all the members it was decided finally to fight the issue out in the courts. This was regarded by many as the final surrender of the principle of love, the acknowledgment after several compromises that the ethic of nonresistance was not an adequate standard for meeting the issues of a complex social situation. Such a discrediting of their faith, with the consequent weakening of morale, was probably an important reason for the final dissolution of the Christian Commonwealth. In an unpublished novel based on the history of the colony, Albertson writes of the effect of this decision to resort to legal defense to save Commonwealth. Hugh, the founder of the colony (Ralph Albertson), has just left the meeting where the decision was made.

Hugh was stunned, silent. He knew now that the die was cast. There would be no withdrawing the case. It would have to go through the court. He rose from the table and staggered out of the house. He walked, aimlessly, uncertainly, for a time thoughtlessly, and he had walked miles up the mountain path before he did think much. His emotions were boiling. The wickedness of it! The falseness of it.

Failure! Utter, irrevocable failure! Ignominious failure! The triumph of lies! The loss of his ideal! The wreckage of his dream!

Jesus? Yes, they had crucified him. They had lied about him. They had proven him wrong. The meek should not inherit the earth. That was worse than nails and spears—to have your faith refuted. They had certainly rejected the gospel of Jesus. It had not been resurrected. It would not come back. Love was crucified. Was always crucified. Herron had said that only crucifixion could await any man who undertook to do as Jesus did in his life. No man could live and love his neighbor as himself. He could only talk about it—cheap, hollow talk!

So this was crucifixion. The land would be sold. The libels would stand. The gospel would be disbelieved. Overfed preachers would stand in their pulpits and read pompously: "Go, sell all thou hast and give to the poor . . . " The words would echo against the blank walls. Smug capitalists would continue to expound Christianity. They would even talk about Jesus as a good business man.

. . . Hugh had been hours in the mountain . . . He reached a rock from which the great Cherokee Valley came into distinct view . . . There at the near end like a few white dots was Fraternity. So puny! So insignificant! Until now so precious! Why had he staked so much on it? How could it be so important? . . .

The struggle in this man was all because he had clung to absolutes.

Truth, righteousness, love, brotherhood, peace, had been enthroned in his mind as absolute realities. His only interest in following Jesus was in going the last mile, in giving the uttermost farthing. He would never be a half-way Christian, a word-follower, a hypocrite! He would either follow Jesus or he would definitely honestly acknowledge that he could not follow Jesus. To follow Jesus now meant to let the Christian Commune be sold out and wiped out. To let them hang it on the cross. Nothing happened after that, except what happens to all of us. And a lot of quibbling and war and competition and darkness and cruelty. How real the crucifixion! All the world on the cross! And Jesus is still there. The Sermon on the Mount is still there. Hugh Cotton's dream is there. Hugh Cotton himself, the idealist, the prophet, the consecrated soul is there. On the cross.

. . . Strange that he had not realized before that Jesus was still on the cross! Why shouldn't the world fight, and be cruel? What else could have awaited him? Herron had seen it clear.

He did not fall asleep as he lay on that rock with his chin in his hands, but something in him fell asleep—forever. And something was born. Hugh Cotton had resolved to fight.[60]

The lawsuit was easily won by the colonists; then in the summer came the greatest catastrophe of all, an epidemic of typhoid fever. Before this the colony had been quite free from sickness, with the exception of a few cases of malaria in the early days of the enterprise. About the middle of May the first case developed. Some fifteen members were down. There were two deaths. Almost the last case was that of Ralph Albertson who was sick from August to October. One night he was left for dead. On his recovery he weighed only eighty-five pounds. During his illness many of the most loyal members had become discouraged and left. Commonwealth never regained its strength physically and spiritually from this succession of trials. Broken in health, undermanned, the leaders gone, a little band of co-operators held on for a brief period. In the spring of 1900 the last contingent of about twenty-one members left together for South Jamesport, Long Island, N. Y. Only one member and his family, a French-Canadian by the name of De Brabant, remained in Georgia.[61] A petition in voluntary bankruptcy was filed and a list of members entitled to a share in the proceeds was given to the court, includ-

---

[60] Albertson, *The Passion that Left the Ground.*
[61] Twenty-five years later his family was still living in the neighborhood of Commonwealth.

ing all those who had been members of the colony within the past six months, although in leaving they had forfeited all legal claims.[62] After the mortgage of $2,000 had been paid, and all accounts settled, something like $8.50 per family was distributed by the Georgia court.

Dr. Alexander Kent attributes the failure of the colony to the fact that the leaders "lacked business sense." [63] On this point Albertson says that one must distinguish between the starting of the colony and its subsequent management. Acknowledging that the initial judgment was "poor business," the management of the colony speaks for itself in the fact that it endured through almost four years in the face of most obstinate difficulties, such as the maintenance of the open-door policy, poor soil, a large initial debt, an epidemic; yet winding up its affairs after caring for all its needy members, without indebtedness. But the important fact, he states, is that it was not a "business" at all. Professor Bushee lays the dissolution of the colony to the open-door policy and to the influx of low-grade colonists which this encouraged.[64] On this point John Chipman, the son of a founder of the colony, wrote:

Reading between the lines of the *Social Gospel* it is easy to see that the colony was plagued by a lot of lazy and thoroughly worthless individuals, that they could not be made to work, and that the leaders of the enterprise were too sincerely Christian to expel them. This would seem to be one of the main causes which contributed to the failure of the Commonwealth. This conjecture coincides with what I remember of my father's statements concerning the enterprise.[65]

While the open-door policy was undoubtedly one of the primary reasons for the breakdown of the colony, because of the economic strain it placed upon the Commonwealth; yet without it the leaders felt that there would have been no excuse for the colony's existence.[66]

[62] Dr. Kent states that the creditors of the colony applied for a receivership, while Mr. Albertson states that it was the colonists themselves who voluntarily took this step.

[63] Kent, *Co-operative Communities in the United States.*

[64] Frederick A. Bushee, "Communistic Societies in the United States," *Political Science Quarterly,* XX (1905), 625-64.

[65] John Chipman, in a letter to the author, November 16, 1932.

[66] ". . . it was the spirit of the open door—the spirit that gave its all to everybody—that was the one excuse for the enterprise."—Albertson, "Commonwealth in Retrospect," in *The Commons,* July, 1901.

How do the colonists themselves regard the experiment, looking back across the intervening years? Their opinions vary; some consider it a purely fantastical and visionary scheme, others regard it reverently as the one interlude in their lives that revealed some of life's deepest secrets.

My experience with the colony was very slight, for while my parents were there during the few years of its existence, my time was spent in studying in Boston or teaching during practically all that period; and I was there only during vacations—and that time I strove to forget as quickly as possible. It was a wild, impracticable dream of Utopia, which could not possibly succeed.[67]

Another member writes:

There are a few people who will look back upon it as the happiest experience of their lives . . . they realized a joy of fellowship elsewhere unknown to them . . . We love our ideals with the whole persistency of life, and we love their concrete expression, their symbols . . . to those whose labors were unceasing, whose sacrifices were considerable . . . Commonwealth will stand for holy things.[68]

Seven years after the disbanding of the colony, Professor Damon, who entered educational work in the Philippines, wrote to Mr. Gibson.

My dear Brother Gibson:
    Your very kind and interesting letter of October 7th has been too long awaiting an answer. We wish you a Merry Christmas, and a happy and prosperous year 1908.
    How differently our lives have flowed on from what we thought when we were toiling at Commonwealth to solve the great problem of a Christian Brotherhood put into practical operation before the wondering eyes of skeptical men.
    If we had been as wise then as we are now, perhaps we might have succeeded in our undertaking.
    And we did succeed in a degree. I have never regretted the efforts we made at that time. It was unselfish and altogether Christian—and I believe we are better and stronger men and women for the experience we then gained.

[67] Mrs. J. V. Fothergill, in a letter to the author, October 19, 1932. It is interesting to compare this estimate of the colony with a judgment made by this same person in 1900. Writing from the New England Conservatory of Music, she said, "since I am deprived of the Commonwealth atmosphere it seems ten times dearer than ever, and now that I am in the midst of the competitive strife, the living of the Gospel at Commonwealth seems more than ever the noblest and highest thing in all the world."

[68] Albertson, *The Commons*, July, 1901.

I still hold, and preach, that Christ was a Socialist, and Christianity is socialism. The world is coming, and not very slowly, into the belief and practice of our ideas. We cannot be held in anything but respect for holding ideas in advance of our time, and which we feel sure that the world must, ere long, approve and adopt.

It would be very pleasant to meet a goodly number of our Commonwealth brotherhood in a reunion. It would certainly revive many pleasant old-time memories. I think it would be a great improvement on the average G.A.R. rallies.

But we shall doubtless have to defer any such gathering until we cross over the river. Then surely both we and the rest will enter along upon a long and straight career of our pure socialism. And this will be vindication enough for us. Praise the Lord for the prospects!

How glad we shall be to meet your dear family once more.

With much love to you,

W. C. DAMON.

By what standards shall we judge a human achievement to be a success or a failure? Is it merely the material evidence of activity—so much cement, stone, and wood assembled in more or less pleasing patterns? Is it the time element which is important—that is good which endures? But everything eventually must perish, and only in death is there life. Are there other quantitative standards? Certainly when the rod of the acquisitive society is applied to the record of Commonwealth it must be judged a failure. But perhaps it should be judged by a standard in quite another category, the functional one for example. How adequately does an event fulfill its essential purpose? Yet even when tested by this formula, the colony must be judged a failure. Its avowed purpose was to demonstrate that the absolute ethic of love is an adequate rule of behavior in an industrial society. And their experience indicates that a society which rigorously follows the logic of such an absolute ethical standard must eventually face extinction at the hands of a world in which individuals may be redeemed by love, but which is still too weighted down and calloused by brutality and selfishness for the multitudes to yield to the spiritual appeal of vicarious suffering. The one supreme example of self-effacing love was crucified within three years of the start of his ministry, which was to have been a personal demonstration of the law of love; and this humble society of his professed followers lasted only three years and eight months. But was Jesus on the cross a failure? Is the spiritual exaltation that comes from the struggle to attain a lofty goal its own reward? Does the striving after a high-flung ideal become a worth-while end in itself? Jane Addams felt something of this after her visit to Commonwealth.

Yet as we drove away we had the curious sensation that while the experiment was obviously coming to an end, in the midst of its privations it yet embodies the peace of mind which comes to him who insists upon the logic of life—whether it is reasonable or not—the fanatic's joy in seeing his own formula translated into action. At any rate, when we reached (Columbus) the commonplace Southern town of workaday men and women, for one moment its substantial buildings, its solid brick churches, its ordered streets, divided into those of the rich and the poor, seemed much more unreal to us than the little struggling colony we had left behind. We repeated to each other that in all the practical judgments and decisions of life, we must part company with logical demonstration; that if we stop for it in each case, we can never go on at all; yet, in spite of this, when conscience does become the dictator of the daily life of a group of men, it forces the admiration as no other modern spectacle has power to do. It seemed but a mere incident that this group should have lost sight of the facts of life in their earnest endeavor to put to the test the things of the spirit.[69]

And Graham Taylor gave expression to a similar thought in his editorial in *The Commons* written shortly after the dissolution of the Christian Commonwealth.

A more pathetically heroic adventure of faith than that which at least outwardly failed in the attempt to establish The Christian Commonwealth in Georgia, we know not of . . . The brave men and women who dared to fail may issue their challenge to those who come after them in the words which Bunyan puts into the mouth of Mr. Valiant-for-Truth as he answers his summons: "My sword I give to him that shall succeed me in my pilgrimage and my courage and skill to him that can get it, marks and scars I carry with me to be a witness for me that I have fought His battles.[70]

[69] Jane Addams, *op. cit.*, pp. 277-79.

[70] It is an odd coincidence that his quotation was used by Walter Lippmann, whose wife was born in the colony, in his editorial for the last issue of the New York *World*, an obituary notice marking the end of what was, for many, another spiritual adventure. At least three people had an active interest in both.

XIII

GEORGE D. HERRON; REVOLUTION AND RELIGION

THE most influential and dramatic character in the Christian socialist movement and the intellectual leader of social Christianity during the last decade of the nineteenth century was George D. Herron.

The life of George D. Herron, professor, minister, statesman, prophet, and poet would provide rich material for a romantic novel. Professor Herron was born in Montezuma, Ind., in 1862, the son of a poor and pious Scotch family. Like Henry George, he worked in his youth as a compositor apprenticed to the printing trade, where he had a working-class background. Except for a brief period at Rippon Academy, Wis., he had but little formal education. It is probable that like so many of his contemporaries, interest in radical social thought was stimulated by his two years of travel and study abroad. In 1883 he entered the Congregational ministry. Eight years later he was brought into national prominence by an address to the state convention of Congregational ministers. His address "The Message of Jesus to Men of Wealth" was widely quoted in the press. One immediate result was a call to the First Congregational Church of Burlington, Iowa. There he met for the first time Mrs. E. D. Rand and her daughter, Carrie Rand, who were to play an important rôle in his life. In the summer of 1892 Herron conducted a retreat at Iowa College, later Grinnell College, and the following year the Rand Chair of Applied Christianity was founded for him at that institution. Mrs. Rand and her daughter took up their residence at this time in Grinnell. Later Miss Rand became Dean of Women at the College.

For seven years Professor Herron was in demand in many parts of the country as a platform speaker. He was a vigorous protagonist of Christian Socialism, tending more to the scientific socialism founded on the work of Karl Marx than to the prevailing Utopian socialism. He addressed student assemblies, church groups, and delivered lectures in many cities including a series of lectures at Princeton and at Union Theological Seminary. Between 1892 and 1899 he published eight books, for the most part sermons and lectures on social Christianity. A conviction of messiahship colored his entire life, having the effect of raising him above envy, hate, ambition, and concern for public opinion. In the words of William Allen White, it made him "one of God's pedestal dwellers, always moving about in bronze or marble . . . yet a kindly and some way sweet and gentle soul withal." [1]

Iowa College was dependent for its financial support upon an unimaginative agricultural group which objected from the first to the progressive thought of Professor Herron. There was a nation-wide controversy over the issues he raised, precipitating persistent demand for his resignation. The difficulty of raising funds for the college so long as it continued to sponsor a man of such radical views was a decisive factor in subsequent events. President Gates gave Professor Herron loyal and courageous support at all times, even during later personal difficulties. In October, 1891, Professor Herron resigned. His letter of resignation was a remarkably restrained and generous document.[2]

In March, 1891, Professor Herron's first wife secured a divorce. In May of the same year he was married to Miss Carrie Rand in a ceremony wherein each chose the other "to be my companion," thus dramatizing his opposition to all "coercive institutions." The ceremony was performed by William T. Brown, an associate editor of the *Social Gospel*. Professor Herron's attitude toward marriage ended his professional religious career. He was deposed from the Congregational ministry on June 4, 1891, by a council of Congregational churches at Grin-

[1] William Allen White, in a letter to Professor Briggs.
[2] In contrast to the violence of his attack upon capitalism Professor Herron seems to have been unusually gentle and considerate in his personal relationships. During the heat of the controversy surrounding his Pacific Coast tour, President McLean stated that although under constant attack and beset hourly by a swarm of interviewers determined to "wring from him some sort of sensational rejoinder," he remained "unperturbed in spirit, calm of demeanor, kindly in expression towards all his detractors."—*Professor George D. Herron; the Man and His Work on the Pacific Coast*, pp. 3-4.

nell, Iowa. Professor Herron's views on marriage were set forth
in a letter addressed to the council mentioned above. In view of
the importance attributed to these views a lengthy quotation
from that letter is included here. He had married, he stated, at
the age of twenty-one, and his children had not been deserted, as
charged. They had now almost reached the point of maturity
and had chosen to remain with their mother, a decision, he said,
probably for the best, for a

man given to the social revolution cannot fail to be more or less an
outcast, as the revolution intensifies and arrays a ruling class against
a working class in a final issue and crisis. . . . I might suggest to you
that a court decree granting a separation of this kind, is based on a
technicality, as you must know. Our laws are so made that a man
and woman legally united cannot get apart save upon some nominal
charge of wrong doing. I did not know the wording of the charge until
I read it in the papers. I suppose it was the least charge upon which
a decree could be issued by an Iowa court . . . I thoroughly believe
in the vital and abiding union of one man with one woman as a true
basis for family life . . . Lives that are essentially one, co-operate
in the love and the truth that make oneness, need no law of state or
church to bind them together . . . On the other hand, no law of
the universe has a right to keep together those who are not vitally
and essentially one . . . And if church and society may visit upon
me, in making a protest against a system that seems to me destructive
to all true morality, and to the very citadel of the soul's integrity,
then my protest has earned its right to be heard . . . Our sayings
and doings, or the things we do not and say not, are guided by the
desire to be respectable, to be approved: hence action and thought
are alike dishonest; and without beauty . . . I cannot speak what I
seem to see as truth, without living out all the truth about myself,
even though the living of truth destroy my opportunity to speak . . .
It seems useless and hopeless to say it, but the crisis which brings
me under your judgment springs from a moral agony to be true to
what I take to be truth. I may be mistaken, or stupid, or mad, or
anything you like, but I have acted from the highest right I know
. . . And in the long run that is enough—enough that a man be
conscious of the rectitude of his soul. In the reach of the centuries, it
does not matter what the world thinks a man is, what a man actually
is—what he knows himself to be—is all that matters. Sometime and
somewhere, if the universe be sincere, be rational, the truth will care
for its own . . .

The same generosity to those who differed from him and the

lack of acrimoniousness which characterized his letter of resignation to the college trustees, is to be found in the subscription of this letter.

In conclusion let me say out of justice to you, and to myself, that I shall not misrepresent you as, dismissing me for socialism, or heresy, or for attacks upon the church . . . I am dismissed from the church and its ministry—for what you consider to be conduct unbecoming a minister and a gentleman . . . With only fellowship in my heart for you all, I remain, Faithfully yours, George D. Herron.[3]

Professor Herron was associated for a time with Stitt Wilson in his "Social Apostalate." He later tried to organize a group within the Socialist Party favorably disposed to religion. To promote this objective he edited a department of "Socialism and Religion" in the *International Socialist Review*. In 1904 he made the nominating speech for Eugene Debs as candidate for the presidency of the United States.[4] Largely through his influence a part of the Rand fortune was used to establish in 1906 the Rand School of Social Sciences. Following his second marriage Dr. Herron moved to a villa near Fiesole, Italy, where he maintained his permanent residence.

He entertained in generous style. A steady stream of men from all walks of life called upon him, but for the most part he moved in a middle-class world of intellectuals. The positive nature of his convictions and his unwillingness to compromise prevented him from being identified with any sect or group.[5] Professor Briggs states that he had an "acquaintanceship with intellectual Europe, probably unsurpassed by that of any other American." [6] He also maintained a correspondence with men and women prominent in American life, including financiers who were impressed with his grasp of European affairs. An interesting exchange of letters passed between Dr. Herron and C. W. Barron, editor of the *Wall Street Journal*. On one occasion Mr. Barron sent Dr. Herron a copy of a book by Calvin Coolidge to which he attached this note:

[4] Herron, *To the Committee Appointed by the Congregational Church of Grinnell, Iowa, to Call a Council of Churches to Inquire into My Ministerial Standing and Church Membership* (pamphlet).

[4] Karsner, *Debs, His Life and Letters*, p. 12.

[5] Briggs. *op. cit.*   [6] *Ibid.*

I take pleasure in sending you a recently published book giving brief addresses of Calvin Coolidge just re-elected governor of Massachusetts . . . I wish you would read it, because it is the only book by a man in political life I ever found that rang true from beginning to end. And Coolidge may be the successor of Woodrow Wilson.

In reply Dr. Herron wrote:

I read Governor Coolidge's book with profound interest. It is, as you say, utterly sincere. On the other hand it is utterly without vision as to the real world we are now living in. You cannot anchor the world in Massachusetts Bay. It is reaction to-day that is making for Bolshevism.[7]

Dr. Herron played an important part in World-War diplomacy, a story which has been ably told in a recent study published by Professor Mitchell P. Briggs. Because of Woodrow Wilson's achievement in domestic reform, Dr. Herron became his ardent admirer, and he did more to establish the popularity of Wilson in central Europe than any other person. He was known as "Wilson's confidence man." Largely because of his dislike for the Hegelian conception of the State and especially because of his antipathy for the Prussian military system, he early became anti-German. He broke with European socialists and supported the Bavarian revolution against the German Republic. President Wilson appointed Dr. Herron and William Allen White as his personal representatives at the abortive council of Prinkipo and thus called forth from the American press a storm of disapproval based on Dr. Herron's socialism and his earlier attitude toward marriage, always caricatured in the press as "free love." The *New York Times* in a two-column leading editorial stated that William Allen White's appointment was fairly satisfactory, since he had gone through the Populist movement in Kansas, "a milder form of Bolshevism." But Herron was out of the question. "As a teacher of socialism and of the loose views of the marriage relation which many socialists hold, Mr. Herron has been in close sympathy with the principles which have guided Lenin and Trotsky in their war upon capitalism and upon society."[8] Dr. W. T. Manning (now Bishop)

[7] *Ibid.*, pp. 158-60.
[8] *New York Times*, February 10, 1919, quoted by Briggs, *op. cit.*, p. 142.

speaking in the chapel of Vassar College said: "There is small use in trying to stem the divorce evil if we have no word to say against the official recognition of a notorious advocate of free love." [9] The Presbyterian Brotherhood of New Jersey meeting at Paterson, passed a resolution condemning the appointment. One speaker said: "this advocate of free love is an insult to the womanhood of America. . . . the IWWism of the Pacific Coast could be traced back to the teachings of Dr. Herron," and another lamented that the responsibility for this appointment rested with President Wilson, a "staunch Scotch-Irish, stubborn Presbyterian who probably would pay no attention to what they said." [10]

As President Wilson's representative, Dr. Herron is said to have persuaded Kurt Eisner to advocate acknowledgment by Germany of her war guilt, a sad rôle for a socialist.[11] His disappointment over the Treaty of Versailles, with its note of revenge and its background of chicanery, intrigue, and bartering for the spoils of war, was the most disillusioning event of his life, for into his work for peace had gone considerable life blood, with the result that the end of the negotiations found him in broken health.[12] Professor Briggs in concluding his book on the war work of Dr. Herron writes:

Why did he fail? Partly because he demanded too much . . . It was nothing less than the millennium that he asked for . . . The habits of theological thinking and homiletic writing never left him: the spiritual fervor that, in his youth, sent him tilting against the windmills of sin and capitalism remained with him to the end. His nature demanded for its very life the belief that the Sermon on the Mount would some day triumph over the selfishness of this world, and he dared to believe that he might do something to hasten the coming of the Kingdom of God in this life. And so he labored and hoped, and failed—and hoped on. And almost at the close of his life could write to a friend: "But after the long and awful night the morning

[9] *Ibid.*   [10] *Ibid.*
[11] *Dictionary of American Biography.*
[12] Of his work for Peace, Dr. Herron wrote: "I did my utmost, but failed. Now certainly it is true that everything that I labored for during the war, and the time of the making of the Peace, has turned into disastrous and apparently unqualified failure."—*Berlin Herald,* April 15, 1922, quoted by Briggs, *op. cit.,* p. 195.

cometh—and a brighter morning than humanity has ever known. In that faith we must live—and create." [13]

But even this experience, which left its mark on a war generation ridden with cynicism, was not able to break the religious faith of Dr. Herron that ultimately justice and brotherhood would be established as the base of society. Almost his last act was the editing of a little volume of his own verse intended as a memorial for Carrie Rand, who had died some years previously, in which he reaffirmed the faith by which he had lived. He died in 1925.

Professor Herron was received gladly by workers, who came in large numbers to hear him wherever he spoke in the East and the West. Some clergymen, especially the Congregationalists and the Unitarians, gave him support, but for the most part organized religion regarded him with suspicion. The capitalist press was enthusiastic in denouncing him. In Montreal the ministers were more concerned about his theology than his sociology, but the theological students from McGill were among his most eager listeners. He stirred the city as much as if a "dynamite bomb had exploded in the square of the city." [14]

Every age has its epithets which its priests and apologists use to stigmatize the views held by those who dare to challenge the pretensions of the ruling class: Philistines, Jacobins, reds, free-lovers, communists. In the nineties "anarchists" was the favorite word with which to brand those with whose views you disagreed. An editorial in the *New York Evening Post* "Offenders Must Not Escape," linked Professor Herron with Richard T. Ely.

Their offence differs little in its essence from that of Parsons, the Chicago anarchist, who was convicted and hanged for inciting others to murder . . . rather than for actual participation in the killing . . . It is the Elys, the Herrons . . . who are responsible for such men as Debs and his host of ignorant followers.[15]

An Iowa paper said of one of his addresses:

This is the first time our people have had a chance to listen to a first class anarchistic lecture right from the depths of a college. It was

[13] Herron, in a letter to Professor William F. Badé, August 23, 1922, quoted by Briggs, *op. cit.* p. 166.
[14] *The Kingdom*, May 4, 1894.
[15] *New York Evening Post*, quoted in *The Kingdom*, September 7, 1894.

undisguised anarchy from beginning to end. He said that it was a crime for the individual to own property. He arraigned *en masse* all railroads, all bankers, all employers of large numbers of men, as criminals of very dark type. He held up lovingly the first eleven centuries of the Christian era with the Crusades as samples of the blessed time when he said all things were owned in common, and declared in a deep down voice and a distressed countenance, and a great effort to be tragic, that unless a division was speedily made, and a return to the good old times where all things were owned in common, the whole civilization of the age would go to an eternal smash-up.[16]

A Chicago paper reporting his commencement address in 1894 at the University of Nebraska carried the headlines:

SHOCKS HIS HEARERS

PROFESSOR HERRON DECLARES

THE NATION IS A FAILURE

IS A POLITICAL ANARCHIST

SO ASSERTS A MEMBER OF THE SUPREME COURT

GOVERNOR CROWSE OPENLY REBUKES A

COMMENCEMENT SPEAKER AT LINCOLN

Professor Herron had been invited by Chancellor Canfield to deliver the Commencement sermon on the subject "The Christian State, or a New Political Vision." Governor Crowse, who followed Professor Herron on the program, had been invited to deliver the commissions to graduating cadets. He utilized his time to deliver a "vulgar and venomous attack" upon Professor Herron, "vulgar in that he attributed his own contentment with social conditions to a difference in their organs of digestion," and implied that Herron was an anarchist by identifying him with Herr Most and Lucy Parsons. Oï the ministers on the platform on that occasion "two doctors divine made haste to shake hands with the governor; four slipped away quickly; and three came to Dr. Herron with hearts greatly stirred and grasped his hand."[17]

A vigorous debate was aroused over the proposal to invite

[16] *Iowa State Register*, January 17, 1898.
[17] *The Kingdom*, June 29, 1894.

Professor Herron to address the Monday Club of San Francisco. The invitation was extended. After an extensive lecture tour in California, Professor Herron closed the tour with an address in the Metropolitan Temple of San Francisco to an audience of more than three thousand persons who listened to him for more than two hours, frequently breaking into applause. The Pacific Coast tour was attended by vigorous controversy. Professor Herron had been invited to address the Congregational Club of San Francisco. At the close of his address, C. O. Brown, pastor of the First Congregational Church, arose and made a virulent attack upon the speaker, denouncing him as an anarchist. When called to a point of order by the Chair, he said "I shall preach against this man in my church next Sunday" and left the hall.[18] Brown's subsequent sermon and a statement by a group of trustees of the First Congregational Church were widely distributed throughout the state. An abridged version of the trustees' statement was written by the Reverend James G. Clark, of Pasadena.

The trustees of the First Congregational Church believe that the time has come when some voice should be raised against the socialistic propaganda now actively at work among the Christian pulpits and churches of America. No more striking proof could be given than the fact that numbers of evangelical pastors welcome the unbridled socialism of Professor Herron and hail him as a prophet inspired of God. Our city and state has suffered quite enough from such agitation in the past. To have such proclaimed in the name of religion seems to us quite unendurable. Such words, as many of Professor Herron's ought to stir the indignation of every loyal citizen . . . The laity of our churches do not approve of socialism and will not follow its leadership. Hitherto, Professor Herron has gone from association to club and from place to place, frequently leaving behind him a number, who have been influenced to propagate his views. We believe that Dr. Brown has done wisely in calling the attention of our churches throughout the land to this tendency, and squarely forcing the issue as to whether the churches are to furnish the platform for destructive socialism.[19]

In answer to this attack upon Professor Herron, the *Arena*, of Boston, published a pamphlet, *Professor George D. Herron; the*

[18] *Ibid.*
[19] *Professor George D. Herron; the Man and His Work on the Pacific Coast.*

Man and His Work on the Pacific Coast, containing a number of statements by California clergymen defending Professor Herron. A few excerpts from the pamphlet indicate the response of some of the clergymen to Christian Socialism as interpreted by Professor Herron. Elder M. J. Ferguson, pastor First Christian Church, San Francisco, summarized Herron's lectures:

Competition is *not* the law of life, but a contradiction of every principle of Christianity. The liberty of the individual consists, not in protection in social antagonisms, but in association in social sacrifice. The progress of democracy cannot stop where it is without disaster, but must go on until fulfilled in direct self-government by the people. Property must be made subordinate to the interests of man . . . the wage system is economic slavery, "a profane traffic in human flesh and blood." The failure in present institutions is plainly pointed out and even revolutionary changes are declared to be necessary to redeem the state from anarchy and make it an organ of justice, but these changes will be effected gradually, not by destruction.

Much of the acerbity against the Professor arises from his denunciation of competition as a principle suicidal in itself and alien to Christ as the prophet of the right social order.—J. Cummings Smith, pastor of Trinity Presbyterian Church, San Francisco.

Professor Herron seeks a new principle for theology;—Calvin made the sovereignty of God, Arminius the free will of man their redemptive principle. Neither is sacrificial or redemptive; both emphasize power and will, the one of the Creator, the other of the creature. In both the cross is a segment of the divine plan, rather than a great law of the divine nature underlying the entire being and activity of God.—W. W. Scudder, pastor Congregational Church, Alameda, California.

"Our economic system is organized social wrong." True to the letter in every word, and the class is exceedingly small, and generally rich, who are foolish enough to deny it.—J. E. Scott, San Francisco.

I can see how . . . there may be Christians, so-called, who in a railway company push the business, not as servants of God, but as servants of Mammon, "for all the traffic will bear," or, who in some great monopoly look more to dividends than to public welfare . . . But how any disciple of Jesus—seeking actually to carry out his precepts—can deride or oppose Mr. Herron, I cannot in the least understand.—R. M. Webster, Pasadena.

The Kingdom issued a special edition of 25,000 copies containing a defense of Professor Herron prepared by Dr. R. F. Coyle, pastor of the First Presbyterian Church, Oakland; President J. K. McLean, of the Pacific Theological Seminary; the Fabian Society of San Francisco; and others. W. W. Scudder, pastor of the Congregational Church of Alameda, said that it was Professor Herron's "advocacy of Christian Socialism that drew most of the fire."

Professor Herron was not a systematic theologian. He frequently criticized organized religion for its preoccupation with theology to the exclusion of concern for social justice. Yet he felt the need of a rational justification for both his personal and social religious interests. He believed in God as both transcendent and immanent, manifested in the universe of nature and in human history. God manifested Himself in the world of nature as mutual aid, and in history as the tendency toward brotherhood, co-operation, and justice. In the universe one may find something which is continuous with and which sustains the highest insights of the soul. If it is otherwise, then is the world merely a battleground for special privilege, and our hope is to escape some of the misery we find about us.[20]

Since God is immanent in the universe he is to be sought in terms of actual life in the facts of history. Religion functions primarily in social relationships. Religion, in fact, may be defined as "relations." To be in the right relationship with God is primarily a right relationship with human life. Religion is valuable to God and to man insofar as it changes and exalts the actual facts of life.[21]

The essence of religion is not mystery, is not worship or theology, but righteousness. "The world by wisdom knows not God . . . Great spiritual facts are not apprehended but distorted by the intellect—not the clear in head, but the pure in heart shall see God." [22]

Biblical religion was always social and only incidentally theological and mysterious, said Professor Herron. The great religious prophets had revelations concerning sanitary laws, architecture, marriage relations, land ownership, and good government. This was true pre-eminently of the religion of Jesus,

[20] Herron, "The Social System and the Christian Conscience," *The Kingdom*, August 25, 1898.
[21] Herron, *Social Meanings of Religious Experience*, p. 70.
[22] Herron, *The Larger Christ*, p. 45.

who was for Professor Herron essentially a prophet whose teachings were more economic than religious, if that term is restricted to a personal subjective connotation. The ideal of Jesus was a social one, and his work was to redeem men for the righteous society called the "kingdom of heaven." He revealed God in the simple facts of nature and in everyday life. Christianity as it comes to us from Jesus is not a theological and ecclesiastical system but a "revelation of life," not a cult of worship but a social ideal to be realized in a human order in which all shall live for the common good.[23]

As a religious prophet and social reformer Professor Herron tended to look with disfavor upon every aspect of religion which diverted its energies away from the struggle to achieve a just society. Theology, ritualism, worship all were waived as nonessentials which people have in the past mistaken for religion. Mystery in religion whether theological or ecclesiastical has been the handmaiden of the tyranny of wealth and corruption which explained why the powerful in commerce and politics have for the most part supported the established religion. Institutional religion has been the stanchest supporter of the prevailing social order, giving the *status quo* religious sanctions. Religious values, like all other values, must be subjected to social pragmatic tests. This is the chief criticism of mysticism; it tends toward self-intoxication, exhausting itself in a cult of worship. Even the most personal and profound experience must have for its ultimate test of value its redemptive significance for common life.[24]

The central thought in all of Professor Herron's work is the social significance given to the doctrine of the atonement. The cross is the fact of supreme importance in Christianity supplying the key to all personal and social problems. "The ethical instructions of Jesus and the apostles were all based upon and developed from the cross." And the secret of the cross for practical living is to be found in selfless living. Man is to live for others. The death of Jesus was not the accident of sin, but the manifestation of the "eternal principle for all divine and human action."

[23] Herron, *Social Meanings of Religious Experience*, p. 69.
[24] *Ibid*, p. 74.

Life can be found in no other way than in losing it. In this paradox is to be found the deepest meaning of religion.[25]

Since society is organically related, there can be no salvation for the individual apart from that of the entire race. Professor Briggs speaks of Dr. Herron as an "individualist." It is difficult to understand how one can get this impression from his work, especially his earlier work published between 1890 and 1900. It is true that he stressed the importance and value of the individual, but his view of the social basis of personality made the fullest development of the individual rest upon right social relations. The individual as a discrete entity is a pure abstraction. The individual is always limited by the social group. Thus the goal of Professor Herron is expressed in social terms. He sought to establish the Kingdom of God on earth, which was for him the symbol of a society of free souls, free, because they had found liberty in the bondage of the group.

> Not back, as loud the foolish cry,
> To nature's unreturning youth,
> But on, to love's collective man—
> This is the quested way to truth;
>
> The way by which, at last, we reach
> Yearned benedictive social forms . . .[26]

Sin is a social as well as a personal fact. In a very real sense all men are guilty of the sins of society. All are caught in the grip of an unethical economic order and must share its responsibilities. Since the existing civilization is largely organized warfare, none is innocent. A teacher paid by funds raised through interest or profit on endowments is in the same category with the capitalist, for he is profiting by the labor of others. Everyone is forced to buy sweatshop clothes, use monopolized industries and utilities, support adulterated food, and it is no excuse that such support is often given unconsciously. All men are caught in the machine of civilization and the "only solution is to capture the machine and make economic facts the expression of the highest spiritual forces." [27] Granting that he is participating in an unethical

[25] Herron, *A Plea for the Gospel*, p. VI.
[26] Herron, "A Fragment of a Philosophy," in *A Lover's Memorial*, p. 80.
[27] Herron, "The Social System and the Christian Conscience," in *The Kingdom*, August 25, 1898.

anti-Christian society which is taking its daily total of lives and from which there is no escape short of self-destruction, what recourse has the Christian? He must look to the cross for his answer. His life must be literally a bearing away of the sins of the world. He must stand for a way of life "which men together must accept or together be lost," and the first prerequisite is a consciousness of partial hypocrisy, for the life of the most earnest Christian in such a society is a

hideous compromise and evasion tangled and broken by all things he hates. Seeking to save others, he is unable to save himself; in order to make possible a better human future, he must literally take part in the sins and oppression of the present. It is this daily dying and hourly crucifixion of all one's ideals of life and love, that the social problem brings unique significance and suffering to the Christian conscience.[28]

The cross is the answer that Christianity gives to all social problems. The essence of these problems is self-interest; the answer is the self-giving symbolized by the cross. This symbol is to be interpreted also in economic terms; its significance must be the touchstone by which we judge all our daily acts if we are to take Christianity seriously. Among other things it means the giving of all property for common use. It implies the ethic of communism. "Individual wealth is absolutely inconsistent with the teachings of Jesus." [29]

This rule of self-giving must become the rule of all societies and institutions as well as of individuals. It is the object of the Church and the State and of nations, to be used in serving the entire community of the beloved society. For no person or institution has a moral right to exist apart from the principle "which moved Christ up Calvary." [30]

Under the conception of ethical theism, faith in God is manifested by the tangible evidence of social relationships. Salvation is attained through living, not through mere believing; it is "divine-human character." [31] The religious life is one which makes brotherhood a dominant quality, thus demonstrating a

[28] *Ibid.*
[29] *The Kingdom*, February 19, 1897.
[30] Herron, *The Larger Christ*, pp. 32-33.
[31] *Ibid*, p. 29.

conviction that love is at the heart of the universe. This is the significance of believing in God. Conversely atheism is the denial of God in one's way of life, a "God-out-ness" life. The religious life is a "God-in-ness" which makes of every relationship a religious rite." [32] Usually the error against which religion storms is theological error, "while a refined brutality practices under the church's protection a conscienceless and defiant atheism." [33] In all the details of common life there lie religious potentialities. That the banker does not open his doors with prayer, that the doxology is not sung at the convening of court, and that the legislative acts are not written in religious phraseology, does not make these activities less religious sacraments and rituals of religion. When the banker, the judge or the factory worker excludes the "social shrine" from the bank, the court, or the factory he exhibits himself as an atheist.[34] "For the denial of God in life and history is the most hopelessly infidel position a man can take." [35]

Professor Herron called himself a "pessimist" with regard to the Church and an "optimist" with regard to the kingdom. He had little confidence in what the Church would do because of its close affiliations with powerful business interests, and its large vested interests which need protection. If the Church is to be saved, it must be willing to be despised and rejected by the rich and powerful in order to seek social justice. All institutions, including the Church, must be sacrificed in Christ's stead for the redemption of the world, but the Church, while accepting the message of Christ, has rejected his cross.[36] The chief charge against the Church is that it has concerned itself with everything except social justice. It has forgotten its responsibilities to the poor and the oppressed, and has given itself to discussion, great conferences, aesthetic indulgences, and the building of costly church buildings, with the result that those who most need help have lost all confidence in the Church and look upon it as one more appendage of a bourgeois world.

[32] Herron, *Social Meanings of Religious Experience*, p. 72.
[33] Herron, *A Plea for the Gospel*, p. 26.
[34] Herron, *Social Meaning of Religious Experience*. p. 72.
[35] *The Kingdom*, August 25, 1898.
[36] Herron, *The Larger Christ*, p. 65.

The jubilees which the church holds in honor of so-called benefactions of stock-gamblers and railroad wreckers, of trust monopolists and oppressors of the poor, are but a ridiculous and ill-disguised religious hoodwinkery. Christ did not send his church into the world to get the money of mammon, but to defend the oppressed, denounce wickedness, establish justice, and work righteousness.[37]

Philanthropy is the "greatest peril that confronts and deceives and endangers the life of the church," for it diverts attention from the fundamental task of religion of transforming society.[38] Merely to assuage the needs of a few, to distribute a few crumbs passed on from the table of plenty cannot take the place of a society where property has become spiritualized, has become the instrument for achieving the common good, not a means for the accumulation of profit by the few. It must not be overlooked that the missionary and benevolent funds of the Church have for the most part come from treasuries filled in the first place by "extortion and social cruelty," by speculation upon economic necessities." [39]

Social reformers are doing their work outside, and often with the opposition of, the Church. Many of them have come from, but are no longer of, the Church. The main task of organized religion is the "Christianizing of industry, the gospelizing of commerce, the moral enforcement of the Sermon on the Mount, and the proclamation of the cross as the basic principle of society." [40] If the Church does not accept the challenge before it of righting the wrongs which have become ingrained in society, that are setting class against class and making enemies of men who should be brothers, God will destroy the Church and raise up a new institution to do his work.[41]

God is pressing for a deeper incarnation of himself in the race. He calls for souls who shall make themselves of no reputation, seek not their own, be not anxious for the morrow's food and property . . . (to) go out into this great, starving, striving, staggering, doubting humanity, to be beaten with its stripes, bleed with its wounds, stricken, mangled, poor and lonely with its sins, taking no thought of

[37] Herron, *A Plea for the Gospel*, p. 44.
[38] Herron, *The New Redemption*, p. 61.
[39] *Ibid.*
[40] Herron, *A Plea for the Gospel*, p. 41.
[41] *Ibid.*

reward, popular churches, of church year-books, in order to become divine righteousness in its life, and Christ builders of its character; in order to become the strength of God to the weak, the joy of God to the wretched, the wealth of God to the poor.[42]

Many, if not most, of the sins usually attributed to the human heart, belong rightly to the economic order. At heart man is not altogether selfish and grasping. It is only that the necessity of making a living, of keeping his family in a fair state of comfort, demands as a prerequisite that one lives selfishly. Capitalism is based on individualism, competition, profit-seeking. Under such a system it is folly to counsel people to live according to the law of love. "How can we obey Christ's law of love, when every industrial maxim, custom, fact, and principle renders that law inoperative." [43]

Capitalism uses property and human beings to make profit rather than to serve the common good; it is therefore the antithesis of the Christian society based on mutual service. A business man is no more justified in making profit the final aim of his store, shop, factory, railway, or capital, than Jesus would have been in accumulating profit by the working of miracles.[44]

Capitalism permits wealth to be withdrawn from the common storehouse without regard to social service rendered. There is no relationship between economic reward and skill or between income and contribution to the general welfare. Society does not scrutinize the balance between what it pays and what it collects in return. Under such a system reward is the result of a "commercial legerdemain" by which one appropriates the labor of others.[45] A just society would insist that all wealth should represent honest socially useful work.

It is not an accident that oppression, exploitation and unemployment are thrown up by the capitalistic system, for these evils are a logical result of that system; they are inherent and inevitable.

The inevitable result of the system of wages and competition will be to increase social inequalities; to increase the wealth of the few and

[42] Herron, *The Larger Christ*, p. 69.
[43] *The Kingdom*, August 25, 1898.
[44] Herron, *The Christian Society*, p. 115.
[45] Herron, *The New Redemption*, p. 26.

the poverty of the many . . . [Capital seeking its own interest will] keep a large class of unemployed men who must work or starve. The present industrial system could not exist were it not for the fact that great multitudes of the unemployed have been brought to this country systematically and purposely, for the sake of reducing wages and producing a state of poverty. By this method the clothing trade of the United States thrives upon the sweating system. By pitting the unemployed against the employed, by reducing men and women and children to a condition of poverty, where they must work at any price or starve, competition has prospered by the blood of women.[46]

It follows that such a system operates to prevent even the ethically inclined from doing the good they would. The wage levels and general labor policy of the business world must be set by the unscrupulous minority, for if the benevolent employer were to treat his employees much better than his competitors, he would ruin those whom he sought to help by certain bankruptcy.

Justice is impossible, furthermore, under the capitalist system, in which the means of production are in the hands of the few; it is industrial oligarchy, in which the workers are reduced to "servitude."

All that can be said against slavery can also be said against the private ownership of economic sources and tools; for the private ownership of the common sources and machinery of life is nothing less than a substantial ownership of human beings. No man is free so long as he is dependent upon some other man for the chance to earn his livelihood. If a man owns my bread, or that which I must have in order to get my bread, he owns my moral being, unless I choose to revolt and starve. He who sells his labor-power for wages sells himself; for his labor-power is his life. The wages system is merely an advance in the slave system, but it is no fit system for free men.

There can be no freedom for the individual soul so long as some people own that upon which all people depend for bread.

We have discovered that no spiritual freedom can achieve or maintain itself without economic freedom. Private property in the natural resources upon which all men depend, and private property in that capital which all men create, is nothing less than private property and traffic in human souls . . . The liberty of the soul can be achieved

---

[46] *Ibid*, p. 28.

only through the passing away of the capitalistic form of society, and the coming in of the free and co-operative state.[47]

Justice demands that the community as a whole must own that upon which life depends.

And if the economic order is wrong judged by ethical and rational standards, it is useless to try to maintain it, either through force or law.

No law or custom is mighty or sacred enough to bring forth peace and order out of injustice and elemental disorder . . . There is no God in the universe almighty enough to make right out of sheer economic might; and there is no civilization strong enough to prevent that which is elementally right from becoming the ultimate and universal might.[48]

Thus it is the first duty of all religious people to destroy capitalism without regard for their own welfare. They must seek justice knowing that the forces of entrenched interests will vent their wrath upon such as challenge their prerogatives, but all professed spiritual leaders will follow the truth as they see it, turning not aside if they find a cross, rather being certain that there is no other way. "We must lay the axe at the root of the tree of social wrong. Whether we keep our pulpits or collegiate chairs or not is a matter with which we have absolutely nothing to do." [49]

Christianity and socialism are mutual allies because they seek to achieve certain mutual moral values which are of universal validity. Both Christianity and socialism fight for a socialized world in order that a co-operative society may replace a competitive profit-seeking order, freeing men to labor for the common welfare; that material goods may be devoted to the material and cultural development of all the workers rather than to the creation of profits for the few; that a classless world may be established, with no divisive social lines to destroy the spirit of brotherhood which can only operate in a profound manner in a society which approaches an egalitarian principle; in a word, that the good life may be made available universally and human beings, wherever found, may be assured of opportunity for the

[47] Herron, *Why I Am a Socialist*, pp. 11, 21-22.   [48] *Ibid*, p. 23.
[49] Herron, in a letter to W. C. Stiles, *The Kingdom*, April 20, 1894.

fullest development of all latent potentialities. Socialism is based on the actual operation of the law of love and may take the place of religion for those who look upon religion as brotherhood, mutual support in seeking the good life.

Professor Herron was one of the few Christian Socialists who accepted the class struggle as a fact of history and who tried to elaborate a philosophy of social change which would do justice to that fact. As a result he rejected the notion that justice is handed down from above. The workers themselves must be organized to demand justice. A class-conscious movement of workers must achieve its own salvation. "All history demonstrates how the people have had to achieve for themselves each inch and gain of liberty, and how they have been again and again betrayed when those liberties have been committed to those above them in worldly condition." [50] Some people are offended at the appeal of socialism to class consciousness, but this is due to a misunderstanding, said Professor Herron. "Class-consciousness does not mean class-hatred." [51] Socialism does not seek to develop hatred in individuals or in classes even when the individuals and classes are the exploiters. But it does make legitimate use of hatred of injustice, while distinguishing between the system which produces injustice and those who are its victims. In one sense even capitalists are victims of a system. The aim of socialism in developing a class-conscious labor movement was to educate concerning the cause of their condition those who suffer from an unjust economic order, that they might realize that their fight is against a system and not against individuals, and to unite them in the common purpose of establishing a new social order free from all class lines.

. . . In meeting the issues of life and society, we must begin with fact and not with sentiment. The class question is not as to whether we like to have classes or not; the question is: Are there classes in society? No one disputes the affirmative answer to this question . . . There is no language realistic enough . . . to lay bare the chasm between the class that works and the class that reaps the fruit of that work . . . And until the working class becomes conscious of itself as the only class that has a right to be, until the worker understands

[50] Herron, *Why I Am a Socialist*, p. 27.   [51] *Ibid*, p. 25.

that he is exploited and bound by the power which his own unpaid labor places in the hands that exploit and bind him, until we all clearly see that what we call civilization is but the organized and legalized robbery of the common labor, until we have a revolutionized comprehension of the fact that our churches and governments, our arts and literatures, our education and philosophies, our morals and manners, are all more or less the expressions and deformities of this universal robbery, drawing their life and motives out of the vitals of the man who is down and underprivileged, out of his unpaid labor and exhausted life—until then, I say, our dreams and schemes of a common good or better society are but philistine utopias, our social and industrial reforms but self-deceit.[52]

The recognition of the need of an oppressed group to unite their strength in a militant organization for the assertion of their interests and as a defense against the depredations of an exploiting group is to renounce the principle of the law of love as the all-sufficient solution for social conflict. It means that the emphasis of Professor Herron's early teaching was qualified but not totally rejected. Conflicts of interest in social groups were not caused entirely by matching of power against power and of interest against interest. In the appeal of religion to renunciation there is an important approach to social change which does justice to the ethical demands of the personal conscience and which also recognizes the historical facts that in the class struggle individuals were able to transcend their personal interests and those of their class, and were able to throw in their lot with the oppressed group. In his earlier writing Professor Herron tended to place entire confidence upon this individualistic appeal to the good will of the ruling class, relying upon their capacity for renunciation and upon the appeal of redemptive love; but as he grew older in the struggle itself and studied the historical facts his position changed. In his earlier work Professor Herron was under the influence of Mazzini, Maurice, and the English Christian Socialists. Mazzini he called "my best beloved master, next to Jesus." [53]

Impressed by the power of economic interests to shape and condition ethical attitudes and by the constraining force of eco-

---

[52] Herron, *From Revolution to Revolution*, pp. 9-11.
[53] Herron, "Italian Shrines," in *The Kingdom*, February 24, 1898.

nomic practice in the formation of habits, he held to a dual approach to the problem. Religion should continue to make use of the appeal to good will and renunciation, but it should also expect to use coercion. In his acceptance of the fact of the class struggle went the implicit recognition of the necessity for coercion. He did not expect to get very many brethren to the altar of economic sacrifice, at least not enough to ward off the revolution. He found sufficient evidence to indicate that a struggle for economic power was not too distant.

Beneath the selfishness and apparent peace of this age there is the rumble of uprising revolutions, which threaten to disrupt society . . . The insurging woes of centuries of wrong are swelling the great heart of humanity.[54]

In the social organism it takes a Spanish Inquisition to usher in religious freedom, and a French revolution to translate this into political freedom; God knows what it may yet cost to translate both into the freedom of economic equality.[55]

And at the beginning of his *Message of Jesus to Men of Wealth* is a quotation from Mazzini in the spirit of Professor Herron's early writing. Man must

not be taught to enjoy, but rather to suffer for others; to combat for the salvation of the world . . . (not) To each according to his wants . . . but, rather, To each according to his love. To invent formulae and organizations, and neglect the internal man, is to desire to substitute the frame for the picture.[56]

Our hope for social freedom will reach its fulfillment, not through social mechanisms, but through our acting as Frederick Maurice says, "in the faith that the constraining love of Christ is the mightiest power in the universe." Society is to be saved by men and women who shall pour out their lives and possessions as streams of love and service into the great currents of Christ's redeeming life, whose onflowing is healing the nations.[57]

But in his later years Professor Herron combined with these ideas notions which show the influence of Marx, and as a result he placed less and less importance upon a subjective approach to social change.

[54] Herron, *The Larger Christ*, pp. 21-22.
[55] Herron, *Social Meanings of Religious Experience*, p. 14.
[56] Herron, *The Christian Society*, p. 98.
[57] *Ibid*, p. 119.

While not advocating direct action, Professor Herron did not think that violence was inimical to a religious approach to social change. Peace at the expense of justice was not a religious solution to social problems. And resorting to his social interpretation of the cross, according to which all moral progress is made at the expense of suffering and sacrifice, he looked upon a revolution by violence, provided it promised a more just society, as a possible technique for social change worthy of the sanction of religion. "It will not do to say that revolution is not coming, or pronounce it of the devil. Revolutions even in their wildest forms, are the impulses of God moving in tides of fire through the life of man." [58] Even though it involve violence, a workers' revolution establishing a co-operative society is essentially constructive, not destructive, for it provides the only possible basis for a just and peaceful world.

John Rae's *Contemporary Socialism* was quoted with approval:

They [the most dangerous social revolutionists] are actuated by no love of destruction for its own sake; it is impossible to conceive any considerable body of human beings so actuated. They would destroy, that others who come after them may build up. They sacrifice themselves for a cause, in whose triumph they shall share; they work for a generation they shall not live to see. [59]

[58] Herron, *The New Redemption*, p. 15.
[59] *Ibid*, p. 19.

BIBLIOGRAPHY

Abbott, Lyman, The Evolution of Christianity (New York, 1892).
—— Christianity and Social Problems (New York, 1896).
Addams, Jane, Twenty Years at Hull House, with Autobiographical Notes (New York, 1910).
Aiken, Charles Augustus, Christian Ethics, edited by the Class of 1879 (Princeton University).
—— Charles Augustus Aiken, D.D., Inauguration of (New York, 1872).
Albertson, Ralph, The Christian Commonwealth. Unpublished MS.
—— The Passion that Left the Ground. Unpublished MS; a novel based on the history of the Christian Commonwealth Colony.
—— "The Christian Commonwealth, the Story of a Community Modeled after the Communism of the Early Church," *The Ram's Horn*, February 1, 1897.
—— "The Christian Commonwealth," *The New Christianity*, July, 1897.
—— "Christianizing Property," *Twentieth Century*, May 22, 1897.
—— "Communist Society," *The New National Era*, April 31, 1897.
—— "Commonwealth in Retrospect," *The Commons*, January, 1901.
Allibone, Samuel Austin, New Themes Condemned; or, Thirty Opinions upon New Themes and Its Reviewer (Philadelphia, American Economics Association, Publication of the (1886).
American Fabian, The, II-V (Boston, 1896-1900).
Andover Review.
Atkins, Glenn Gaus, Religion in Our Times (New York, 1932).
Ballou, Adin, Practical Christian Socialism (New York, 1854).
—— Autobiography (New York, 1896).
Barnes, Harry Elmer, "Two Representative Contributions of Sociology to Political Theory; the Doctrines of William Graham Sumner and Lester Frank Ward," *American Journal of Sociology*, XXV (July, 1919).
Bascom, John, Sociology (1887).
—— Ethics or Science of Duty (1879).
—— Growth of Nationality in the United States (1889).

Batten, Samuel Z., "Great Need—Sociological Seminary," *The Kingdom,* June 14, 1895.
———— "The Brotherhood of the Kingdom," *The Kingdom,* July 19, 1895.
Behrends, A. J. F., Socialism and Christianity (New York, 1886).
Bellamy, Edward, The Duke of Stockbridge.
———— Looking Backward (New York, 1889).
———— Equality (New York, edition of 1910, with Introduction by Wm. D. Howells).
Bernard, L. L., "The Social Sciences as Disciplines," in Encyclopedia of the Social Sciences, I (1930), 321 ff.
Bliss, W. D. P., editorials and articles in *The Dawn.*
———— Socialism, by John Stuart Mill, ed. (New York, 1891).
———— What is Christian Communism? (Boston, 1890).
———— American Trade Unions (Boston, 1896).
———— Ed. Encyclopedia of Social Reform.
Briggs, Mitchell P., George D. Herron and the European Settlement (Stanford University, 1932).
Brotherhood of the Kingdom, Annual Report, 1895.
Buckham, John Wright, Progressive Religious Thought in America (New York, 1919).
Bushee, Frederick A., "Communistic Societies in the United States," *Political Science Quarterly,* XX (1905), 625-64.
Chamberlain, John, Farewell to Reform: Being a History of the Rise, Life and Decay of the Progressive Mind in America (New York, 1932).
Chevrin, Henri Georges, Socialisme Chrétien; ou, Christianisme Social, etude comparative entre Herron et Sheldon (Paris, 1901).
"Christian Socialism," in Encyclopedia of Social Reform (rev. ed., 1908), pp. 203-4.
Colwell, Stephen, New Themes for the Protestant Clergy: Creeds without Charity; Theology without Humanity; Protestantism without Christianity; with Notes on the Literature of Charity, Population, Pauperism, Political Economy, and Protestantism (Philadelphia, 1851).
———— Politics for American Christians; a Word upon Our Example as a Nation; Our Trade, Elections, Education, and Congressional Legislation (Philadelphia, 1852).
———— The Position of Christianity in the United States and Its Relations with Our Political Institutions, and Especially with Reference to Religious Instruction in the Schools (Philadelphia, 1854).
Coming Nation, The (1896-1900).
Commons, John R., History of Labor in the United States (New York, 1918).

Commons, John R., A Popular Bibliography of Sociology (Oberlin College, January, 1892).

—— Social Reform and the Church (New York, 1894).

Commonwealth Details; an Illustrated Account of the Community of Christian Socialists Located at Commonwealth, Georgia (Commonwealth, Georgia, 1899).

Communist, The, I (St. Louis, 1868).

Converse, Florence, Children of Light (New York, 1912).

Crosby, Ernest, Plain Talk in Psalm and Parable (New York, 1899).

Dawn, The, I-VIII (Boston, 1879-86).

Ely, Richard T., Competition; Its Nature, Its Permanency, and Its Beneficence, an Address Delivered December 27, 1900 (Detroit, 1901).

—— An Introduction to Political Economy (New York, 1889).

—— "The Past and the Present of Political Economy," Johns Hopkins University Studies, Vol. III (Baltimore, 1884).

—— French and German Socialism in Modern Times (New York, 1883).

—— The Labor Movement in America (New York, 1886).

—— Social Aspects of Christianity (New York, 1889).

—— Socialism; an Examination of Its Nature, Its Strength, and Its Weakness, with Suggestions for Social Reform (New York, 1894).

—— The Social Law of Service (1896).

Equity (Boston, 1874-75).

Faulkner, Harold U., "American Christianity and the World of Everyday," Essays in Intellectual History (New York, 1929).

—— Economic History of the United States (New York, 1928).

Fremantle, W. H., The World as the subject of Redemption (London, 1885).

Fries, Horace L., and Herbert W. Schneider, Religion in Various Cultures (New York, 1932).

Gates, Isabel Smith, The Life of George Augustus Gates (1915).

Geiger, George Raymond, The Philosophy of Henry George (New York, 1931).

George, Henry, Complete Works (New York, 1904).

Gibson, George Howard, articles and editorials in *The Social Gospel*.

—— "Why Commonwealth Failed," *The Commons*, January, 1901.

—— "Communism Again," *The Kingdom*, January 17, 1896.

Gillen, John Lewis, "The Development of Sociology in the United States," Publications of the American Sociological Society, XXI (1926), 1-25.

Hall, Thomas C., The Religious Background of American Culture (Boston, 1930).

Hendricks, Robert J., Bethel and Aurora; an experiment in Communism as Practical Christianity (New York, 1933).
Herron, George D., The Message of Jesus to Men of Wealth (New York, 1891).
—— The Larger Christ (New York, 1891).
—— The Call of the Cross (New York, 1892).
—— A Plea for the Gospel (New York, 1892).
—— The New Redemption (New York, 1893).
—— The Christian Society (New York, 1894).
—— The Christian State (New York, 1895).
—— The Social Meanings of Religious Experience (New York, 1896).
—— Between Caesar and Jesus (New York, 1899).
—— Why I Am a Socialist (New York, 1890).
—— Social Democratic Party. Speeches of E. V. Debs and G. D. Herron, Delivered at the Formal Opening of the National Campaign (Chicago, 1900).
—— To the Committee Appointed by the Congregational Church of Grinnell, Iowa to Inquire into My Ministerial Standing and Church Membership.
—— The Day of Judgment (New York, 1904).
—— A Lover's Memorial and Related Earlier Poems (New York, 1925).
Herron, Professor George D.; the Man and His Work on the Pacific Coast (Boston).
Hibben, Paxton, Henry Ward Beecher; an American Portrait (New York, 1927).
Hicks, John D., The Populist Revolt (Minneapolis, 1931).
Hill, David J., The Social Influence of Christianity (New York, 1888).
Hillquit, Morris, History of Socialism in the United States (New York, 1903).
Hinckley, Sue Fay, Diary (1900). Unpublished.
Hinds, William Alfred, American Communities and Co-operative Colonies (1902).
Hitchcock, Roswell D., Socialism (New York, 1897).
Howells, W. D., "Edward Bellamy," *Atlantic Monthly* (1898) pp. 253-56.
Jacobs, Leo, Three Types of Ethical Movements of the Past Half Century (New York, 1922).
Karsner, David, "Debs, His Life and Letters."
Kent, Alexander, Coöperative Communities in the United States. Bulletin of the Department of Labor, No. 35 (July, 1901).
Kingdom, The, VII-XI (Minneapolis, 1895-99).

Labor-Balance (Boston and North Abington, 1877-79).

Laidler, Harry W., Socialism in Thought and Action (New York, 1920).

Laubenstien, Paul F., A History of Christian Socialism in America, 1925. An unpublished S.T.M. thesis, Union Theological Seminary.

Lewis, William L., Ten Blind Leaders of the Blind (Chicago, 1910).

List, Frederick, National System of Political Economy; with Preliminary Essay and Notes by Stephen Colwell (Philadelphia, 1856).

Lloyd, Caroline Augusta, Henry Demarest Lloyd. 1847-1903 (New York, 1912).

Lloyd, Henry Demarest, A Strike of Millionaires against Miners; or, the Story of Spring Valley (Chicago, 1890).

—— Wealth against Commonwealth (New York, 1894).

—— Man the Social Creator (New York, 1906).

—— Men, the Workers (New York, 1909).

—— Lords of Industry (New York, 1910).

—— Mazzini and Other Essays (New York, 1910).

Loomis, S. L., "Modern Cities and Some of Their Problems," *Theological Seminary Bulletin* (Andover, 1897).

McGiffert, Arthur Cushman, The Rise of Modern Religious Ideas (New York, 1922).

McNeill, George E., The Labor Movement; the Problem of To-day (New York, 1887).

Mathews, Shailer, The Social Teaching of Jesus (New York, 1897).

Miller, Spencer, Jr., and Joseph F. Fletcher, The Church and Industry (New York, 1930).

Mitchell, Edward P., Memoirs of an Editor (New York, 1924).

Monfort, F. C., Socialism and City Evangelism (Cincinnati, *ca.* 1885).

Munger, Theodore T., Freedom of Faith (1883).

Nash, H. S., Genesis of the Social Conscience (New York, 1897).

Nationalist, The, I-III (Boston, 1889-91).

Niebuhr, H. Richard, The Social Sources of Denominationalism (New York, 1929).

Niebuhr, Reinhold, Moral Man and Immoral Society (New York, 1933).

—— Reflections on the End of an Era (New York, 1934).

Northwestern Congregationalist, I-VI (Minneapolis, 1889-94).

Peabody, Francis G., "The Philosophy of Social Reform," *Andover Review.*

—— Reminiscences of Present-Day Saints (New York, 1927).

Post, Louis F., The Prophet of San Francisco. Personal Memories and Interpretations of Henry George (New York, 1930).

Prentiss, George L., The Bright Side of Life (New York, 1901).
Randall, John Herman, and John Herman Randall, Jr., Religion and
the Modern World (New York, 1929).
Rauschenbusch, Walter, The Brotherhood of the Kingdom (New
York, 1895).
—— The Kingdom of God (New York, ca. 1895).
—— Christianity and the Social Crisis (New York, 1907).
—— Christianizing the Social Order (New York, 1912).
Reckitt, Maurice B., Faith and Society (New York, 1932).
Reply to Roswell D. Hitchcock, D.D., On Socialism, by a Socialist
(New York, 1879). Published anonymously.
Roberts, John B., Christ and Our Country; or, A Hopeful View of
Christianity in the Present Day (Nashville, 1892).
Rowe, Henry Kallock, The History of Religion in the United States
(New York, 1924).
Ruffner, E. W. H., Charity and the Clergy; Being a Review by a
Protestant Clergyman of the "New Themes" Controversy (Phila-
delphia, 1853).
Rylance, J. H., "Social Inequalities and Social Wrongs"; a sermon
preached in Saint Mark's Church, New York, 1878, in Commu-
nism Not the Best Remedy (New York, 1878).
Sanborn, F. B., "The Commonwealth of Social Sciences," Journal of
Social Science, IX (1884), 4 ff.
Schaff, Philip, Theological Propaedeutic; a general Introduction to
the Study of Theology, Exegetical, Historical, Systematic, and
Practical, Including Encyclopedic, Methodology, and Bibliogra-
phy, a Manual for Students (New York, 1893).
Schneider, Herbert W., The Puritan Mind (New York, 1930).
Scudder, Vida D., "Christian Socialism. The United States," Encyclo-
pedia of the Social Sciences, III (1930), 451-52.
Seminary Student, The, Union Theological Seminary (New York,
1893-94).
Small, Albion W., "Fifty Years of Sociology in the United States,"
American Journal of Sociology, XXI (1915-16).
—— "Origins of Sociology," American Journal of Sociology, XXI
(1915-16).
Smyth, Newman, Christian Ethics (New York, 1882).
Social Gospel, The (Commonwealth, Georgia; South Jamesport, New
York, 1898-1901).
Sprague, F. M., Socialism from Genesis to Revelation (Boston,
1893).
Sprague, Philo W., Christian Socialism; What and Why (New York,
1891).
Standard, The (New York, 1887-92).

Strong, Josiah, The New Era or the Coming Kingdom (New York, 1893).

—— The New World-Religion (New York, 1915).

—— Our Country (New York, 1885).

Stuckenberg, J. H. W., The Age and the Church (Hartford, 1883).

—— Christian Sociology (1880).

Sumner, William Graham, What Social Classes Owe to Each Other (New York, 1883).

—— The Challenge of Facts and Other Essays (New Haven, 1914).

—— War and Other Essays (New Haven, 1919).

Sweet, William Warren, The Story of Religions in America (New York, 1932).

Taylor, Graham, Pioneering on Social Frontiers (Chicago, 1930).

Theological Seminary Bulletin (Andover, 1882-91).

Ticknor, Caroline, Glimpses of Authors (New York, 1922).

Thompson, R. E., De civitate Dei; the Divine Order of Human Society (1891).

Tolman, Frank L., "The Study of Sociology in Institutions of Learning in the United States," in *American Journal of Sociology*, VII-VIII (1901-2).

Tucker, William Jewett, My Generation; an Autobiographical Interpretation (New York, 1919).

—— "The Church of the Future," The New Puritanism (New York, 1897).

Visser 't Hooft, William A., The Background of the Social Gospel in America (Haarlem, Holland, 1928).

Ward, Harry F., "American Christianity and Social Idealism," *American Review*, I (July-August, 1923).

Ward, Lester F., Dynamic Sociology (1883).

Weigle, Luther A., American Idealism (New Haven, 1928).

INDEX

Individualism, 17, 18, 183, 187
Iowa College, 71, 72
Ivins, William M., 47

James, William, 3, 69
Jesus, 132, 133, 140, 141, 181-82
Johnson, Tom, 138
Johnson, W. Preston, 98
Jones, "Golden Rule," 137
Jones, Jesse H., 77, 82, 83
Justice, 141; impossible under capitalism, 188; can only be achieved by organized labor, 190

Kelley, Florence, 134
Kelley, James P., 161-62
Kent, Alexander, 167
Keyes, E. T., 138
Kingdom of God, 15, 20, 112, 125, 132, 133, 139, 176, 183
Kingsley, Charles, 5, 71, 102
Kinsley, Alfred, 124
Knights of Labor, 3, 4, 52, 74, 93, 96, 97, 102
Krammer, John W., 43

Labor movement: influence on social Christianity, 3; development from 1870-1900, 3
Labor Reform Party, 3
League for Social Service, 99
Lenin, 27, 175
Lewis, William L., 6
Liberalism, 20, 30
Linton, E. D., 77
Lippmann, Walter, 170
Little, Thomas, 77
Lloyd, Henry Demarest, 3, 31, 105, 111, 119, 121-31, 138
Loomis, S. L., 4
Love: as an agent of social change, 130, 133, 140; redemptive power, 140, 191
Lutheranism, 15

Macauley, Jerry, 111
McDermott, Ida, 150, 152
McDowell, Mary, 138
McGill University, 176
McGlynn, Edward, 43-45

McGuire, P. J., 93
McKensie, Alex, 110
McLean, J. K., 181
McNeill, George E., 5, 77, 78, 102, 104
Macy, Jesse, 110-11
Manchester School, 51
Manning, W. T., 175
Marchant, Mrs., 143
Marx, Karl, 3, 10, 15, 67, 85, 104, 122, 133, 134, 141, 144, 156, 161, 192
Mathews, Shailer, 10, 18, 20, 22, 27
Maude, Aylmer, 138
Maurice, Frederick, 3, 5, 16, 102, 191
Mayo-Smith, Richard, 72
Mazzini, 127, 191-92
Meadville Seminary, 9
Millard, Nelson, 110
Miller, Spencer, Jr., 98
Mills, B. Fay, 110, 113, 123, 138, 161, 164
Mitchell, Edward P., 86
Morgan, Thomas J., 72
Morris, William, 147, 156
Munger, Theodore T., 3, 14, 64, 110

Nationalist Movement, 84-95, 101
Nelson, N. O., 72, 137
New Churchmen's Single Tax League, 43
Newton, R. Heber, 43, 44, 95, 101
Newton Theological Seminary, 9, 71
Nordhoff, Charles, 77
Noyes, John H., 77

Oakley, Henry A., 98
Oberlin College, 72, 133
Owen, Robert, 3, 77

Pacifism, 7, 130, 141
Parsons, Frank, 105, 111, 138, 160, 163
Parsons, Lucy, 134, 178
Pattee, W. S., 110
Peabody, Francis G., 14, 18, 22, 28, 63, 69, 70
Pease, A. H., 150
Phillips, Wendell, 5, 28, 102
Pomeroy, Eltweed, 138
Pomona College, 111
Populist Party, 3, 110, 114